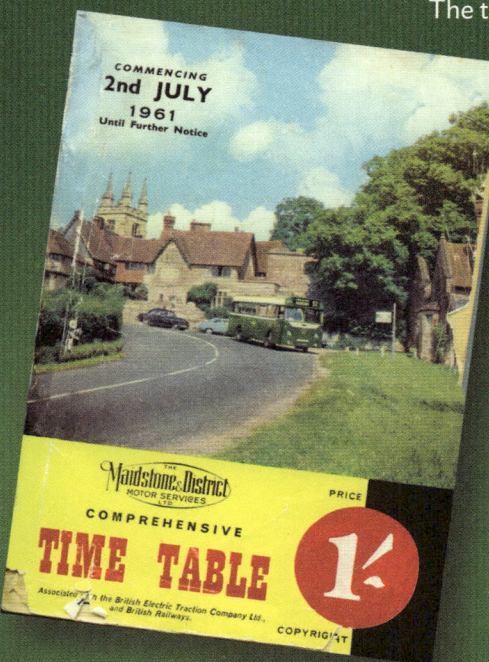

Like most bus companies during this era, Maidstone & District published a comprehensive timetable book of all its services. Each issue usually included a map, although maps were sometimes a bit vague as to where the buses actually went. Maidstone & District in its later books merely used straight lines between towns and villages.

However, for their day these books had attractive covers featuring scenic delights from around the company's territory, as these examples show.

The earliest timetable here is that for the winter of 1955 above on the right. The scene here is Ightham village with the George and Dragon Inn on the left, although the inn sign is on the opposite side of the road. Dating from the 16th century, it's said that Queen Elizabeth I once stayed here. The bus is one of the Weymann Orion bodied Leyland Titans described on page 28.

The timetable for the summer of 1960 shows an open-top Leyland Titan outside All Saints Church at Eastchurch on the Isle of Sheppey.

The charming village scene on the left on the cover of the summer 1961 timetable book is Penshurst, towards the western extremity of Maidstone & District's empire. The village is famous for Penshurst Place, dating from the 14th century and first owned by Sir John de Pulteney.

After passing through the hands of two of Henry IV's sons, it was owned by Henry VIII, who used it as a hunting lodge and gave it to Anne of Cleves as part of her divorce settlement from him. Briefly in the hands of Sir Ralph Fane, it was finally gifted by Henry VIII's son, Edward VI, to his loyal steward and tutor Sir William Sidney in 1552. It has been in the Sidney family ever since.

The single-decker bus is Weymann bodied AEC Reliance SO303 on the 93 route from Edenbridge to Tunbridge Wells.

Lastly, the larger format timetable book for the summer of 1965 shows iconic Kentish oasthouses, built for drying the hops used in making beer. Interesting that the price of the booklet remained at 1/-.

At a number of towns on the edge of its territory Maidstone & District bus services could be seen alongside those of other bus companies. At East Grinstead M&D was joined by fellow BET operator Southdown and the green Country Area of London Transport.

Maidstone & District had three bus routes from the town. The 91 ran to Tunbridge Wells, the 135 to Edenbridge via Cowden and the 137 paralleled the 91 as far as Withyham then turned off to Crowborough. In this picture Weymann bodied AEC Reliance 3212 of 1957 had arrived in East Grinstead on the 137 with a Southdown single decker on the 92 from Eastbourne and Uckfield behind.

The story of the 135 and 137 routes is told on page 136 in this book.

RAY STENNING

written by
David Toy & Ray Stenning

edited & designed by
Ray Stenning

cartography by
Ray Stenning

printed by
Lavenham Press

published by
Best Impressions
15 Starfield Road London W12 9SN

© copyright 2020
David Toy & Ray Stenning
image copyrights shown throughout the book

David Toy and Ray Stenning gratefully acknowledge the considerable help from members of the M&D and East Kent Bus Club in producing this book.

All rights reserved. No part of this book may be reproduced or utilised in any form or by any means, electrical or mechanical, including photocopying, scanning, transmission across a network, or by an information storage and retrieval system without the written permission of the copyright holders.

a superb **Classic Bus** production

ISBN 978 0 9565740 5 3

One of Maidstone & District's calls to fame was its well-known trio of open-top AEC Regal III single deckers that were used on the Round the Town Tour in Hastings. These are dealt with on pages 120-121 of this book, in the section that looks at Hastings and Bexhill.

In this picture by Jeremy Williams we are already into the era really beyond the scope of this book, after ownership of Maidstone & District had passed from the BET Group to the state-owned Transport Holding Company in late 1967, leading to the formation of the National Bus Company on 1 January 1969.

Decimalisation of UK currency happened on 15 February 1971 and the cost of a ride on the tour had become 20p (equivalent of 4/- in 'old' money) by the time of this photograph of 8002, originally OR2, on Hastings seafront.

Like many other bus companies, Maidstone & District ran a programme of touring holidays by coach during the summer months, and in the picture above Harrington Wayfarer IV bodied AEC Reliance CO382 had stopped to let its patrons enjoy some scenic delight, or perhaps give them a bit of time to look round a town, while on a holiday tour of East Anglia and the Broads. Very nice, too. In the background you can see a distinctive British Railways station name sign.

This was one of the 13 coaches delivered in 1957 with seating for just 37 and glazed roof cant panels. Bought specifically for holiday touring, they were largely replaced on such duties by the Harrington Cavalier bodied Reliances of 1962.

Whether this aspect of the company's operations ever returned a real profit is a moot point, as often coaches would be laid up delicenced for the winter months doing nothing.

The section on coaching starts on page 50.
JEREMY WILLIAMS COLLECTION

We've put this book together to give an insight into the character and personality of the bus company that was Maidstone & District. We did not set out for this to be a chronological look at the fleet or of the operations of the company, although the journey we take you on is largely chronological and you get a good feel for the company's operations. Nor is it a forensic study of management decisions and policies, although the repercussions of those decisions have had a major influence on the story we present.

We start by telling how it all began and take the story briefly through the earlier part of the 20th century to the start of the Second World War. This gives historical context and sets the scene for the time period we are focusing on, which more or less starts in the Second World War and takes us up to when Maidstone & District became part of the National Bus Company in 1969, although we've not religiously adopted a hard cut-off date.

We've taken various themes and specific aspects of the company to draw out its intrinsic character, and these are listed on the right with the page numbers where you can find them.

We hope you get as much pleasure from discovering that character as we have had in digging it out and presenting to you.

contents

	page	
the early years	4	from the early years of the 20th century through to the 1930s
into the Second World War	10	hard times and hard seats with utility buses
the road to recovery	13	new buses and boom times
the post-war re-body programme	16	new bodies replace war-worn utilities with sound chassis
the Beadle rebuilds	24	getting new coaches quickly using old running units
the ones that went to Yorkshire	26	M&D's utilities with Yorkshire Woollen
the last front-engined double deckers of the 1950s	27	a switch to the Leyland Titan, then the AEC Regent
the post-war single-deck story … and the spread of one-man operation	30	the engine moves to under the floor and, later, to the rear, and buses get longer
over the hills & far away	50	coaching and coaches in the post-war years
development of the Harrington Wayfarer	76	evolution of a style closely associated with M&D
moving the engine to the back	80	first the Leyland Atlantean, then the Daimler Fleetline
a day at the seaside	91	always popular in M&D's excursion programmes
around the patch	92	In this section we explore Maidstone & District's territory, depot by depot, looking at the towns it served and the nature of the routes it ran to, through and in those towns. We also take a few diversions to look at other interesting aspects of the areas served, to put things into perspective, add context and extra flavour, enriching the fascinating story of what Maidstone & District was all about.

Maidstone	94	Edenbridge	134
The Medway Towns	100	Rye	139
Hastings	114	Tenterden	140
Round the Town Tour	120	Ashford	142
Bexhill	122	Borough Green	144
Tunbridge Wells	124	Isle of Sheppey	146
Tonbridge	131	Gravesend	150
Hawkhurst	132	Faversham	161
		Sittingbourne	162

	page	
travels to my Aunt's	163	a personal recollection by David Toy
joint operations	164	where the company shared its routes with others
the Heathfield Pool	166	an intriguing, intricate piece of timetabling
keeping the wheels turning	170	inside the engineering department
behind the scenes	176	a brief look at service vehicles
a tale of two superintendents	178	Alan Price's experiences as a trainee in 1959
along the Medway Valley	190	a scenic bus ride through pretty villages
August Bank Holiday 1956	192	when Tunbridge Wells was covered by the white stuff
a personal story	194	one man's war-time experiences
the rule book	196	what staff should do and what they mustn't do
a thorn in the side	198	Dengate to Rye and Hastings
the network	199	a map of routes in 1965
the fleet	200	a table of new vehicles
the final years	202	the end of Maidstone & District and a final flourish
a Maidstone & District legacy	204	Maidstone & District lives on in preservation
M&D in adverts	206	using the company to sell other products
Knightrider House	208	a shiny coach and a famous resident

the early years

A brief look at how Maidstone & District came about and how it grew before the outbreak of the Second World War.

The Maidstone & District Motor Services was formed as a limited company in 1911 with a capital of £4,000 by Walter Flexman French and Colonel H I Robinson. The company had seven chain-driven Hallford chassis with detachable double-deck bodies, one charabanc and two lorry bodies.

But to understand its origins we need to go back to three years earlier. In 1908, following trials with a steam bus, a motorbus service between Maidstone and Chatham was started. The road between the two towns was not to a high standard and there were two long hills, a challenge for a steam bus; in fact, for any type of bus at that time. This operation was managed by A W Austen, who had started a bus service at Maidstone, operating from Maidstone's North Ward to the Athletic Ground. Alas, all did not go well as financial troubles arose. The Hallford motorbuses, on hire purchase from J E Hall of Dartford, were repossessed in 1909, when Austen was unable to make the repayments. With the buses being returned, Hall's decided to operate the Maidstone to Chatham service itself, and start a service of its own between Chatham and Gravesend too, with the new title of the Maidstone, Chatham & Gravesend Omnibus Service.

A fatal accident occurred in Chatham: a young boy was struck by one of the Hallford buses and died. This put a different outlook on the company's business and it decided to move away from bus services and sell that part of the operation. The rescue came when Walter Flexman French bought the company in May 1910. The sale included the buses and also the booking offices in Chatham Military Road and Maidstone. The buses were garaged in a yard near St Peter's Street in Maidstone. In the same month a new service was introduced to West Malling. This was the beginning of Maidstone & District.

a growing business

The population of Maidstone in 1911 was 35,000 and growing. There was a need to expand bus services and have a network to other towns in Kent and Sussex. Buses by day and lorries by night was how Walter French kept the business going, until it became profitable to operate solely as a bus company. At the end of the bus working day the bodies were removed and a lorry body bolted onto the chassis. On their night journeys the lorries carried hops and fruit for Covent Garden in London, then in the morning the bodies had to be changed ready for the next day's bus services. Over the next two years new services were introduced, including Maidstone to Rochester via Eccles, Burham and Wouldham, which were villages on the banks of the River Medway; also Maidstone to Sutton Valence and longer services to Faversham, Hastings, Hawkhurst, Sevenoaks and Ashford.

With the company expanding into nearby major towns, it was not surprising that interest was growing from other quarters. In 1913 the British Automobile Traction Co. Ltd, a subsidiary of the British Electric Traction Co. Ltd, was looking to invest into bus companies and it thought that Maidstone & District was an ideal candidate, so injected capital into the company and thereby secured a place on the board.

By the following year, 1914, the company had outgrown its roots and moved to new offices in Upper Stone Street, Maidstone, with a new garage being built on the same site. The company had invested in new buses and the fleet had now grown to 21. Maidstone & District was operating over half a million miles per year and carrying one and a half million passengers. But in 1914, of course, the First World War broke out.

the First World War

Those four years, 1914-1918, were difficult days for transport operators all over the country, and Maidstone & District faced tough times. Staff left to join the armed services and buses were requisitioned by the military authorities to help with the war effort. This was the time when bus companies up and down the country began employing women conductors for the first time and Maidstone & District was no exception. Another problem was obtaining fuel for the fleet, so the alternative of using gas was introduced, and Maidstone & District tried this novel method. Buses had gas bags fitted onto their roofs but this didn't always work out, as in high winds they could be blown off with the crew in hot pursuit to recover the bag. That certainly didn't help the reliability of services.

In the war years there were some positive moves as well. In 1916 the company bought Straker Squire chassis with Tilling open top bodies. These new buses were put onto the Chatham service. The operations of Ernest Neve were bought, and this included premises at Sutton Valence and Tenterden and three Leyland buses. So, by 1917 the company had the bus routes shown on the map on the next page, all carrying letters introduced in 1915 for identification purposes.

new depots, new routes and a bus station

After the First World War expansion in the Medway towns and Hastings meant that there were not going to be enough route letters for further services, so the company turned to using numbers in 1920 after the acquisition of North Kent Motor Services. Its routes were Gravesend to Dartford, Chatham to Meopham and Chatham to Hoo, Cliffe and West Malling, so Maidstone & District's operating area now reached Dartford. The assets of the North Kent Motor Services included 10 buses (nine Daimlers and an AEC).

By 1920 Maidstone & District's fleet had grown to 74, so there was an increasing need to have new operational centres away from Maidstone. The first was at Hastings for 18 buses, opened in 1920, followed by Nelson Road at Gillingham with 26 buses.

The driver and conductor were standing in front of their charge at the bottom of the opposite page. This very early Maidstone & District saloon, KT 873, dated from 1913 and was a Daimler 40hp with a Birch body.

Note the driver's splendid boots and that they are both wearing period flat caps. The bus disappeared from the fleet in 1915, thought to have been requisitioned and transferred to the War Department.
M&D AND EAST KENT BUS CLUB

Above, at White Rock in Hastings in the early 1920s, conductors were standing by their buses waiting for passengers. The bus nearest the camera was a Leyland N with a Tilling body, ready for the service to Maidstone.

Due to the condition of roads in those days and a journey undertaken on solid rubber tyres, passengers would have had a rough old ride in front of them, especially if any were going all the way between Hastings and Maidstone.
M&D AND EAST KENT BUS CLUB

With the growth of services from Maidstone it was becoming essential to have a central terminus in the town and the company's first bus station was opened in 1922 at Palace Avenue. This was not just a first for the company, it was also the first to be built in the United Kingdom.

With the fleet still growing there was the requirement for a separate central engineering works, so in June 1922 Postley Works opened on a two acre site on the outskirts of the town. Maidstone & District now had facilities to carry out major overhauls to its fleet. The works had the latest machinery to overhaul major units, plus a well-equipped machine and body shop.

Another milestone in 1922 was when M&D became a public company, which would assist it financially to expand further. There had been new depots built at Faversham, Gravesend, Hastings and Hawkhurst and, after having had the experience of operating to the Wembley Exhibition in London, the company moved into running express services. These first started between Maidstone and London and soon afterwards from Gillingham. These were a success and soon other express services were started from other major towns in the company's territory. Stage carriage operations were also expanding, connecting more local villages to the main towns, although there were still gaps in the Tunbridge Wells and the Isle of Sheppey areas.

Fleet investment continued, with new buses being bought on a regular basis; for example, 13 in 1922 (Guy and Leyland) and nine in the following year (Leyland and Tilling Stevens).

Letters were introduced to identify routes in 1915. The map above shows the network in 1916. To get to Tunbridge Wells you actually had to change to an Autocar service at Mereworth. The B was worked jointly with North Kent. The O between Hastings and Eastbourne was added in June 1919.

Maidstone's Mill Street bus station must have seemed revolutionary when it opened in 1922. This posed photograph was taken in 1931 with a line up of Leyland and Tilling-Stevens buses and coaches.
M&D AND EAST KENT BUS CLUB

expansion and new depots through the 1920s

Acquisitions continued with the purchase of Carter & Lidstone of Little Common, Bexhill, in July 1926. This included eight buses, a mixture of Ford Model T, Vulcan and Morris chassis. These only stayed with Maidstone & District until they could be replaced by more suitable types. There was further investment in premises with, for example, new depots at Bexhill, Ashford, Dartford, Tenterden, Borough Green and Battle.

In 1930 the Southern Railway acquired a financial interest in the company, leading to agreements to co-ordinate some road and rail services within the area. This came about through Tilling and the BET forming a new joint company, Tilling & British Automobile Co. Ltd (TBAT). With this the big four railway companies agreed not to operate bus services, but instead could buy shares in local TBAT companies and thereby have a place on the board.

At Gravesend the tram system lumbered on until BET decided to close it in 1929. The trams were replaced by a fleet of Maidstone & District Leyland Titan TD1s in a red and cream livery, which M&D ran as a subsidiary for the rest of the year. More purchases were made; in 1929, in a joint venture with neighbouring East Kent, Cambrian Coaches was bought (the Folkestone operations transferring to East Kent). This included the subsidiary Buck's of Maidstone, although M&D did not operate any of Buck's vehicles, which were sold on to a dealer.

1930 Road Traffic Act

This introduced formal licensing for bus and coach services and the certification of buses and coaches by a Ministry of Transport certifying officer with regular re-certification. Each area of the country was regulated by Traffic Commissioners who had the power to authorise bus services, agree timetables and fare structure. The commissioners also had the authority to remove operators who did not conform to the new legislation. For smaller operators this was a step too far and large numbers sold to the larger companies within their area.

As a result, Maidstone & District's expansion was very rapid. The following were purchased by the company:

T Standen, Sheppey Motor Transport Co. Ltd
Sheerness Enterprise Motor Services
Theresie Safety Coaches Ltd of Chatham
H Sands of Wouldham
Sittingbourne, Milton and District Motorways
Orange Coaches of Chatham
Medway District Bus Owners Association
Huck Brothers of Burham
Weald of Kent Transport Company of Tenterden

These all had a variety of bus and coach types and not all entered service with Maidstone & District, many being disposed of immediately.

Services in the Medway Towns could now expand when the Chatham & District Traction Company was set up in 1930 as a subsidiary company to take over the routes of the Chatham and District Light Railway Company. The trams were replaced by a fleet of new Leyland TD1s.

The top picture is of Gillingham depot in the 1920s, built on farm land with the office being an old farm cottage. The neat chalk boards were advertising tours and on the wall was a list of stage services. Outside waiting to go on a tour was KN 7105, a 1920 Leyland N with Harrington charabanc body.
M&D AND EAST KENT BUS CLUB

By 1928 roller destination blinds and pneumatic tyres were standard on new buses like 262, a Leyland Titan TD1 with a Short 48-seat open-top and open-platform body, shown in the middle picture.
DAVID TOY COLLECTION

On the seafront at Hastings on a circular tour was 490 on the right, a 1928 Tilling Stevens B10A2 with Harrington 31-seat rear-entrance body. This was from a batch that was also used on express services. In inclement weather the tarpaulin roof would be pulled over to make a more enjoyable ride.
M&D AND EAST KENT BUS CLUB

Above is a photograph of Knightrider House taken during the Second World War. Note how both people in the Ovaltine advert were in military uniform.
M&D AND EAST KENT BUS CLUB

Below is a pre-war photo of 319, a 1936 Leyland Titan TD4 with Weymann lowbridge body on route 9 at the bottom end of Maidstone High Street, and a fine example of bus design of the time.
M&D AND EAST KENT BUS CLUB

With the company growing at a substantial rate there was a need for a new larger head office, so in 1928 a large private house that stood in its own large grounds in Maidstone was bought. The house was converted into offices and within the grounds the company built a new depot for the Maidstone fleet. The house had its own history, beginning as the residence of William Shipley who founded the Royal Society of Arts - see page 208.

some losses but many gains through the 1930s

With the formation of the London Passenger Transport Board in 1933 bus operators in the capital and over quite a large surrounding area were combined to form London Transport. Its operating area went out as far as Dartford and Gravesend and this led to Maidstone & District having to relinquish its Dartford operations. Dartford and Northfleet depots, together with 55 buses and coaches, were transferred to the new Board but the company kept the Gravesend operation with limited services into London Transpot's country area.

In the following year A Timpson and Sons of London sold its Hastings bus and coach operation, including 67 vehicles, to M&D for £106,488. This included the large garage that adjoined the M&D Hastings depot. Timpson's service to Pett Level was transferred to East Kent.

Maidstone & District had had a financial interest in Redcar Services of Tunbridge Wells since 1928 and Redcar was effectively operated as a subsidiary. In 1935 Redcar became part of the parent, bringing 54 buses and coaches to the fleet. Within months Autocar in Tunbridge Wells, which M&D had owned since 1933 but also run as a subsidiary, was absorbed into the company with 43 vehicles. And in Tunbridge Wells again, and in the same year, Victor Motor Transport was bought with 13 buses.

Maidstone & District now had a network of services radiating from Tunbridge Wells, linking Uckfield, Edenbridge, Maidstone, Cranbrook, Gravesend, and Heathfield as well as many rural villages. The last major company to join Maidstone & District was Hastings Tramways in November 1935, with M&D acquiring a majority shareholding. Hastings Tramways operated 58 trolleybuses from depots at Silverhill and Bulverhythe. With this acquisition M&D could now start to rationalise its services in the Hastings area.

In 1934 M&D turned to Harrington for eight 48-seat double-deck bodies on Leyland Titan TD3 and TD3c chassis. They were to a higher specification with a front entrance with sliding door and better seating for the longer routes from Maidstone. Two of them, 344/5, were M&D's first double deckers to have oil engines. Above, in Mill Street bus station in the 1930s, the first of the batch, 338, was waiting to load its passengers for the 5 to Hastings. This bus was rebodied by Weymann in 1942 and withdrawn in 1954.

M&D AND EAST KENT BUS CLUB

A batch of the new AEC Regent double deckers was delivered in 1935, ordered by Autocar but coming to M&D after the takeover. They had either Weymann or Short 48-seat rear-entrance bodies. Below, leaving the bus station on time on the 7 to Tunbridge Wells was 125, a Weymann bodied example. Later renumbered DH309, its running units were used in the Beadle semi-chassisless programme, fitted to CO204 (see page 24).

OMNIBUS SOCIETY

The Second World War wasn't easy for any bus company, but possibly Maidstone & District had more to deal with than many others, being virtually on the front line with military ports and airfields in its territory an easy target for Nazi bombers.

With so many male staff being called up into the armed forces, more and more women were taken on, especially as conductresses. Several vehicles got requisitioned for war service and a number of single deckers converted to ambulances with doors fitted at the back to enable stretchers to be loaded on easily. Lots of things were soon in short supply, but the spirit of the people was indomitable and, as elsewhere in the land, there was an overwhelming sense of pulling together for the common good. After all, there was an enemy to be defeated and freedoms to be protected. Although the company's express services were suspended for a period during the war years, many vehicles were still needed for troop movements and transport to army camps for entertainers and the like (see page 194).

The company did not get through the war unscathed by any means. For example, there was the total destruction of the Hastings offices. But the most serious incident happened on the night of 27/28 August 1940, when Gillingham depot at Nelson Road was attacked from the air. Several of the bombs hit the depot, and the force of the explosions destroyed major sections of the buildings; 51 buses were completely beyond repair and many more damaged. The depot had to be rebuilt and this was carried out during 1941/42.

In 1940 the company brought in a new fleet numbering system with separate class prefixes.

- **CO** Coach Oil engine
- **CP** Coach Petrol engine
- **DH** Double Deck Highbridge
- **DL** Double Deck Lowbridge
- **SO** Saloon Oil engine
- **TC** Twenty seat Coach
- **OT** Open Top
- **SP** Saloon Petrol engine

into the Second World War

The 10 Leyland Titan TD7s with Weymann 54-seat bodies that were delivered in 1940 were the last double deckers for Maidstone & District with 'normal' bodies until after the war. Subsequent wartime deliveries would all be to the much more severe-looking utility specification.

DH8, on the right, was photographed after the war. This was a Gravesend based vehicle, working on route 23 to nearby Cobham. This bus gave 16 years' service with the company before being sold to Taylor of Bicester in 1956.

SOUTHDOWN ENTHUSIASTS' CLUB

RAF airfields in Maidstone & District's area

In 1940 10 Leyland Titan TD7s with Weymann bodies were delivered, these being the last of the 'standard' bodies until after the war. These buses were the first to carry the new fleet numbering system, being numbered DH1-10. In the same year a new single-deck chassis also appeared in the fleet, the Dodge 84, and eight were delivered with Duple 24-seat coach bodies that year, followed by four more in 1941. These were numbered TC1-12.

Once the war started to bite, shortages and restrictions began to be noticeable in everyday life more and more, and government control of so many things was a necessity. For example, a bus company needing new buses could no longer just go out and buy what it wanted, nor specify them in any way; it couldn't even choose the vehicle manufacturer. It had to apply to the Ministry of War Supply and, if it got buses, the bodies would be built to what was called a utility standard.

These bodies were very basic and had stark interiors with slatted wooden seats. They were constructed from unseasoned timber and on the majority of bodies there were no window pans, windows being fixed by a wooden beading. Interiors were single-skinned and had just a few half-drop windows. The bodies would prove generally to have a limited life span.

The first three to this standard arrived in late 1941 on single-deck Bristol L5G chassis, one having a Burlingham body and the other two with Strachans.

The picture below, taken in Sevenoaks bus station during the Second World War, shows TC2, one of the batch of 12 Dodge 84s with 24-seat Duple coach bodies delivered in 1940 and 1941. Note the wartime restricted headlamp shields. They were to be used for high quality coach tours but the war stopped those plans, so were used on bus services instead.
M&D AND EAST KENT BUS CLUB

The first utility bodied buses for Maidstone & District were three Bristol L5Gs, SO1-3, delivered in 1941. SO1 had a Burlingham 36-seat body and the other two 35-seat Strachans bodies. The picture at the bottom of this page shows the last of the three, SO3, in Globe Lane in Chatham with a very obscure destination screen. The lorry parked on the left was a Fordson. These three Bristol L5Gs were not in the re-bodying programme and were withdrawn in 1955.
DAVID TOY COLLECTION

In 1945/6 six of the 1942 delivery of Bristol K5Gs were transferred from Maidstone & District to Chatham & District in exchange for the same number of Guy Arabs.

One of the three transferred in 1945, Chatham & District 917 (previously M&D DH16), was on route 2 in the picture on the left. The 56-seat utility body was built by Bristol and got replaced by a new Weymann body in 1951.
M&D AND EAST KENT BUS CLUB

Below you can see the interior of the Weymann utility body of Daimler CWA6 DH34. Note the less than comfortable wooden seats and dim, shielded internal lighting.
M&D AND EAST KENT BUS CLUB

The picture at the bottom shows DH22, a Guy Arab from 1943 with queues of people to shift in Chatham.
M&D AND EAST KENT BUS CLUB

By 1942 more buses were desperately needed, especially to replace the destroyed vehicles at Gillingham depot, which had been mainly double deck. Providing transport for workers at Chatham Dockyard was a priority in the war. In 1942 seven Bristol K5Gs with a mixture of Strachans and Bristol bodies were allocated to the company, followed in 1943 by Guy Arabs and Daimler CWs with either Gardner 5LW or AEC 7.7-litre engines and utility bodies built by Weymann, Duple and Brush. There's a chart showing wartime deliveries on page 17.

Around this time there was increased pressure to save fuel, so in 1943 several gas producer units were bought that could be towed behind buses. These went to Sheerness depot for use with early Leyland Titan TDs. The thinking was that if the Kingsferry Road Bridge was destroyed and cut the island from the mainland, and therefore fuel could not be delivered, the buses could continue in service using gas.

More utility double-deckers came in 1944, a mixture of Guy Arabs, Daimler CWA6s and 12 Bristol K6As. Several Guy Arabs with Gardner 6LW engines were exchanged for Daimler CWA6s with Yorkshire Woollen in 1944/45 - see page 26.

Bristol K6As (and one K6B) with HKR registrations and Weymann bodies arrived in 1946/7.

Tunbridge Wells based DH202, a 1947 delivery, was photographed on the right on a local service in May 1960, the year it was withdrawn. DH202 gave 13 years of service with M&D before having further life with Contract Bus Services.
G MEAD

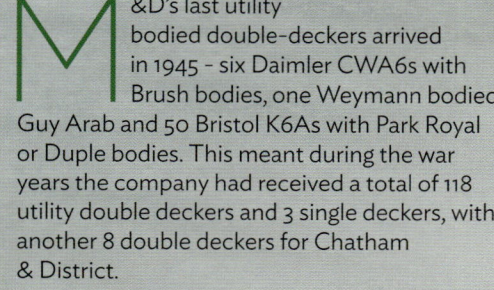

Below, DH50, a Brush bodied Daimler CWA6, was one of the last batches of utility double deckers delivered in 1945. Here it was on local Hastings route 27.
SOUTHDOWN ENTHUSIASTS' CLUB

the road to Recovery

M&D's last utility bodied double-deckers arrived in 1945 - six Daimler CWA6s with Brush bodies, one Weymann bodied Guy Arab and 50 Bristol K6As with Park Royal or Duple bodies. This meant during the war years the company had received a total of 118 utility double deckers and 3 single deckers, with another 8 double deckers for Chatham & District.

The problems the company would now face in peacetime were going to be very challenging. Not only were there a lot of inferior utility bodies but the rest of the fleet had suffered from a lack of spares and a lack of maintenance. In 1945 the fleet total - Maidstone & District and Chatham & District combined - was 681, and over 17% had utility bodies. There were still petrol-engined vehicles in the fleet and large numbers of elderly buses and coaches dating from the early 1930s.

Like other large bus companies there was the need to start a fleet renewal programme. However, the high demand for new buses and coaches that manufacturers were experiencing immediately after the war gave rise to long waiting lists and long delays.

The war may have ended but fuel rationing was still in force for private motoring and car ownership was still low. So with restrictions on travel lifted, Maidstone & District needed to reinstate bus services, as ridership was about to increase. In the short term there was need to improve the utility bodied vehicles.

Due to shortage of materials at the time, buses had been delivered with boarded-up upper-deck emergency windows and these were replaced with glass during 1945. The wooden slatted seats on many of these utility bodies were replaced with upholstered seats at the same time.

Bristol was to become the main chassis suppler for the double-deck fleet in early post-war years. 37 Bristol Ks with Weymann 56-seat bodies were taken into the fleet in 1946, DH 163-199, the first non-utility bodies for five years. All but one had AEC 7.7-lite engines; DH176, the odd one out had a Bristol AVW engine. These Weymann bodies had 5 window bays with top sliding windows on both decks and the characteristic Weymann flared skirts.

New single deck buses also came into the fleet in 1946/7 32 AEC Regals with Beadle 36-seat front entrance bodies - see page 31.

The large number of buses and coaches on order at this time, not just from Maidstone & District, was giving several bodybuilders a major problem with too many chassis to body. So when M&D bought six AEC Regent chassis in 1947, the delivery time was shortened by transferring bodies built in 1942 that had been fitted in that year to older AEC Regents. These late 1933/early 1934 AEC Regents had been acquired when Maidstone & District took over the Timpson operations in Hastings in 1934, becoming 105-110 in the M&D fleet. In 1942 their Harrington 56-seat double-deck bodies were replaced by brand new 54-seat Weymann ones. These Weymann bodies were then fitted to the new AEC Regent III chassis in 1947. DH244-249, as they were numbered, were non-standard by having AEC 9.6-litre engines, pre-selector gearboxes and air brakes, and spent their working lives at Tunbridge Wells depot. There's another shot of one of them on page 128.

With increased demand for leisure travel, the coach fleet needed updating too, to allow express services to resume and increase, tours and excursions to run again and to meet the growing demand for private hire. In the three years between 1947 and 1949 no fewer than 116 AEC Regal coaches entered the fleet, as shown here.

	FLEET NO.	CHASSIS	BODY	SEATS
1947	CO 1-23	AEC Regal	Harrington	C32F
1948	CO 24-31	AEC Regal	Harrington	C32F
	CO 32-57	AEC Regal	Beadle	C32F
	CO 62, 64-65, 67-72	AEC Regal III	Harrington	C31F
	CO 85-96, 98	AEC Regal III	Harrington	C32F
1949	CO 58-61	AEC Regal	Beadle	C32F
	CO 63, 66, 73-84	AEC Regal III	Harrington	C31F
	CO 97	AEC Regal III	Harrington	FC32F
	CO 99-112	AEC Regal III	Harrington	C32F
	CO 113-116	AEC Regal III	Harrington	FC32F

The Harrington bodies on these 23 coaches had been built in 1936 and were taken from AEC Reliance chassis built in 1929 that M&D had acquired with the Timpson business in Hastings in 1934 and rebodied.

The Harrington bodies were refurbished by Portsmouth Aviation before fitting to CO62-84.

A new livery for coaches was introduced in 1948, now mainly cream below the windows with a green flash descending from the waist rail to the rear corner; also a green roof. The practice of having the company name above the front destination screen continued. Even in 1950 there were still nearly 90 coaches and 34 single-deck buses in the fleet with petrol engines but by now the double-deck fleet was all diesel.

DH245 on the 87 in Tunbridge Wells, on the left, was one of the six AEC Regent IIIs delivered in 1947 that stayed at Tunbridge Wells all their lives, until withdrawal in 1958. The story of these buses and their secondhand bodies is told on this page.
M&D AND EAST KENT BUS CLUB

In November 1948 the coaching livery was effectively reversed to become mainly cream. Harrington bodied CO7 at the top of the opposite page was showing off the new style.
M&D AND EAST KENT BUS CLUB

CO108 in the middle of the opposite page was one of the 1949 Harrington bodied AEC Regal IIIs parked in the far corner of London's Victoria Coach Station on layover.

You can see here the increased amount of cream on subsequent repaints and removal of the green flash.
JEREMY WILLIAMS COLLECTION

Five of the KKK-registered AEC Regal coaches had fully-fronted Harrington bodies. Although this gave a more modern appearance, the simple slats for airflow to the radiator didn't look very elegant, and access to the engine was more restricted.

Surrounded by Southdown coaches on a busy day at Victoria coach station was one of them, CO115, in the picture at the bottom of the opposite page.
DAVID TOY COLLECTION

More Bristol K6As appeared in 1948, 1949 and 1950, the majority with Weymann bodies, although Maidstone & District turned to Saunders on the Isle of Anglesey for bodies for 40 of them in 1948, DH204-43. Several of these spent their entire lives on the Isle of Sheppey, and you can see one there on page 147.

At the 1948 Commercial Motor Show in London Weymann bodied Bristol K6A DH256 was on display, one of the first buses with fluorescent lighting, although that didn't last long; it got conventional bulbs in 1950. Similar Weymann bodied DH264 became the first M&D bus to carry a 3-track number blind above the destination screen, which then became standard, as it was more practical.

The very last Bristol double-deckers for Maidstone & District, before Bristol products were only available to the nationalised BTC fleets, were a further 21 K6As with 53-seat Weymann lowbridge bodies, DL2-22. The cab had less room than their highbridge counterparts and was disliked by the drivers. There's one on page 98.

There were also Bristol L single deckers and these are described on page 30.

Winter Excursions by Maidstone & District Motor Services Ltd.

Every M. & D. Depot operates a certain number of tours and excursions — some to London Theatres, Ice Shows and Pantomimes, Football Matches (including international games), Race Meetings and events of importance or interest. Ask for programme at your local office or watch for announcements in the press or on the boards at local offices.

the post-war re-body programme

The deprivations and hardships sustained through five long hard years of war, and the necessity of make-do-and-mend rather than thorough programmed maintenance, meant the Bristol, Guy and Daimler chassis delivered during the war still had more years in them but their utility bodies definitely did not.

Utility bodies were not only built simply and without frills but the almost alacrity with which they had to be built using unseasoned timber - all that was available then - soon gave problems with warping and other issues after just a few years. However, the first buses to be rebodied after the Second World War were not any of the utilities but, rather, six 1935 Leyland Titan TD4c types in 1945/6 that originally had Beadle 48-seat lowbridge bodies, DH251/253/256/284-286. With replacement bodies also by Beadle, these chassis gave the company an impressive total of 23 years' service.

Between 1942, when the company got its first utility bodied buses, and its last ones that arrived in 1945, a grand total of 129 had entered the fleet, including those for subsidiary Chatham & District

Maidstone & District decided that its utility bodied Bristol Ks, Daimler CWs and Guy Arabs should be rebodied by Weymann, a programme to be rolled out over several years. The body style would have been more-or-less the same on the three chassis types, except that the last 25 of the Bristol K6As ended up with Weymann's new lightweight Orion body and there were variations along the way. This was at the same time as other brand new double deckers were being bought, Weymann bodied Bristols followed by Leyland Titans with first Leyland bodies then Weymann Orion bodies.

Six Leyland TD4s were rebodied by Beadle with 48-seat lowbridge bodies in 1945/6. Parked in Maidstone Lower Stone Street bus station, above, was DL253 showing the distinctive lines of the Beadle body.
DAVID TOY COLLECTION

On the right, similar DL256 was photographed on a short working of the Maidstone-Gillingham via West Malling route 20 to West Malling only.
M&D AND EAST KENT BUS CLUB

double deckers with utility bodies and those that were rebodied

new			rebodied by Weymann				
1942			1949	1950	1951	1952	1953-4
◆ DH 11-12	Bristol K5G	Strachan	DH 11 rebodied by Saunders		DH 12		
◆ DH 13-17	Bristol K5G	Bristol			DH 13-17		
■ 907-909	Bristol K5G	Bristol			907-909		
■ 910-911	Bristol K5G	Park Royal			910-911		
1943							
DH 18-20	Guy Arab I	Weymann				DH 18-20	
● DH 21-28	Guy Arab II	Weymann				DH 21-24, 27	
DH 30-31	Daimler CWG5	Duple		DH 30-31			
DH 32-33	Daimler CWA6	Weymann		DH 32-33			
DL 1	Daimler CWG5	Brush		DL 1 renumbered DH 378			
1944							
● DH 29	Guy Arab II	Weymann					
DH 34-40	Daimler CWA6	Weymann			DH 34-40		
DH 41-44	Daimler CWA6	Duple		DH 41-44			
● DH 61-66	Guy Arab II	Weymann				DH 65, 66	
DH 67-71	Guy Arab II	Park Royal				DH 67-71	
DH 72-80	Guy Arab II	Weymann	DH 76 ■			DH 72-75, 77-80	
DH 100-111	Bristol K6A	Park Royal			DH 100-111		
912-914	Guy Arab II	Weymann	transferred to M&D in 1945 as DH 82-8			DH 82-84	
1945							
○ DH 45-50	Daimler CWA6	Brush					DH 45-50 all in 1953
DH 81	Guy Arab II	Weymann				DH 81	
DH 112-149	Bristol K6A	Park Royal			DH 112		DH 113-149
DH 150-162	Bristol K6A	Duple					DH 150-162

- ◆ these buses were transferred to Chatham & District and apart from DH 11 were rebodied as Chatham & District vehicles
    1945   DH 15-17   (Chatham & District 915, 917, 916) - in return M&D got Chatham & District 912-914 (M&D DH 82-84)
    1946   DH 12-14   (Chatham & District 918-920)
    1952   DH 11   (Chatham & District 912)

- ■ new to Maidstone & District but transferred to Chatham & District without being operated by Maidstone & District rebodied as Chatham & District vehicles

- ●○ DH 25-26, 28-29, 61-64 went to Yorkshire Woollen in 1945 and later rebodied by Roe
    These were in exchange for 6 Daimler CWA6s DH 45-50

- ■ DH 76 was rebodied after the original utility body was badly damaged following a collision in March 1949 with Leyland coach 629 at Rochester

Weymann's standard 5-bay construction with flared skirt was continued on these last rebodies except for:
4-bay body style (no flare)   DH 114, 121-123, 128, 129, 133, 139-141, 143-145, 150-161
lightweight Orion style   DH 113, 115-120, 124-127, 130-132, 134-138, 142, 146-149, 162

Although the exterior styling had many Weymann hallmarks, like the shape of the roof mouldings above the upper-deck windows and the flared skirt, features like the radiused window corners gave a more modern appearance. Interiors were a vast improvement, too. Seats were covered in green swirl moquette and the floors had lino. Access to the driver's cab was through a sliding door and all the bodies had a single destination screen with a 3-track number blind above.

All the chassis were overhauled before being re-bodied. The 1942 wartime deliveries of Bristol K5Gs (with GKR and GKT registrations) kept their high-mounted radiators but the later wartime deliveries of K6As (the 'HKEs') were given the Bristol's new post-war lower-mounted radiators, which gave them a more modern appearance, as you can see on the following pages.

The rebodied Guy Arabs would be based at Gillingham depot and operate the local services and to the outlying smaller towns and villages. Maidstone was the home for the majority of the Daimlers with Ashford and Tenterden having the rest. The Bristol K6As were the mainstay of the double-deck fleet and operated from the majority of the depots; they could be seen on any type of duty including the longer stage services.

The first utility double decker to be rebodied under Maidstone & District's post-war rebodying programme was DH11 in June 1950. Although all the rest were sent to Weymann at Addlestone in Surrey to be rebodied, this one uniquely went to Saunders Engineering & Shipyard Works at Beaumaris on the Isle of Anglesey off the north coast of Wales.

Saunders was at the time building 300 RT bodies for London Transport, which explains its overall similarity to the RT in terms of its basic 4-bay appearance and general architecture. Note the high positioned radiator on this rebody and some subsequent ones. Later rebodies had the tall radiators replaced by lower post-war style ones.

Carrying this body, DH11 was transferred to Chatham & District in 1952, where it got renumbered 912, but returned to the Maidstone & District fleet when Chatham & District was absorbed into the parent company in 1955. Its new number was then DH445. Above it was still in Chatham & District colours though carrying a Maidstone & District scroll fleetname. It was withdrawn in 1960.

BRUCE JENKINS

In pristine condition, DH65 had been parked in Dock Road in Chatham in the picture above. This Gillingham based Guy Arab had been new in 1944, rebodied by Weymann in September 1949 as here and withdrawn in 1965.

It was on route 19 from Gillingham Green to Hoo Five Bells.

M&D AND EAST KENT BUS CLUB

On the left is the lower deck of Guy Arab DH67 with the new Weymann body it got in May 1952. Notice the lino floor, chrome top-rail seats with soft seat trim in the M&D swirl design, green window surrounds and top sliding opening windows, a vast improvement over its original utility body.

M&D AND EAST KENT BUS CLUB

On the opposite page in Military Road in Chatham was DH444, a Bristol K5G rebodied by Weymann in March 1951, on the 140 from the Earl Estate to Luton Burma Way. This bus had been new to Chatham & District in 1942 as 911. At that time it had carried a Park Royal utility body.

M&D AND EAST KENT BUS CLUB

The final batch of rebodied Bristol K6As, DH112-162 (known as the 'HKEs'), had three types of Weymann bodies, as listed in the chart on page 17. This included the more modern-looking 4-bay version that no longer had the flared skirt.

Gillingham bus station was redeveloped with drive-through bus stands in the early 1960s. On the new stand in the picture above, on a short working of the 65, was DH144, one of the 4-bay versions. It hadn't many years left, as it was withdrawn in 1967.
DAVID TOY COLLECTION

On the left, leaving Maidstone Lower Stone Street bus station on the 1 to Gillingham and ending up at Hawthorne Avenue, was DH111, one of the 13 rebodied with the 5-bay design.

Note that this one has had its lower-deck windows modified with bottom fixed glass section having radiused top corners instead of square - compare with the upper deck style. Some 'HKEs' had this on both decks.
OMNICOLOUR

DH126 was on Gravesend Overcliffe in the picture to the left, waiting to leave on the 2-hour journey down through the Medway Towns and on to Faversham, although this could take considerably longer when traffic through the Medway Towns was congested, an ever-increasing problem in the post-war years.

Here, the bus was still carrying its utility body, so the photograph must have been taken before 1954.
SOUTHDOWN ENTHUSIASTS' CLUB

It would have been confusing for passengers at Gillingham bus station in the view below, since DH115 was displaying route 20 in the number box, which it could not have been on as this was a lowbridge route to Maidstone. It was, in fact, on the 8 to Wigmore, Fairview Avenue, as the destination blind correctly showed.

The bus was a Bristol K6A rebodied with a Weymann 56-seat Orion body.
M&D AND EAST KENT BUS CLUB

This Leyland Tiger TS7 coach on the left, CO564, was photographed at London Victoria and was one of the 26 rebodied by Harrington in September 1950.

M&D AND EAST KENT BUS CLUB

Three petrol engine Leyland Tigers dating from 1931 gained new Harrington 32-seat coach bodies in 1946. This was odd, as the company had moved away from petrol-engined coaches before the Second World War.

In the picture immediately below, CP679 had been delicensed and was parked up for disposal at Bulverhythe.

M&D AND EAST KENT BUS CLUB

As well as the big influx of new coaches in the early post-war years, a number of older ones were rebodied, too. Three 1931 petrol-engined Leyland Tiger TS1s - 677, 679, 680 - were rebodied in 1946 with new 32-seat Harrington bodies, becoming CP677, 679 and 680 in 1950.

Then in 1949/50 26 Leyland Tiger TS7s dating from 1936/7 had their original Harrington bodies replaced by new ones from the same manufacturer. These were CO553, 555-559 and 560-579, the chassis being refurbished at Postley Works before they were re-bodied.

There was an odd body within the batch. CO554 had been new to M&D in 1937, then went to Samuelson's New Transport London in 1938, eventually returning in 1947. The new Harrington body CO554 received in 1950 was of all-metal construction and without a canopy, and did look out of place when compared to the standard Harrington design.

not so much a rebodying... as a re-chassis-ing!

Maidstone & District with Chatham & District became the largest user of Bristol buses outside the Tilling group - 323 were bought in total over 31 years, with the largest number in the fleet at any one time being 306.

Its first came at the end of 1936, although Chatham & District had a GO5G demonstrator, CHW 835, on loan for several months around the same time. This was actually painted into Chatham & District colours and got numbered 356 in the fleet.

Of the 16 GO5Gs the company bought, all with Weymann bodies, 12 were lowbridge for the Maidstone & District fleet, 270-282, and four highbridge for Chatham & District, 352-355.

Unfortunately, these buses proved less than ideal for M&D's territory, so were returned to Bristol in November 1938 to have their bodies transferred to an equivalent number of new K5G chassis. Although they had new registration numbers in the FKL series, they kept the same fleetnumbers that the GO5Gs had.

The K5G proved to be a much more satisfactory chassis than the GO5G and these 16 had a service life with the company of between 14 and 18 years - not a bad testimonial.

Showing its unusual all-metal 1950 Harrington body without a nearside canopy, CO554 was unloading its passengers in Victoria Coach Station in the picture above. This was after a three and a half hour journey from Bexhill on the E4 express service.

M&D AND EAST KENT BUS CLUB

The Bristol K5G chassis was better suited to the company than the earlier GO5G, so Maidstone & District returned the 16 buses it bought in 1936 to Bristol in 1938, in exchange for the same number of K5Gs. The Weymann bodies were simply transferred to the new chassis.

On the left was K5G no. 280, based in Maidstone and here was leaning to the nearside on the adverse camber of the road on its way cross-town to Ashford Road Yeoman from West Malling. There's more about this route on page 98.

Being lowbridge, this bus was always with Maidstone & District.

M&D AND EAST KENT BUS CLUB

In the middle on the left is 278, one of the 16 original Bristol GO5Gs when new.

This one was 278, one of the 12 with lowbridge bodies for Maidstone & District. The other four for Chatham & District had highbridge bodies.

M&D AND EAST KENT BUS CLUB

The picture on the right was taken in Globe Lane in Chatham and shows at least two of the four Chatham & District highbridge bodied 're-chassised' Bristols.

Those Gardner 5LW engines had to work hard on the routes within the hilly Medway towns.

P M PHOTOGRAPHY

the Beadle rebuilds

As new, more modern underfloor-engined coaches entered the fleet in the mid-1950s, the Beadle/AEC coaches and Leyland CO241 were converted to 39-seat buses in 1954/55 becoming SO69-110. Photographed passing Warrior Square in St Leonards on a local service was SO106, which always had this slightly different grille.
DAVID TOY COLLECTION

In the picture below, Gillingham based CO270, one of the shorter Beadle rebuilds, was parked in London on a private hire.
ROY MARSHALL COLLECTION

Even with the addition of new AEC Regal coaches and older ones being rebodied, in the early post-war years Maidstone & District was still in desperate need of coaches, and modern ones at that. There were still expensive-to-run petrol-engined coaches and ones that had not returned from war services that had to be replaced, too.

Beadle of Dartford had developed an economical to buy integrally-constructed single-deck vehicle for some of the BTC companies by taking the mechanicals and chassis parts from buses and coaches that were time expired and building a new body around them. A few BET group subsidiaries also turned to Beadle for the same concept. Maidstone & District was one of them, using running units initially from its pre-war AEC Regent double-deck fleet. The donor vehicle would have the chassis cut in the middle to make into two sub frames, which would be incorporated into the new Beadle body frame. This gave a 30ft long coach body with a good seat pitch for 35 passengers.

The first conversion for M&D was CO200, which had donor units from DH310, a 1935 AEC Regent which had an AEC 7.7 litre diesel engine fitted in 1937. This was the first 8ft wide vehicle for the company and with this a new practice was started of having a white steering wheel on any bus or coach of this width. The interior of these Beadle rebuilds was to a high standard. The front bulkhead had a clock with fan-shaped lights each side and there were varnished wood cappings. The driver had a glass partition with a sliding window at the top to communicate with passengers.

A further 40 conversions took place in 1951 and 1952, using units from old AEC vehicles. These became CO201-240. There was one created as a 39-seat bus, SO67. Then 19 more followed in 1952, CO241-259, using Leyland TD4 running units, then 12 shorter 26-seat versions, CO260-271. The last three arrived in 1954, CO301-3, these using Leyland Tiger TS7 running units.

The coaches were allocated all round the company and could be seen on express services, day tours and private hire duties. Subsequently, when new and better underfloor-engined AEC Reliance coaches joined the fleet in large numbers, all the AEC-based Beadle coaches and Leyland CO241 were converted to 39-seat buses in 1954 and 1955 and repainted into the bus livery, becoming SO69-110.

There were further Beadle rebuilds in 1955/6, and the interesting story of these is told on pages 60-61.

Converted to a 39-seat bus in 1954, SO89 was here in Maidstone Mill Street bus station waiting to leave on the 61, which only took 17 minutes to get to Bearsted. The route was converted to one-man operation on 3 May 1959.
MICHAEL DRYHURST

the ones that went to Yorkshire

A total of eight Guy Arab IIs with 6-cylinder Gardner 6LW engines and Weymann utility bodies got sent to Yorkshire Woollen District at Dewsbury in the first few months of 1945.

DH25, 26 and 28 had been new to Maidstone & District in 1943, and DH29 and 61-64 in 1944. Like many of the M&D wartime buses, with Yorkshire Woollen they all got rebodied, in this case by Roe. Here are their new fleetnumbers and when they were rebodied.

DH25	Yorkshire Woollen	506	rebodied	1953	withdrawn 1967
DH26	Yorkshire Woollen	507	rebodied	1956	withdrawn 1965
DH28	Yorkshire Woollen	508	rebodied	1953	withdrawn 1967
DH29	Yorkshire Woollen	510	rebodied	1953	withdrawn 1965
DH61	Yorkshire Woollen	509	rebodied	1952	withdrawn 1967
DH62	Yorkshire Woollen	511	rebodied	1955	withdrawn 1967
DH63	Yorkshire Woollen	512	rebodied	1953	withdrawn 1965
DH64	Yorkshire Woollen	513	rebodied	1954	withdrawn 1965

511 was later renumbered 34

An extra five Arab IIs with Gardner 6LW engines and Weymann utility bodies were intended for Maidstone & District in 1944, but instead these also went to Yorkshire Woollen as its 498-502 and similarly were rebodied by Roe in the early 1950s. Some were also renumbered.

Eight Daimler CWA6s, which had been allocated to Yorkshire Woollen by the Ministry, were intended to go to Maidstone & District in exchange for the eight Arabs listed above, and five more Daimlers in exchange for the other five Arabs just mentioned that never went to M&D. In the end, only six Daimlers appeared in exchange in 1945, these being DH45-50.

At the top of this page is former DH25 with Yorkshire Woollen but still with its original Weymann utility body, and to the left is former DH26 carrying the new Roe body it acquired in 1956. Former DH61 in the picture below was rebodied by Roe slightly earlier, in 1952. Note the window to illuminate the staircase better. The top picture was taken by Alan Cross. The photographers of the others are not recorded.

Of the wartime double-deck deliveries listed in the table on page 17, a handful of Guy Arab buses got sent north to Yorkshire during the final months of the Second World War in 1945 to work for Yorkshire Woollen District.

the last front-engined double deckers of the 1950s

With Bristol chassis no longer on the open market, (being nationalised, it could only sell to other state-owned companies), Maidstone & District turned initially to the Leyland Titan, then the AEC Regent.

Leyland double-deck back in favour

When the upgraded Leyland Titan PD2 was announced in 1951, the British Electric Traction group began to order chassis for its subsidiary companies. Quite common in many BET company fleets up and down the country was this chassis with the nicely-proportioned Leyland built body. Maidstone & District took delivery of 41 of these handsome beasts in 1951 to PD2/12 specification with 58-seat highbridge bodies, DH379-419, although five of them, DH415-419, were PD2/3 types with 56-seat bodies and believed to be originally intended for another operator. A further 12 had 55-seat lowbridge bodies, DL23-34.

M&D's PD2 chassis had the Leyland O.600 engine rated at 125bhp at 1,800rpm, and a synchromesh gearbox with vacuum brakes. All of the chassis were 8ft wide but the PD2/3s had a slightly shorter wheelbase. Also, these five buses had half-drop windows in place of the company's standard sliders.

Leyland's body was tapered at the cab to give a width of 7ft 6ins; for Leyland this avoided having separate front end jigs for the two widths of bodies, 7ft 6in and 8ft. Maidstone & District's Titan PD2s were to become the mainstay of the longer services, with many achieving very high mileages during their time with M&D. DH380 was exhibited at the Festival of Britain on London's South Bank in 1951. The highbridge Leylands were allocated to Ashford, Faversham, Hawkhurst, Maidstone, Sittingbourne, Tenterden and Tunbridge Wells. During 1954 most had rear platform doors fitted. The lowbridge ones were sent to Hawkhurst, Maidstone, Tenterden and Tunbridge Wells.

Parked at Whiffens Avenue car park above Chatham Town Hall was DH417, one of the five PD2/3s. It shows the well-proportioned lines of the Leyland body and also how half-drop windows could show wear and tear after a while.
CLASSIC BUS COLLECTION

DH436 on the right was one of the 1953 Weymann Orion bodied Leyland Titans, here in April 1967 in Maidstone Mill Street bus station about to leave on route 10 to Folkestone, a journey that took two hours and was run jointly with East Kent.
JULIAN BOWDEN

In December 1951 OKM 317, an AEC Regent III with a London RT-style Saunders 56-seat highbridge body, was with Maidstone & District on demonstration. It was given fleetnumber DH500 and stayed until March 1952.

This bus operated from Tunbridge Wells depot and in the photograph below it was on local route 98 from Tunbridge Wells Ramslye Estate to Tonbridge Cage Green.

It was then bought by AA Motor Services' member Charles Law of Prestwick, and subsequently passed to Dodd's of Troon in 1953. Amazingly, this bus stayed in service until July 1979 and was then preserved.
M&D AND EAST KENT BUS CLUB

The last front-engined Leyland double-deckers bought by M&D were 20 more PD2/12s with Weymann Orion 58-seat bodies delivered in 1953, DH420-439, These had similar bodies to some of the final rebodied Bristols and the new Guy Arabs of Chatham & District. Unlike the cab doors on the Leyland bodied Titans, which were hinged, these slid open. Although delivered with open platforms, platform doors were added in 1958/9. Like the Leyland bodied buses these were also used on the longer services, the first going into service at Faversham, Maidstone, Tunbridge Wells and Hawkhurst.

back to AEC

An AEC Regent III demonstrator with a Saunders-Roe 56-seat body had been on loan to Maidstone & District between December 1951 and March 1952, running out of Tunbridge Wells depot. As we've seen, M&D was buying Leyland Titans then for its new double decks but in 1956 a switch was made to AEC. There had been 22 more Leyland Titan PD2/12s on order but in March 1955 that order was changed to AEC for the same number of chassis. The AEC Regent V MD3RV with a Park Royal body was specified. It's believed this came about because general manager Percy Graefe had retired at the end of 1954, to be replaced by William Dravers. Dravers had come from fellow BET company South Wales Transport, and South Wales had been a loyal AEC buyer.

There were 14 with highbridge bodies seating 59, DH476-89, and eight lowbridge versions seating 56, DL35-42, all with platform doors from new. The MD3RV Regent was a lightweight chassis with vacuum brakes and AEC's AV470 7.68-litre engine rated at 103bhp at 1,800rpm coupled to a 4-speed synchromesh gearbox.

With a concealed radiator behind an imposing AEC grille and a well-proportioned, modern-looking Park Royal body, these buses did look smart in M&D's livery. Seven of the highbridge Regents went to Hastings, one to Bexhill, three to Maidstone and three to Gravesend. The lowbridge examples were split between Tunbridge Wells, Ashford, Tenterden and Hawkhurst, essentially for the long cross-country 97 route.

Between the last Titans and these Regents, in 1955 eight Guy Arabs intended for the Chatham & District subsidiary instead entered the M&D fleet, the result of Chatham & District being absorbed into M&D - see page 106.

Three years later a whole new type of double decker appeared in the fleet, but you'll need to turn to page 80 to read all about that.

The 119 and 122 routes down to Brighton could get very busy during the summer months. In the top picture on the right AEC Regent V DH480 was loading with passengers in Pool Valley in Brighton ready for the long return journey to Lewes, Uckfield, Tunbridge Wells, Tonbridge, Borough Green and Gravesend.
M&D AND EAST KENT BUS CLUB

AEC Regent V DH478 had just unloaded its passengers in Canterbury bus station in the picture on the right, with the blind already turned ready for its return to Maidstone, a journey of 1 hour 25 minutes. The 67 was run jointly with East Kent - see page 165.
M&D AND EAST KENT BUS CLUB

Gillingham depot was rebuilt during the Second World War after being badly damaged by bombs - see page 102. Poking out of it in the picture below was Regent V 5484, which began life as DH484.
THE BUS ARCHIVE/ROY MARSHALL

the post-war single-deck story...

and spread of one-man operation

Following the 1930 Road Traffic Act, one-man operation was restricted to buses with no more than 20 seats or, under certain conditions, 26. Before the Second World War Maidstone & District had taken over several small operators that ran one-man operated buses, although not all of these acquired buses continued in service with M&D. The only one-man buses the company bought new before the war were 12 Dennis Aces in 1934, 750-761, and these were used on routes like the 31 between Hawkhurst and Rye and the 48 between Bexhill Gold Club and Hooe.

Although after the war Maidstone & District did buy four new 20-seat one-man Dennis Falcons in 1950 for Tonbridge area routes 130/1/2, routes acquired from Ashline, its early post-war single deckers were initially 32 Beadle bodied AEC Regals seating 36 in 1946/7, followed by 16 ECW bodied Bristol L6A 35-seaters in 1949/50, and later in 1950 more ECW bodied Bristols, this time 1 longer LL6A and 14 LL5Gs, all with 39 seats.

Before the company's initial foray into underfloor-engined buses with SO68, a solitary Saunders-Roe integral in 1953, its next single-deck bus was SO67 delivered in 1951, one of the Beadle chassisless vehicles using pre-war double-deck running units but fitted out as a 39-seat bus.

When the legislation changed in 1955 to allow buses with seats up to 45 to be one-man operated, Maidstone & District was quick to respond to the challenge. The company had a high proportion of rural services, and on some the revenue did not even cover the crew costs. M&D was using profits from the urban routes in the Medway Towns, Hastings, Tunbridge Wells and Gravesend to subsidise rural routes. And of course there were other changes that were beginning to affect bus operation - for example, car ownership was growing and the new medium of television meant that people were beginning to travel less than in the past to cinemas and local theatres in the evenings.

Later, in 1961, General Manager Mr A J White was interviewed by the trade press and stated that if M&D had not gone to one-man operation on its rural routes it would have had to cut the mileage by 14.2% to save costs. By 1961 the company had 25% of its stage mileage operated by one-man buses, which equated to 20% of its routes. The annual stage carriage mileage of the company then was 22,870,000, with contracts accounting for a further 1,270,000 miles.

In the big picture opposite, ECW bodied Bristol L6A SO45 was waiting its next turn on Hastings local route 153.
JEREMY WILLIAMS COLLECTION

Above, Beadle bodied AEC Regal SO8 was loading up in Tunbridge Wells for the run out to Wadhurst on the 78. These buses were the company's first post-war single-deck bus purchases in 1946/7. Three of them were converted to open-top in 1957/8 to replace similarly de-roofed Dennis Aces on the Hastings Round the Town Tour.
SURFLEET

It must have been a hot day on the far left as the driver of S053 had his windscreen open. This 30ft Bristol LL5G was working the Tonbridge local route 100 between Trench Wood Estate and Dowgates Close.
OMNICOLOUR

In 1950 four Dennis Falcons with Dennis 20-seat bodies were bought, mainly for the local bus services taken over from Ashline in Tonbridge. On the left was TS3 in Tonbridge.
DAVID TOY COLLECTION

The first concerted move into this new world of one-man buses was on 14 September 1955, when the 47 (Gravesend-Higham-Cliffe), 102 (Tenterden-Wittersham-Rye) and 111 (Gravesend-Chalk-Shorne Ridgeway) went over to one-man operation. To run these routes the company bought its first vehicles designed specifically for OMO, but they were an unusual choice, 42-seat Harrington/Commer integrals. There were 11 of them, SO200-10. Their Rootes TS3 horizontally-opposed 2-stroke 3.26-litre engines developed 105bhp at 2,400rpm. These engines had three cylinders with two opposed pistons in each cylinder; a supercharger was also fitted.

The driver's cab was accessed from the outside through a sliding door. There was a 2-piece destination screen. These green buses had a cream roof and a cream band at waist level and, soon to be standard, the distinctive cream 'moustache' below the windscreen. Although launched in a blaze of publicity, they were not to be the most reliable of buses, being very underpowered on hills. Ticket machines were a mixture of the new Almex and the older Setright. These Harrington/Commers were allocated to the following depots: SO200/01 (Gravesend), 202 (Tenterden), 203-8 (Tunbridge Wells) and 209/10 (Edenbridge). The next one-man conversions in October 1955 were at Tunbridge Wells, involving the 78 to Wadhurst, 90 to Crowborough, 94 to Burwash and the 110 to Mayfield.

On the right you can see how one-man operation was flagged up in timetable books by the company.

The first underfloor-engined buses bought specifically for one-man operated services were 10 Harrington/Commer T48Bs. These had Commer horizontally-opposed 3-cylinder TS3 engines and seats for 42.

Tunbridge Wells had five of this batch allocated, and SO207 on the left was photographed in the original livery with a cream roof. Note the driver's sliding cab door which for M&D was only specified for this batch.

Route 80 from Tunbridge Wells to Hawkhust or Hurst Green was converted to one-man in June 1957. The complete journey took just under an hour.
M&D AND EAST KENT BUS CLUB

It is believed that Maidstone & District was involved with the design and development of the Saunders-Roe integral single-deck bus, although SO68, delivered to the company in 1953 as its first underfloor-engined bus, remained a one-off in the fleet. It had a Gardner 5HLW engine and seated 43.

SO68 was converted to be able to run as a one-man bus in April 1956 and sent to Rye to work on route 31 to Hawkhurst in June. A year later it was sent to Tunbridge Wells, where in the picture at the bottom of this page it was showing clearly the small illuminated PAY AS YOU ENTER notice on the front and the larger illuminated rectangular one on the side.
SOUTHDOWN ENTHUSIASTS' CLUB

On ONE MAN Operated Buses, Pay Driver as you Enter, and Tender Exact Fare whenever possible

On the left was S205 on the 150 in Penshurst. It was working out of Tunbridge Wells depot in its revised livery in the early 1960s. This bus was withdrawn in 1965.

Penshurst was also served by the 93 but that went via Bidborough and continued through Four Elms to Edenbridge.

OMNICOLOUR

As there was no conductor to help people with pushchairs climb on to one-man buses, for a while the company offered a free push chair loan scheme for bona fide passengers travelling on a one-man bus.

Amazing that if you wanted to book one in advance you had to first send a postcard!

To help customers get used to paying the driver, these vehicles had a round PAY AS YOU ENTER disc behind the entrance at waist level. Later, a second disc was placed on the nearside front of the bus. These were soon superseded by the panels on the front and nearside as shown above.

Any service operated by OMO buses was identified as such in timetables, and passengers were asked to have the correct fare ready. A problem that arose was reversing at remote destinations. If a crew-operated bus had to reverse to turn round, the conductor assisted to ensure that all was clear at the rear. An audible and visual warning was fitted to these OMO buses when reverse gear was engaged, with an isolation switch so the horn could be turned off in urban areas at night.

The remaining OMO conversions in 1955 were at Edenbridge with the 135 and 137 (see page 136), followed by the 96 at Tunbridge Wells. To convert the 31 Hawkhust to Rye back to OMO as it once had been, SO68, the one-off Saunders Roe integral, was converted to OMO in 1956.

PUSH CHAIRS ON LOAN

A number of Push Chairs are available for loan without payment or deposit at the following places.

MAIDSTONE — — Omnibus Station
TUN. WELLS — — Opera House
TONBRIDGE — — Quarry Hill Road, Booking Office
HASTINGS — — Wellington Square
BEXHILL — — Marina
SHEERNESS — — Bus Station
GRAVESEND — — Overcliffe, Booking Office

The Push Chairs are available between the hours of 8.0 a.m. and 5.0 p.m. (except Hastings and Bexhill which will be between 9.0 a.m. and 5.0 p.m.) to passengers presenting a valid ticket issued on a "PAY AS YOU ENTER" bus for a journey on the day that the push chair is required.

Passengers requiring to reserve a push chair may do so by postcard to:— District Superintendent, Maidstone & District Motor Services Ltd. at the above Stations or Offices.

For further details apply to the Inspectors on duty.

SO68, on the right, was again working from Tunbridge Wells depot, but this time as a crew-operated bus before it was converted to OMO. It was on the 91 between Pembury, Tunbridge Wells and East Grinstead, a route more usually operated with lowbridge double deckers.

Note no cream 'moustache' on SO68 when first delivered.

M&D AND EAST KENT BUS CLUB

Maidstone based S214, a 1956 AEC Reliance with a Weymann body was photographed on a 25 working at Wrotham in April 1962 in the picture on the left. The 25 from Maidstone to Borough Green had been one-man operated since March 1959.
OMNICOLOUR

The 9, normally a lowbridge double-deck route, was a quicker and more frequent connection between Maidstone and Borough Green and continued to Sevenoaks.

Possibly having done a relief working, another Weymann bodied Reliance, 3211, was parked on Borough Green depot forecourt in the picture at the bottom of this page.
JEREMY WILLIAMS COLLECTION

On the opposite page is a typical Kent scene with characteristic oasthouses south east of Maidstone.

Beadle bodied Reliance S236 was on its way to Yalding, though some journeys continued beyond the village to Laddingford or Horsmonden.
OMNICOLOUR

During 1957 29 more of the company's routes were converted to OMO: four at Ashford, Tunbridge Wells and Tenterden, two at Gravesend, six at Faversham, eight at Maidstone, and one at Gillingham. To operate these M&D turned to the AEC Reliance, which then became the standard single-deck chassis for the next decade. Between December 1956 and January 1957 SO211-222 were delivered and carried Weymann 42-seat bodies. These 12 Reliances were the MU3RV version, with vacuum brakes and an AEC AH410 engine rated at 98bhp at 2,000rpm, although it was found very early on that the 410 engine meant the Reliance was underpowered. The Weymann body had no driver's external door, entrance to the cab being from inside the saloon. These were delivered in green with a cream waistband and cream 'moustache' like the earlier one-man saloons but above the windows the arced cant panel was cream this time and the rest of the roof green. The Harrington/Commers got repainted into the same style later on, as shown on the previous page.

A second batch of 17 AEC Reliances was delivered later in 1957, SO223-239, with the same chassis but this time with 42-seat bodies built by Beadle. Nine were allocated to Tunbridge Wells, eight to Maidstone, three to Ashford, two each to Tenterden, Gillingham, Faversham and Edenbridge, and one to Hawkhust. In 1958 a further 21 routes were converted to OMO, including some of the longer routes: the 40, which went from Gravesend to Sheerness in summer (some journeys starting at Dartford), but only from Chatham in winter, the 41 from Maidstone to Sheerness, the 3 from Maidstone to Faversham and the 11 from Oare and Faversham to Ashford. The 99 Hastings to Eastbourne during the winter went over to one-man operation but during the summer months it reverted to crew operation with double deckers due to the heavy loadings.

Parked at Maidstone on the right was S239, one of the Beadle bodied AEC Reliance buses. The 33 between Maidstone and Tunbridge Wells via East Peckham was not converted to one-man until September 1960.

Next to it was a Southdown Leyland Tiger Cub with a Beadle coach body on a day trip that had stopped at Maidstone.
DAVID TOY COLLECTION

Within the 1958 programme six routes operated by Borough Green were converted to one-man operation. More vehicles were required for these and 25 more AEC Reliances were delivered in 1958. These had Harrington 42-seat bodies and were numbered SO240-264.

These most recent AEC Reliances replaced the last of the front-entrance AEC Regal buses and the first of the Beadle rebuilds. One-man operation was now well spread around the company and by the end of 1958 the company had one of the highest proportions of one-man services in the country.

In October 1958 an Albion Nimbus NS3N demonstrator with Willowbrook 31-seat body, 143 SMG, was tried in service for a month. Tunbridge Wells local route 89 to Molyneux Park was used to test this bus, so it became a temporary one-man operation for which CO303 had also been converted to one-man operation.

In the summer months it wasn't unusual to see ordinary buses on the company's express service to London, mostly as duplicates, including even the rear-entrance Bristol L6As. The scheduled time of nearly two hours for Maidstone and Medway Towns to London could take a lot longer with the summer traffic and, quite frankly, standard bus seating did not give the best impression of the company's express services.

Meanwhile, the first rather boxy BET Federation standard body design for service buses had begun to appear and Maidstone & District took 20 of these in 1959, all on AEC Reliance chassis. 19 were the company's now standard vacuum brake 2MU3RV model, SO265-283, while SO284 was a 2MU3RA model with air brakes.

Bodies for these were built by Park Royal, but to make them more suitable when used for express service reliefs, 40 dual-purpose, high-back seats were specified. The now more obvious destination box jutting out from the rounded front dome was claimed to make it easer for passengers to read at bus stops. Strangely, the front cream 'moustache' had quite a dip to its shape, unique to this batch of BET-style buses (see page 162). The PAY AS YOU ENTER illuminated sign above the front nearside wheelarch could be changed to EXPRESS SERVICE when needed. Tunbridge Wells, Gravesend and Borough Green got three each of these buses, seven went to Maidstone and one each to Sheerness, Hastings, Sittingbourne and Tenterden. Seven more routes were converted in 1959.

Delivery of these new single-deck buses enabled the withdrawal in 1958 and 1959 of AEC Regent IIIs from Tunbridge Wells and the first of the Bristol K6As and Daimler CWA6s.

In the picture above, Harrington bodied AEC Reliance 3242 was close to Tunbridge Wells Central station, having come in from Maidstone on the hourly 33 via Paddock Wood and Pembury.

Behind the bus on the opposite side of the crossroads was Weeke's department store, later Hooper's.
RAY STENNING

In October and November 1958 M&D had this Albion Nimbus on the left on loan to test its possible suitability for one-man use on low capacity routes.

The bus worked from Tunbridge Wells depot on the 89 between Tunbridge Wells West station and Molyneux Park.
M&D AND EAST KENT BUS CLUB

On the right you can see the very narrow entrance on the 30ft standard BET single-decker and the high steps to the platform. This was Weymann bodied S0339 first allocated to Sheerness depot.
M&D AND EAST KENT BUS CLUB

In peak summer weekends the E19 from London to the Leysdown holiday camps was very busy with over 60 vehicles needed. M&D would hire in independent operators but also re-allocated double deckers to garages that could release single-deck and dual purpose buses. Gravesend based Commer/Harrington SO200 in the picture at the far right was the 43rd coach on the service that day. It shows the PAY AS YOU ENTER sign changed to EXPRESS SERVICE.
DAVID TOY COLLECTION

Below is S296, one of the Weymann bodied Reliances, at the Cooling terminus of the 112 route from Gillingham, showing the squared-off lines of the BET-style body. There are now houses where the bus was standing.
MIKE HODGES

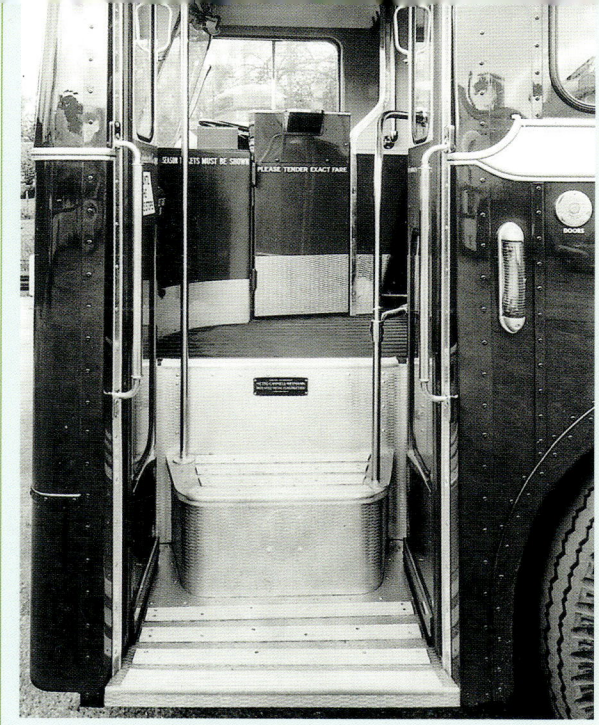

In 1960 only six routes switched to one-man operation, including three longer ones - 6: Maidstone-Goudhurst-Hawkhurst/Kilndown from Maidstone and Hawkhurst depots (some journeys on the 6 had been OMO since 1957), 33: Tunbridge Wells-East Peckham-Maidstone (cut back from Gillingham) operated from both ends, and 84: Tunbridge Wells-Hawkhurst-Hastings operated by Tunbridge Wells, Hawkhurst and Hastings. There were also two routes in Sittingbourne and the Hastings to Rye route 30 operated by Rye depot.

In 1960 20 more dual-purpose seated, early BET-style bodied AEC Reliance 2MU3RVs were bought, SO285-304, although this time Weymann built the bodies and they had the larger 7.68-litre AH 470 engine with an output of 112bhp at 2,000rpm. This became the standard engine for the next three batches of Reliance buses.

The 94 was an early conversion, becoming one-man in October 1955, but it was a prime candidate for Nimbus operation when the type was introduced.

Tunbridge Wells depot's Nimbus 3312 on the opposite page was heading down Mount Pleasant Road in 'The Wells' in 1967, passing the impressive Great Hall built in the French Empire style in 1872.

3312 was on an afternoon through journey to Burwash. As you can see from the timetable there were only two through journeys a day in 1965; mostly you had to change in Wadhurst.
RAY STENNING

Hastings local circular route 155 became one-man in September 1962, along with four other local routes, and all Nimbus buses except S317 were moved to Hastings and Silverhill depots to allow this, but this was only for a year as we shall see on the next page.

S315 was photographed in Cambridge Road in the picture on the right.
JEREMY WILLIAMS COLLECTION

The 53 West Malling local route was one-man operated from March 1958. Borough Green's SO309 was waiting in West Malling's High Street in the picture below.
M&D AND EAST KENT BUS CLUB

For services that required less seating and operating where there were awkward town streets or narrow country lanes, following the demonstrator mentioned on page 36 Maidstone & District decided to buy a batch of 15 Albion Nimbus NS3Ns in 1960, SO305-319. These had Albion's 4-cylinder engine rated at 72bhp at 2,400rpm. The wheelbase was only 11ft 10ins and their neatly-styled Harrington bodies, not too dissimilar from the 30ft BET look, seated 30.

Inside were luggage racks and an opening roof vent. Seven were allocated to Tunbridge Wells, four to Hastings and one each to Borough Green, Gillingham, Sittingbourne and Rye. They were moved around subsequently, as we shall see. For example, when Tonbridge depot opened on 1 January 1961, SO307/8 moved there from Tunbridge Wells, and another went to Edenbridge.

Another 31 AEC Reliances with Weymann 40-seat dual-purpose bodies followed in 1961/2, S320-350, and this large intake of buses allowed the last Bristol L6As and LL5Gs to be withdrawn from the fleet. From the summer of 1961 single-deck fleet classification was changed to just **S**, dropping the **O** for oil engine, and similarly coaches became classified **C** instead of **CO**.

Increase in one-man operation continued with four routes in the Medway towns being converted in 1961. These were the infrequent 42 from Gillingham to Meopham, the 112 to Cooling and 113 Lower Higham out on the Isle of Grain, these last two initially Albion Nimbus operated, and lastly the 70 from Chatham, Rochester and Strood to Upnor.

The following year saw nine more routes converted, including the 29 from Maidstone to Chatham via Aylesford run by both Maidstone and Chatham depots. This route is featured on page 190. Five routes were converted in the Hastings/Bexhill area - 72/74/134/155/161 - for which all except one of the Albion Nimbuses were drafted to Hastings or Silverhill depots. From 30 September two routes were partly converted: the Faversham workings of the 26 to Gravesend and at Sheerness the 52 Rushenden to Shellbeach.

Conversion to one-man operation wasn't always the exact science it was supposed to be. If a one-man bus wasn't available, then a crew would be sent out on a supposed one-man route with a crew-operated bus.

39

The last of M&D's BET-style flat-fronted AEC Reliances were specially built to operate in the Hastings town area. The Albion Nimbus buses drafted in (mentioned on the previous page), although highly manoeuvrable, were too small to give adequate capacity on the routes they ran on. Also, the Nimbuses had problems climbing Castle Hill with a full load; neither were they proving to be the best in terms of reliability.

These ten 2MU2RA Reliances, S190-199, were delivered in 1963 and had monocontrol transmission and air brakes. But what really stood them apart from earlier BET-style deliveries was their Harrington 42-seat bodies which were only 7ft 6ins wide and better able to cope with the very narrow roads in the old town. Although still the basic BET standard design, a number of subtle styling features gave them a more satisfying appearance. For a start there was a subtle but noticeable taper inwards to the skirt panels, which also finished lower and therefore didn't have any guard rail. Foglights were also set into neat recesses.

The two pictures on this page show S191, one of the narrow Harrington bodied AEC Reliances delivered in 1963 for use in routes through the Old Town in Hastings. These buses had route number boxes in the rear dome.

The view on the left in particular shows the awkwardness of some the roads and the hills these buses needed to climb.

M&D AND EAST KENT BUS CLUB

On the 134 Fairlight Glen service, 7ft 6in wide Harrington bodied AEC Reliance 3690 was on the sea front at Hastings in the picture on the left.

In the background perched at the top of the cliff are the ruins of Hastings Castle. This is all that remains of a stone fortress built after William of Normandy's coronation in 1066. Less than half of the original structure remains

During the Second World War an anti-aircraft gun was placed alongside the castle and the steep cliffs were used as a training area for commandos.

GEOFFREY MORANT
courtesy of Richard Morant

rebuilding Harrington Wayfarer IV coaches for one-man bus operation

An interesting part of the story of Maidstone & District's post-war single-deck buses and its quest to convert more and more routes to one-man operation was the strange decision to rebuild a number of mid-life Harrington Wayfarer IV bodied AEC Reliance coaches to make them more suitable for such work in 1963.

Their story is dealt with on page 68, but in the upper picture from the M&D and East Kent Bus Club archive you can see how C394 was being turned into SC394 at Thomas Harrington's factory in Hove, Sussex. The new bus front section was on but awaiting final painting. This was one of the first batch of 10, C390-399.

The lower picture from Jeremy Williams' collection shows SC404, one of the second batch of 10, C400-409, that were rebuilt in 1965. These had this style of lower single line destination box, although this particular conversion, strangely, didn't have the PAY AS YOU ENTER illuminated sign on the front panel. SC404 was initially delivered to Silverhill depot.

Maidstone & District's first 36ft long bus was S1 and was exhibited at the 1962 Commercial Motor Show in London. During the first few months of service with the company it was sent round to be tried out at several depots.

While working out of Sheerness depot, it was caught by the photographer in Gillingham bus station on the left on the 40 route on its way from Gravesend to Sheerness.

You can see it was quite a steep climb up to the saloon floor.
M&D AND EAST KENT BUS CLUB

In 1961 legislation was changed to allow single-deck buses and coaches to be up to 36ft long (11 metres) and 8ft 2½ins wide (2.5 metres) and it wasn't long before manufacturers were producing longer chassis and bodybuilders designing coachwork to fit. At the time the extra six feet made vehicles to the new length look inordinately long and many operators and highway authorities voiced concerns about the suitability or otherwise of vehicles of this length, particularly in older towns and along narrow rural roads.

A new single-deck bus body was developed by the BET Group and this matured quite quickly into a thoroughly modern and rather stylish design that was soon to be seen the length and breadth of the country.

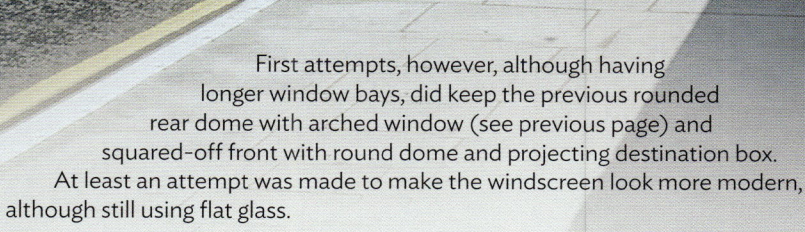

Dual-purpose SC55 was coming down Mill Street passing Maidstone's first bus station in the picture on the right. It was one of 20 AEC Reliance 590s with a very smart Weymann BET-style bodywork, especially thanks to twin headlights and brightwork beading and grille. Note there was no traditional 'moustache' under the windscreen.

These entered service in early 1965 and were used on all aspects of the company's operations, a common one being the E3 from Tenterden, Headcorn and Maidstone to London.
GEOFFREY MORANT
courtesy of Richard Morant

S10 was one of the 1965 batch of 36ft Reliances, photographed on the left on a wet Saturday in Maidstone when it was still quite new.

These later ones had one sliding opening toplight added to the window above the fleetname on both sides, rather spoiling the clean window line but, presumably, highly necessary.

You can compare the modern look presented by these buses with the older squarer BET-style single-deck body on the right of it and perhaps over-curvaceous Beadle design to the left.
RAY STENNING

First attempts, however, although having longer window bays, did keep the previous rounded rear dome with arched window (see previous page) and squared-off front with round dome and projecting destination box. At least an attempt was made to make the windscreen look more modern, although still using flat glass.

Maidstone & District's first 36ft long buses had this early type of body and were built by Willowbrook on AEC Reliance 2U3RA chassis. They had the AEC 590 engine with a 4-speed manual gearbox and air brakes. Vacuum brakes were no longer an option on the chassis and the company now standardized on air brakes. There were to be seven of them. S1 was built first and exhibited at the Commercial Motor Show in London's Earl's Court in 1962. This seated 54, but S2-5 that were delivered in September 1963 seated 53. Of course, this made them unsuitable for one-man operation, as legislation still only allowed a maximum of 45 seats for a one-man bus. What should have been S6 and S7, instead were painted mainly cream and had dual-purpose seats, entering service as SC31 and SC32. One of these is shown on page 67. In 1964 these two had their gearboxes replaced with ZF 6-speed units.

The revised BET-style 36ft single-deck body that appeared shortly afterwards was transformed in its appearance. It now looked extremely elegant and very contemporary. With curved front corners and double-curvature screens front and back, and the front and rear destination screens incorporated into neat, crisp, full-width identical peaked panels, it all looked part of a coherent whole, with no bits added on as previously.

The next 36ft single-decker buses in 1965 were 53-seaters to this new style built by Marshall of Cambridge, 20 more AEC Reliance 2U3RA, S6-25. Twelve were allocated to Sheerness, six to Tunbridge Wells and two to Maidstone. The next 20, also in 1965, had similar bodies by Weymann, S41-60. Four of this batch went to Tunbridge Wells, six to Tenterden, two to Hastings and three to Tonbridge. A single vehicle went to Maidstone for route 10 with East Kent providing one of its own new BET-style 36ft AEC Reliance too. In the following year 10 from this second batch were downseated to 45 to be used as one-man buses on the Heathfield Pool services - see page 168.

1965 was quite a landmark year for single-deck deliveries, for there were also another 20 AEC Reliances with similar BET-style bodywork, except that these were SC38-57 with 49 dual-purpose seats and finished in the dual-purpose livery of green skirt, cream main body section and green above the waist. What also set them apart were twin headlights and a rather splendid slightly V-shaped brightwork grille up front.

Eventually Maidstone & District was to have 95 Leyland Panthers. Of the first in 1965 with Willowbrook bodies, 11 were allocated to the Hastings area to release Leyland Atlanteans to other depots.

In their early days the majority were crew operated, like S29 in the picture on the left on the 151 route on Hastings sea front.
ADRIAN LEWES

Some of the Willowbrook bodied Leyland Panthers were delivered with seating for 45 so they could be used on one-man services.

Chatham based S93 below was a 45 seater photographed when new in 1967 on the 65A approaching Frinsbury on its way to Lower Halstow.
MIKE HODGES

In both these pictures you can see the lower driving position and how the top of the windscreen was lower than the top of the side windows (compare with the Reliances); also the slight dip of the roofline at the extreme front.

It was always intended that the 36ft single-deck fleet would be dual-sourced, and in 1965 15 of Leyland's new rear-engined Panther model were also delivered. These were PSUR1/1Rs with Leyland's O.600 engine rated at 125 bhp coupled to a 4-speed pneumocyclic gearbox. Their BET-style bodywork was built by Willowbrook, easily distinguishable by the larger square mesh grille for the front-mounted radiator and a slightly lower set windscreen and subsequent drop in roofline at the very front. S26-37 had 53 seats, but the last three, S38 and s39, had 45 seats from the outset, enabling them to be used as one-man buses.

Maidstone & District's general manager wanted an updated fleet in the Hastings area, so most of these were allocated to the Sussex coast garages - three to Hastings, four to Silverhill and four to Bexhill. The plan for the Hastings area was to use the Panthers on the lowbridge routes to release Atlanteans to other garages which, in turn, would start withdrawal of the 1951 lowbridge Leyland Titan PD2/12s. One of these new Panthers also went to Maidstone to operate on the 7 route, although later in the year it was transferred to Hastings. Of the three one-man buses, one each went to Tonbridge, Bexhill and Sheerness to trial one-man operation with longer vehicles.

As regards one-man operation, in 1964 only two routes were converted to OMO, Gillingham's 8 from Chatham (White Road) to Bredhurst and the 67 between Maidstone and Canterbury that was jointly run with East Kent (see page 164), but in 1965 there were no conversions at all. Interestingly, those first Commer/Harrington TS3 single-deck buses that had begun the mass conversion to one-man were withdrawn in 1965, having proved somewhat unreliable. Being a 2-stroke, the TS3 engine required extra maintenance when compared to 4-stroke counterparts. Oil technology at the time was not as good as it later became and the engines had to be de-carbonised at regular intervals. In 1966 the 57 between Maidstone, Rochester and Gravesend and the 23 Chatham-Cobham-Gravesend both became one-man operated, and three Silverhill operated routes in Hastings, the 72, 74 and 134, had their summer schedules switched to one-man.

Although M&D had now committed itself to the Leyland Panther in a big way for bus work, it still had more AEC Reliance dual-purpose vehicles delivered, taking 10 with Marshall BET-style bodies in 1966, SC73-82. Then in 1967 no less than 48 more Panthers arrived with similar Willowbrook bodywork as the 1965 examples. S61-80 seated 53 and were crew operated. Five each went to Tunbridge Wells and Gillingham, four each to Hastings and Chatham and one each to Sheerness and Bexhill. The remaining 30, S81-110 had 45-seat bodies for one-man duties and, after an initial settling-in period with a few moving around the depots, the allocation at the end of the year was seven at Chatham, six at Sheerness, two at Tonbridge, five at Tunbridge Wells, four at Tenterden, and three each at Maidstone and Sittingbourne.

With this intake of new buses more routes were converted to one-man during 1967.

Chatham
65 65A	Lower Halstow-Medway Towns-Lower Stoke-Grain
66	Strood (Brompton Farm Road)-Davis Estate
147	Strood (Brompton Farm Road)-Luton (Wagon-at-Hale)

Sheerness
36	to Minster and Eastchurch
37	to Queensway
54	to Queenborough and Rushenden
64 (Sat only)	to Harty

Sittingbourne
51	Kemsing-Snipeshill
124	Homewood Avenue-Murston

Maidstone
7	Maidstone-Hadlow-Tunbridge Wells (joint with Tunbridge Wells)
12	Maidstone-Tenterden-Hastings (joint with Tenterden)

Tunbridge Wells
87 87A	to Paddock Wood & Tonbridge (joint with Tonbridge)

Bexhill
121	Upper Barnhorn-Sidley
160	Bexhill-Mount Idol View

Above is the interior of Willowbrook bodied Leyland Panther S81 showing the gently ramped rising floor layout of these buses.

M&D AND EAST KENT BUS CLUB

S34 was new in September 1965 and below it was photographed the following year at the East Grinstead Station terminus of the 91 route worked by Tunbridge Wells depot. This Panther was was a 53-seater two-man bus at the time, being downseated to 45 seats and converted for one-man use in October 1968.

RAY STENNING

With a Leyland 0.600 engine coupled to a pneumocyclic gearbox, all the weight was at the rear of the Panther so, inevitably, body problems developed with movement over this area and the batch bodied by Strachan had to be rebuilt in the early 1970s. On its way to Battle in the picture on the right was 3140. This bus was withdrawn and sold in 1979.
DAVID TOY COLLECTION

Ten of the 1968 Strachans bodied Panthers were delivered with two doors, which exacerbated the rear end problems and these were rebuilt to singe door in 1973/4 by Willowbrook. Below in original condition was 3119, heading into town along the seafront at Hastings with the pier in the background.
THE BUS ARCHIVE/ROBIN HANNAY

In the small picture, with Hastings Castle in the background, 3113 was in Castle Hill Road on on the local 155 route.
DAVID TOY COLLECTION

There had been legislation since July 1966 for double-deck buses to be used for one-man operation. London Transport, for example, took advantage of this around that time when it experimented with running its Country Area XF-class Daimler Fleetlines one-man with the top deck chained off during the off-peak. Within large company fleets there had been resistance nationally to this by the trade unions, as well as resistance to any increase above 45 seats on a one-man single decker.

It was the municipal sector that had managed to get agreement early on, Brighton Corporation being the first to put one-man double deckers into service in 1966. Then in 1968 the government introduced a 25% bus grant on new buses that were suitable for one-man operation. Double deckers had to meet certain criteria. With this new incentive, agreement was reached nationally with the trade unions for one-man operation to be possible on all buses and coaches.

The Leyland Panthers Maidstone & District ordered for 1968 were bodied by Strachans, this time all suitable for one-man operation. The first 10 were 45-seaters with dual doors, 3111-3120, and the other 20 were 48-seat single-door versions, 3121-3140.

The new numbering was because in January 1968 M&D changed its fleetnumbering to do away with prefixes and instead use a straightforward number only system more suitable for computers.

The Strachans body, although largely conforming to the current BET-style, introduced a stepped waistrail with deeper windows towards the front. The screen was even lower set than the earlier Panthers and this did lead to a less elegant, heavier-looking front. These buses featured twin headlights and chrome bumpers, too.

All the 2-door buses were allocated to Silverhill and Hastings, the single door ones going to Hastings, Tunbridge Wells, Tenderden, Hawkhurst, Tonbridge, Maidstone and Ashford. Like some of the other rear-engined single-decker models hastily brought to market at that time, the Panther fleet developed serious body structure problems at the rear due to unfortunate cantilever action. The 10 with two doors had added problems around the centre door and in the 1970s the bodies on these Panthers needed to be rebuilt and all became single door.

Also entering the fleet in 1968 were 18 more dual-purpose single deckers, 2801-2818, but these were now on the Leyland Leopard PSU3A/4RT chassis. Their Willowbrook 49-seat bodies were similar to earlier dual-purpose BET-style single deckers but featured longer side windows (five instead of six) that were now standard for this body design. They were fitted out for one-man use during 1969.

Turning into White Rock from Robertson Street in the photo above was an unidentified 2-door Strachan bodied Panther on the 75 between St Helens and Crowhurst. The bumpers on these looked added-on, but this picture clearly shows the same-shaped but shallower double-curvature rear screen of this BET-style body design.
THE BUS ARCHIVE/ROBIN HANNAY

Below, in front of one of the Strachan bodied Panther buses in Hastings Coach Station by Hastings Cricket Ground - this is now all the Priory Meadow shopping centre - was one of the dual-purpose Leyland Leopards mentioned on this page trying to drum up business for an excursion to the Bluebell Railway.
GEOFFREY MORANT courtesy of Richard Morant

The 30 single-deck Daimler Fleetlines with Marshall 45-seat 2-door bodies were allocated to the Medway Towns garages. 3816 in the picture below was photographed by The Marquis of Lorne in Mill Road, Gillingham.
M&D AND EAST KENT BUS CLUB

For a week in June 1968 Halifax Corporation Willowbrook bodied Daimler Fleetline single decker 107 was on loan to M&D in the Medway towns. On a wet day below it was on the 144 Earl Estate to Chatham Military Road route worked by Luton depot.

Probably just to stamp his mark on things, Geoffrey Hilditch, then in charge at Halifax, insisted his BET-style single deckers had an old-fashioned rounded front dome with protruding destination box, making them look far less modern.
M&D AND EAST KENT BUS CLUB

There were more route conversions to one-man operation during 1968. The long route 5 from Maidstone to Hastings run by Maidstone, Hastings and Hawkhurst depots was converted in September 1968. In the same month Hastings local 75 and 151 were also converted and five routes in the Tunbridge Wells area, including duties operated by Tunbridge Wells and Hawkhurst on the 97 as far as Hawkhurst. October 1968 saw further conversions within the Medway Towns with Gillingham operated 17 from Hempstead to Cliffe, Chatham routes 144 to Earl Estate, 145 to Borstal and 146 to Cookham Wood.

In June 1968 the company had borrowed Halifax Corporation no. 107, a Daimler Fleetline SRG6LX with a Willowbrook 45-seat single door body. This bus was put to work in the Medway Towns for a week and this was enough to persuade M&D to buy 30 of its own single-deck Fleetlines, having of course double-deck Fleetlines in the fleet and thereby make economies with spare parts stock.

These Daimler Fleetline SRG6LX-36 types, 3801-3830, with Marshall 45-seat 2-door bodies became the last 36ft single-deckers to be delivered in Maidstone & District traditional livery. They were due to be delivered in 1969 but various delays meant they didn't enter service until 1970 when they were sent to the Medway Towns garages. Although to the standard BET design, inside they had leathercloth seat trim instead of the standard moquette.

In an attempt to modernise the livery a little, the scroll fleetname was moved forward to be over the front wheelarch.

3419, photographed on the left on the 84 passing through Ticehurst, was one of the first batch of short Leyland Leopard buses to enter the fleet in 1971. The Marshall bodywork on this first batch had such niceties as aluminium beading, twin headlights and chrome bumpers. The later batches didn't.
DAVID TOY COLLECTION

Below is 3419 from the same batch passing through Wadhurst on its way to Hastings, not exactly loaded to the gunwales.
SOUTHDOWN ENTHUSIASTS' CLUB

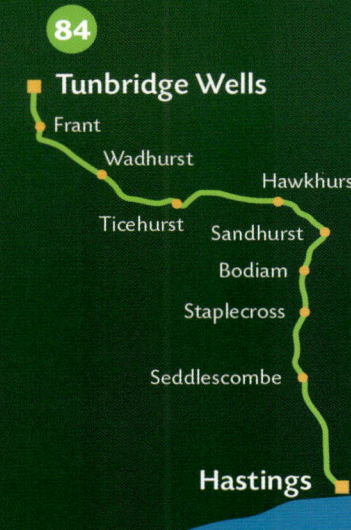

Within a few short years 12 were transferred to Northern General in exchange for double-deck Fleetlines, and the rest to closer fellow National Bus Company operators.

One-man operation continued to spread as the 1960s turned into the 1970s, including the 91 between Tonbridge, Tunbridge Wells and East Grinstead in November 1969 and the long 119/122 from Gravesend through Tunbridge Wells, Crowborough and Uckfield to Lewes and Brighton in January 1970.

The final 'traditional' Maidstone & District single-deck buses, before the Leyland National began its inexorable domination of National Bus Company operators, as Maidstone & District had now become, were no less than 75 short Leyland Leopards with BET-style 45-seat bodywork. The first 20 of these, 3401-3420, were PSU4A/4R models bodied by Marshall and these arrived in 1970. The next 20, 3421-3440, were PSU4A/2R versions bodied by Willowbrook. These were delivered in 1971, the only vehicles bought that year, but were stored and didn't enter service until 1972. The remaining 35 were PSU4B/4R versions, bodied by Marshall again, and these were delivered in 1972 and 1973.

As with the single-deck Fleetlines on the opposite page, these versions of the BET-style eliminated the horizontal moulding at the top of the windscreen that separated the windscreen recess from the destination screen recess and led to something of a 'surprised' look to the front. They also shared with the dual-purpose Leopards shown previously longer side windows - in this case, four and a half bays on these shorter buses.

Over the hills ... & far away

Like many companies within the BET Group, Maidstone & District was heavily involved in coaching.

It had a network of express services, an extensive programme of day excursions and touring holidays, and ran a busy private hire section.

Before deregulation of coaching in 1980, all express services, excursions and tours were regulated by the Area Traffic Commissioners, and a company had to register all services with the commissioners. The licence for an express service would have an agreed route (many of the licences were loosely worded to allow diversions round traffic black spots), picking up and setting down points, and a timetable. Where the service went into another traffic area, as most did, there was the requirement to have a backing licence in order to operate in that traffic area. Any changes to the service had to be agreed beforehand.

Licences for excursions and day tours were the same, giving details of the starting and picking up points, destinations and the routes followed, and fares. Extended (holiday) tours also needed a backing licence and the addition of local excursion licences. Objections could be made to a new or modified service by other operators and by British Railways at the traffic court. Organising and operating any of these services took up a vast amount of management time.

getting going after the war

Before the Second World War coaching activities had been increasing to become an important part of Maidstone & District's business, and the coach fleet had been growing in numbers. During the war, express services were suspended generally, but afterwards, when restrictions on travel had been lifted, the company was quick to get the London services shown on the map on the opposite page up and running again.

These were operated first by AEC Regal or Leyland Tiger TS7/8 coaches, pre-war and early post-war, and later the semi-chassisless coaches built by Beadle using pre-war AEC and Leyland running units.

37-seat Harrington Cavalier bodied AEC Reliances were bought in 1962 for extended tour duties, and didn't they look just gorgeous in Maidstone & District's elegant livery. Here on the Cornish coast, probably at Land's End, C24 had paused during a 6-day tour of the Cornish Riviera to let its clientele enjoy the rugged scenery. This cost £26/5/0 in 1966 with no fewer than 19 departure dates to choose from between late May and late September.
DAVID TOY COLLECTION

Maidstone & District was a loyal customer of bodywork built by Thomas Harrington of Hove, especially for coaches. The Leyland Tiger TS7 above was one of 20 carrying distictive Harrington coachwork delivered in 1936, here waiting to leave Maidstone Palace Avenue bus station on the London express service.

Note the lovely display board on the pavement alongside.
M&D AND EAST KENT BUS CLUB

At London's Victoria Coach Station in the picture below, nearest to us was CO579, another 1936 Leyland Tiger TS7 with its post-war Harrington 32-seat body. It was waiting to leave for Tunbridge Wells, parked alongside CO39, a Sheerness bound 1948 AEC Regal I with a Beadle 32-seat body. Note the full-length luggage container on the roof of the Tiger.
P M PHOTOGRAPHY

The Royal Sovereign was another way to get from London to the Thanet coast down the Thames Estuary. Above, passing London's docks, she was sailing near to her full capacity of 1,800 passengers.
CLEM RUTTER

By now numbered C110, the Harrington bodied AEC Regal on the left was leaving Gillingham depot on a relief express.

After the 1949 Regals, 37 in total, Maidstone & District turned to semi-chassisless Beadle coaches using withdrawn running units from older buses. Within three years the company was buying its first underfloor-engined coaches.
M&D AND EAST KENT BUS CLUB

Soon, summer services to coastal resorts were running again, too. By 1948 they were operating daily between June and late September as, after that long period of wartime travel restrictions, the population wanted to get out and about. Services in 1948, shown on the map at the bottom of this page, were publicised in the booklet also shown on this page.

These longer services would have been operated by the new AEC Regals coming into the fleet. All coastal services had a 5- or 10-minute comfort stop, normally about midway in the journey. There were 63 booking and enquiry offices to promote the company's coaching operations. This included sister companies' offices as well as local shops (mainly tobacconists and newsagents) and early travel agents.

In 1948 there was little alternative to the coach or train to get to the Kent coast, as car ownership was still very low. But more leisurely competition from Gravesend and the Medway towns in 1948 was provided by pleasure steamers. For example, Royal Daffodil (2,060 tons, 2,073 passengers) sailed from Gravesend pier with a fare to Margate of 10/6d return. She had a very fine restaurant on board but the time you could spend at Margate was short.

From the Medway Towns, getting on at Strood Pier, the paddle steamer Medway Queen (316 tons, 980 passengers) could take you to Herne Bay and back for 8/- and Margate for 10/-. However, on a day trip on the E11 to Margate you could have 6¾ hours at the resort before returning home, all for 7/-.

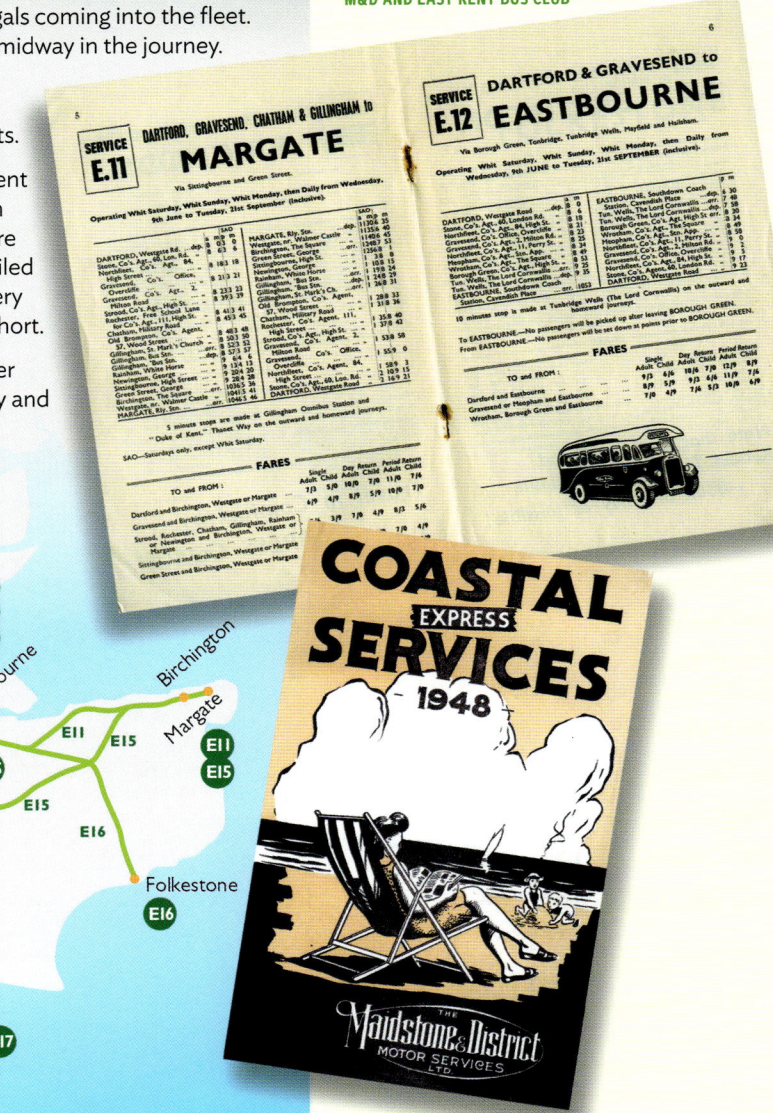

CO271 was a 26-seat Beadle semi-chassisless rebuild using running units from a 1939 Leyland Titan TD5 that was delivered in 1952 in Scout livery, which it kept until withdrawal in 1960.

In the picture on the right it was touting for business on a sunny day in Hastings, with chalk boards propped up against the side and an M&D inspector looking suspiciously at the photographer.

Neighbouring operators East Kent and Southdown had similar Beadle semi-chassisless coaches delivered around the same time. The upsurge in demand for new vehicles in the early post-war years meant chassis were in short supply, so using serviceable older chassis and running parts in a new body structure was a good way of getting 'new' coaches into the fleet quickly.

M&D AND EAST KENT BUS CLUB

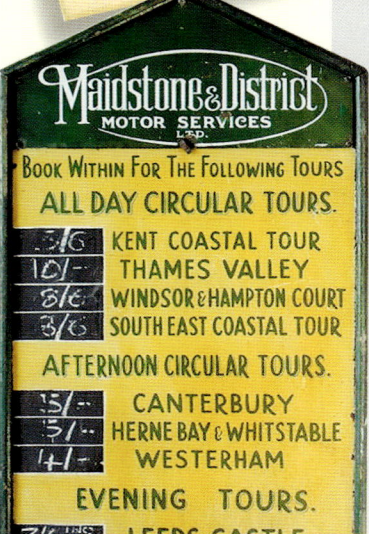

The commitment to coaching in the late 1940s can been seen by looking at the Hastings programme for coach tours in 1949. On a Sunday over 30 coaches were needed to cover the programme, and this would not have included the depot's commitment for the E4 London service with duplicates running as well as the normal service cars.

In 1948 the tours were split into All Day Tours, All Day Circular Tours, Afternoon Circular Tours and Morning and Evening Tours. Of the 48 tours, 26 operated daily except Saturday during the summer peak. The rest were worked on individual days. Sunday was the peak requirement.

The Saturday programme was limited to excursions to race meetings because so many coaches were needed for the express services. All Day Tours included Southampton for 14/-, Eastbourne 4/9d, Canterbury and Margate for 7/- and 10/6d. The Circular Tours had several stopping points. For example, the Kent and Sussex Tour for 10/- stopped at East Grinstead, Sevenoaks or Tunbridge Wells. The Circular Tour of Kent Coast Towns for 11/6d stopped at Ramsgate and Whitstable. Afternoon Circular Tours - 19 in total - had shorter stops and went to destinations such as Bodiam Castle & Rother Valley for 3/6d, Winchelsea & Rye also for 3/6d, and Heathfield 4/9d. 11 of them ran six days a week. Similar programmes were being operated from the majority of the main depots and were expanded as time went on.

Of course, in those days coaches were still limited to a maximum speed of 30mph which was reflected in the journey times. This was to change very little over the next decade. Coaching being very seasonal meant that the majority of the fleet was delicenced and stored during the winter months, although sufficient coaches were left to cover the express and private hire commitments, plus any excursions which were operated all year.

buying Scout

In May 1951 Maidstone & District bought Scout Motor Coaches of Hastings and took into the fleet four elderly coaches - three Bedford WTBs with Duple 25-seat bodies new in 1937/8 and a 1935 Dennis Mace. They were all withdrawn within two years but, to preserve the licences that were acquired with the company, a few coaches wore Scout livery. CO245, a Beadle/Leyland semi-chassisless coach, was painted into the red and cream Scout livery in 1953, although similar coaches CO271 in 1952 and CO301/2 in 1954 were delivered new in Scout livery.

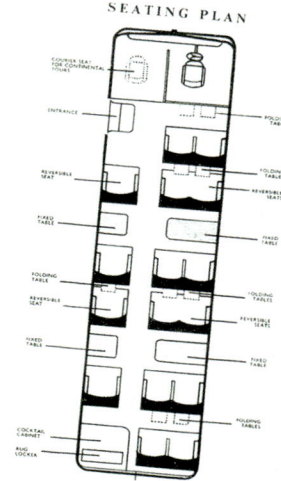

Much care and thought has gone into the design and construction of "The Knightrider" limousine in order to provide a service of the highest possible standard.

The driver, neatly attired in private chauffeur's uniform is proud of his vehicle and seeks to extend the same high standard of *personal* service. His driving ability, like that of all the company's drivers may be taken for granted, but apart from that you will find him a real help in carrying out your arrangements—knowledgeable, courteous and co-operative.

THE Maidstone and District Motor Services Ltd. present with pride "The Knightrider" limousine— an enterprise in design which overleaps the austerity years and regains the threads of progressive development which the events of 1939 so sadly interrupted.

It is conceived and built for the small private party (up to sixteen in number) to standards which can justifiably be described as unique.

Look through this brochure; critically examine "The Knightrider" features and we are confident you will agree that this is the ideal vehicle for the special occasion which demands something out of the ordinary in door to door passenger transport.

Better still, ask us for an appointment to inspect. Opportunity will be gladly afforded.

Bearing in mind the enhanced cost of construction and operation of this unique limousine you will naturally expect the rates of hire to be a little more than the standard rates for an ordinary coach but for the private party seeking perfection, the relatively small extra charge will reap a more than commensurate reward in prestige and luxury.

The Knightrider

An eight foot wide body seating sixteen passengers is mounted on a full thirty-two seater chassis with under-floor petrol engine for smooth running and quietness. The exterior is finished in a distinctive royal blue with only the name unobtrusively superimposed.

The vehicle looks what it is—a private limousine for the conveyance of sixteen passengers in the acme of comfort.

Included in the M. & D. Hire Service is

The Knightrider LIMOUSINE

Designed especially to provide the highest possible standard of luxury travel for private parties the Knightrider carries 16 persons in a body that normally seats 32. Thus plenty of room is available for the many unique features that earned for it the title in the American Press of "Most Luxurious of all."

• Unique Features

Armchair seats upholstered in Dunlopillo, some of which are reversible for seating a friendly foursome. Separate tables. Cocktail and Tea Cabinet with cocktail glasses, tumblers, cups and saucers, and vacuum flasks. Radio—four discreet loudspeakers. Communication by driver to passengers via loudspeakers. Air conditioning and demisting unit. Wide vision windows and roof lights. Sorbo rubber floor with pile carpet. Capacious luggage compartment. Seat for use of Courier on Continental Tours.

Maidstone & District produced an illustrated brochure to help promote The Knightrider for bespoke private hire, and advertised it in its timetable booklets.

Unfortunately, it wasn't a great success in that arena in those early post-war years, with not so much demand as there is today for top end coach hire, so one of its chief uses became ferrying the board of directors around to make head office visits to depots.

Above you can see the sumptuous 2+1 armchair seating and tables inside LC1, the Knightrider.

M&D AND EAST KENT BUS CLUB

On the right is The Knightrider gleaming in pristine condition.
DAVID TOY COLLECTION

In the lower picture it was on Madeira Drive in Brighton taking part in the British Coach Rally.
NA3T

The Knightrider

The company bought its most famous vehicle also in 1951 – LC1 *The Knightrider* (NKN 650), a petrol-engined Commer Avenger with a Harrington 16-seat body. The coach was built to a very high standard with sumptuous armchair seats, some reversible around tables and it even included a bar. The coach was painted a very dark blue and was intended to be used for exclusive private hire duties. Actually, it had rather limited use as such and became a coach used by the company directors for visits around their empire. LC1 has been in preservation for some time and can often be seen at bus rallies in the South of England.

On the left are pages from the brochure printed to extol the extremely de-luxe features of the coach and drum up business for it. Interestingly, it never carried the fleetnumber LC1 on the bodywork

The sharp, modern lines of the Leyland coach body, with its straight waist and lantern windscreen arrangement, are shown to good effect in this picture on the right of CO283 on an E23 express working from Sheerness and Gillingham.
M&D AND EAST KENT BUS CLUB

In the view below of fellow Leyland bodied Leyland Royal Tiger CO285, the sharp rake of the windscreen is clearly visible, along with the thrusting look of this style of body. The rolling tuck-under of the front apron enhances this dynamic. Some other operators had a less elegant vertical lower apron that rather ruined the efffect. A lot of the styling development of this model was done in collaboration with fellow BET company Ribble, which was based in Preston in Lancashire not far from the Leyland factory.
COLIN FROST

a new position for the engine

The last new front-engined AEC Regal III coaches were delivered in 1949 and, with the rebuilt semi-chassisless Beadle/AEC/Leyland entering service in 1950-52, these helped to boost the coaching fleet. The industry was now manufacturing underfloor-engined chassis and the BET Federation began to order chassis for its subsidiary companies. Leyland's new chassis was the Royal Tiger.

This had the new Leyland 9.8-litre O.600 engine with a rating of 125bhp at 1,800rpm and a 4-speed manual gearbox. The front axle was set back by 6ft 5ins to allow an entrance opposite the driver, if required. The chassis had a dropped rear frame extension to accommodate a rear luggage locker. Maidstone & District ordered 15 Royal Tiger PSU1/15 chassis and these were delivered in 1952. They had manual gearboxes and vacuum brakes.

Fourteen had the new Leyland-built coach body with 37 seats and a central entrance; passengers and driver were together inside the saloon, so the driver's external door was also the emergency exit. The Leyland body was modern and distinctive in appearance, with a 24° slope to the lantern-style windscreen. These coaches also had an advanced heating and ventilating system. Passenger seats were well padded and the interior had full length luggage racks. They were numbered CO273-286.

However, the first of the batch, CO272 (PKE 272), had a 37-seat, centre-entrance Harrington Commander body, and was shown at the 1952 Commercial Motor Show at Earls Court in London. This was a one-off for Maidstone & District, although the same body style was later seen on a fleet of coaches for the state-owned airline BOAC, immortalised in a Dinky Toy model.

Above, CO282 was at Victoria Coach Station, about to take up its position in readiness for a trip to one of the holiday camps on the Isle of Sheppey, a popular and inexpensive holiday destination for many Londoners.
M&D AND EAST KENT BUS CLUB

On the right is numerically the first of the Royal Tigers, CO272, with its somewhat Leyland-lookalike Harrington Commander body.
DAVID TOY COLLECTION

This basic style was immortalised in miniature with the Dinky Toys BOAC Commer coach model, a collector's item now.

CO117-119
chassis AEC Regal I
body Harrington C32F

CO120-121
chassis AEC Regal III
body Harrington C33F

CO122
chassis AEC Regal IV
body Gurney Nutting C37C

CP2-3
chassis Austin CXB
body CP2 Harrington C26F
CP3 Kenex FC27F

SP1
chassis Commer N4
body Duple B20F

SP2-3
chassis Bedford WTB
body Duple Utility B28F
(SP3 B32F)

Skinner's joins the company

Skinner's Luxury Coaches of St Leonard's-on-Sea had sold its local stage carriage operation to Timpson's in the 1930s but had carried on with coaching until August 1953 when it decided to sell out to Maidstone & District. This included the goodwill, licences and the 11 coaches listed on the left with their Maidstone & District fleetnumbers. In order to keep the licences the Skinner's name and blue livery were kept.

SP1-3 may not have actually been used by M&D and the Austins were all withdrawn by 1956. CO122 was the only Regal IV operated by the company; the Regal IV was a heavy chassis having the underfloor AEC 9.6-litre engine rated at 125bhp, so was not the best on fuel consumption.

A second batch of 14 Royal Tigers was delivered in 1953/54 with Harrington 37-seat centre-entrance bodies to a new style, the latest incarnation of Harrington's Wayfarer model. These were numbered CO287-300. The first underfloor-engined chassis were heavy when compared to their older front-engined counterparts and the industry was soon to move to producing a lighter chassis.

a move to lighter weight chassis

After buying the heavyweight Leyland Royal Tiger, the company turned to the lighter weight AEC Reliance MU3RV that had AEC's smaller AH470 engine, rated at 112bhp at 2,000rpm, and a 5-speed gearbox. The first batch had Harrington Wayfarer II 37-seat central-entrance bodies, broadly similar to the last batch of Royal Tigers, although the waistline on these was in a more pronounced arc. For ventilation there were six top sliding windows on the offside and four on the nearside. The driver had a large door which was also the emergency exit. 47 entered the fleet during 1954/55 and were numbered CO304-350. These became the backbone of the company's coaching fleet and could be seen in most of the depots.

The new AEC Reliance very soon became a driver's favourite, thanks to the ease of driving with a synchromesh gearbox and the power of the AH470 engine.

Also in 1955, three slightly different Harrington Wayfarer bodied coaches entered the fleet, CO351-3, these being the first to have the entrance ahead of the front axle. They were of integral construction with seating for 41, and had the Commer TS3 2-stroke engine (the same as the service buses SO200-10). They were put to work at Tunbridge Wells and performed better than their bus counterparts; it seems that the TS3 engine was happier on longer journeys.

There was still the need for more coaches in the mid-1950s. Although car ownership was growing it had not yet stopped the large numbers of passengers travelling by coach. Holidays abroad were a rarity and holidays on the Kent and Sussex coast, as well as to the West Country, were still popular. Day trips and afternoon or evening tours also drew in the crowds.

A recognisable design feature pioneered by Harrington, and always associated with it, was the 'dorsal fin' you can just make out on the rear of Skinner's AEC Regal coach shown in the main picture on the left. It was said to aid airflow and ventilation in the saloon but, whether it did or not, this stylish feature looked most impressive.

This AEC Regal III became CO120 in Maidstone & District's fleet and was photpgraphed here on the ramp at the side of Tunbridge Wells depot.
RICK READING

The poor quality small shot on the left shows Skinner's rare Gurney Nutting bodied AEC Regal IV. This stayed in the Maidstone & District fleet until 1965 but didn't get scrapped until the early 1970s.
M&D AND EAST KENT BUS CLUB

On the right is one of the final Leyland Royal Tigers with Harrington Wayfarer II bodywork, CO295. You can see how the otherwise straight waist has a dip at the very rear and a slight dip at the front to flow into the scooped lower windscreen line.
JOHN SHEARMAN

Below is C352, one of the three Harrington/Commer integral coaches, clearly showing the possibly more elegant arced waistline and the entrance ahead of the front axle.
M&D AND EAST KENT BUS CLUB

ONE COACH OR A FLEET
M & D hire dept. can supply them

We can help you to decide destination, settle routes, make catering arrangements, obtain tickets for theatres and sporting events, and generally lighten your planning worries

Finally on this page is one of the large batch of Harrington Wayfarer II bodied AEC Reliances that M&D had in 1954 and 1955, this one being one of the last of the 1955 delivery.

What is interesting here is that you can see how Harrington's Wayfarer coach style developed through the early 1950s out of the straight-waisted Commander seen on page 57 to the more coherent and elegantly flowing style shown on the right.

There's more about this starting on page 76.
SOUTHDOWN ENTHUSIASTS' CLUB

the later semi-chassisless Beadle rebuilds

In 1955/6 the last semi-chassisless coaches were built by Beadle for M&D, CO354-376, the sub-frames and units having come from 23 of the 1948/9 batch of AEC Regal IIIs that had carried older 1936 Harrington bodies.

The new Beadle bodies had 37 seats with a central entrance, and a rather upright but more modern frontal appearance when compared to the earlier batches. They also had a passing resemblance to Maidstone & District's Harrington Wayfarer Mk IIs. As there was no bulkhead between the driver and the saloon, the driver's door was also the emergency exit.

Above is AEC Reliance 154, a former Timpson's coach that carried a Hall-Lewis 30-seat rear-entrance body when it was new in 1929.

Maidstone & District took over the Timpson's Hastings business in 1934, and in 1935 a number of these Reliances had their Hall-Lewis bodies removed, to be replaced with Harrington coach bodies the following year. 154 shows this more modern body.

SOUTHDOWN ENTHUSIASTS' CLUB

These 1936 bodies were then rebuilt by Portsmouth Aviation and transferred to new 1948 AEC Regal IIIs. Below is Regal III CO64, with the Harrington body that actually came from 154, in post-war mainly cream livery near Victoria in London.

The running units of CO64 went on to be incorporated into Beadle rebuild CO361.

M&D AND EAST KENT BUS CLUB

These coaches were used on express, day tour and private hire duties. Of the 23, 12 were allocated to Hastings, with single vehicles each at Bexhill, Rye and Tunbridge Wells, while two went to Sheerness and six to Gravesend.

The picture at the top of the page on the right shows CO373 on an express service to one of the holiday camps at Leysdown on the Isle of Sheppey.

Leysdown was busy in the high summer - hence the perceived need for a bus station - but the area was dead in the winter!

M&D AND EAST KENT BUS CLUB

The interesting line-up on the right in Tenterden Recreation Ground shows Beadle semi-chassisless CO375 flanked by two different versions of Harrington Wayfarer bodied AEC Reliances, with more in the background.

CO324 on the far right was a Wayfarer II, as dealt with on previous pages, while CO395 was a 1958 Wayfarer IV, a style we'll look at on the following pages. The similarities between the Beadle and Wayfarer II can be noted.

Tenterden was always a popular stopping off point for a refreshment break for both excursions and private hire, due to several characterful pubs in the attractive town.

M&D AND EAST KENT BUS CLUB

Leroy Tours to the continent

Maidstone & District had already been operating continental tours for Leroy, a tour operator at Tunbridge Wells, when in late 1955 it applied to the Traffic Commissioner to operate its own continental tours. A 2-day hearing was held in December, where evidence and objections were heard. The application was turned down, as it was felt that the adjoining companies, East Kent and Southdown, who were already operating tours to the continent, provided sufficient capacity and there was not the need for another operator.

The Commissioner also took into account that M&D was already operating tours on behalf of Leroy. It would seem there was a falling out between Leroy and Maidstone & District after this and Leroy went its own way and was soon running its own coaches, Duple Britannia bodied AEC Reliances and later it had at least one Duple Continental bodied Reliance.

M&D used Leyland bodied Royal Tigers for Leroy's continental tours to several European countries. However, problems did arise abroad. The Royal Tigers were prone to head gasket failures owing to engines overheating on mountain roads, and this also put a strain on the relationship between the two companies.

The coach below, on hire to Leroy and either in or on its way to what was then Yugoslavia, was not a Leyland bodied Royal Tiger but one of the company's Harrington bodied ones, CO293.

enter the Wayfarer Mk IV

Mainly for use on the company's holiday tours, 13 more AEC Reliance MU3RV coaches with the higher output AH470 engine were delivered between October and December 1957. Still with bodies built by Harrington of Hove, these were the new Wayfarer IV type, a style to be as closely associated with Maidstone & District as the Wayfarer II was.

These had the entrance ahead of the front axle and seats for 37. The two large grilles in the front were to help give a better air flow over the engine. A new feature for M&D was the curved windows in the roof cant above the side windows, plus two more in the front dome. These all had concertina sun blinds. Inside were full-length luggage racks with a net base, giving good visibility though the roof windows and a very light interior. To improve ventilation in the hot weather there were two lift up roof vents.

Fleetnumbers were CO377-389, and five were allocated to Gillingham, two to Tunbridge Wells, four to Maidstone and one each to Hastings and Bexhill.

The AEC Reliance with Wayfarer IV body had now become the standard coach for M&D and a further 75 were delivered between 1958 and 1961 - CO390-444 and, starting a new numbering series, C1-20.

As by now all vehicles ran on diesel fuel (referred to as oil), other than The Knightrider, that is, there was no longer any need to differentiate between 'oil' and 'petrol', so CO and CP were changed to just C. Older CO numbers gradually changed to just C.

These two subsequent batches of Wayfarer IV coaches were to the same specification but with an increase in seating to 41. The earlier ones with DKK registrations did not have the cant or dome windows, although the later deliveries did have dome windows with blinds. Three of the AEC Wayfarers were not in the standard M&D livery: CO442/443 were in the all-blue Skinners livery and CO444 in the red and cream livery of Scout.

Above right is a publicity shot of the then new CO379 in 1957, a lovely and well-loaded Harrington Wayfarer IV bodied AEC Reliance. The side cant glass panels are clearly visible with some of the blinds in use.
MAIDSTONE & DISTRICT

You can see how these glass panels and the net parcel racks made the interior very light and airy and ideal for admiring the scenery on a Maidstone & District holiday coach tour in the picture immediately to the right. Those Chapman seats were comfortable, too.
M&D AND EAST KENT BUS CLUB

The other picture on the right shows a later Wayfarer IV, CO443, by then numbered 4443, in the livery of Skinners.
M&D AND EAST KENT BUS CLUB

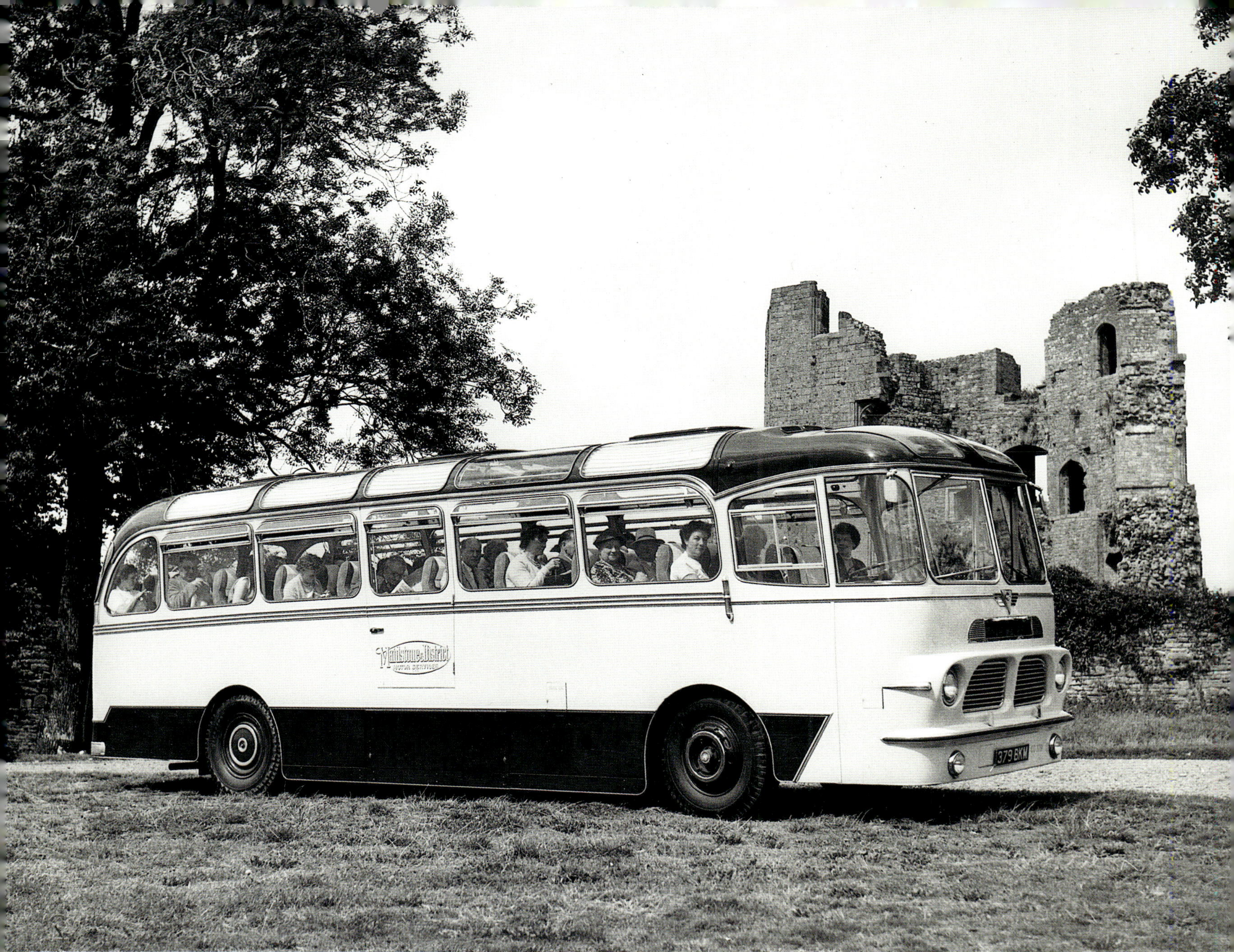
379 BKM

SKINNERS
PRIVATE
443 LKE

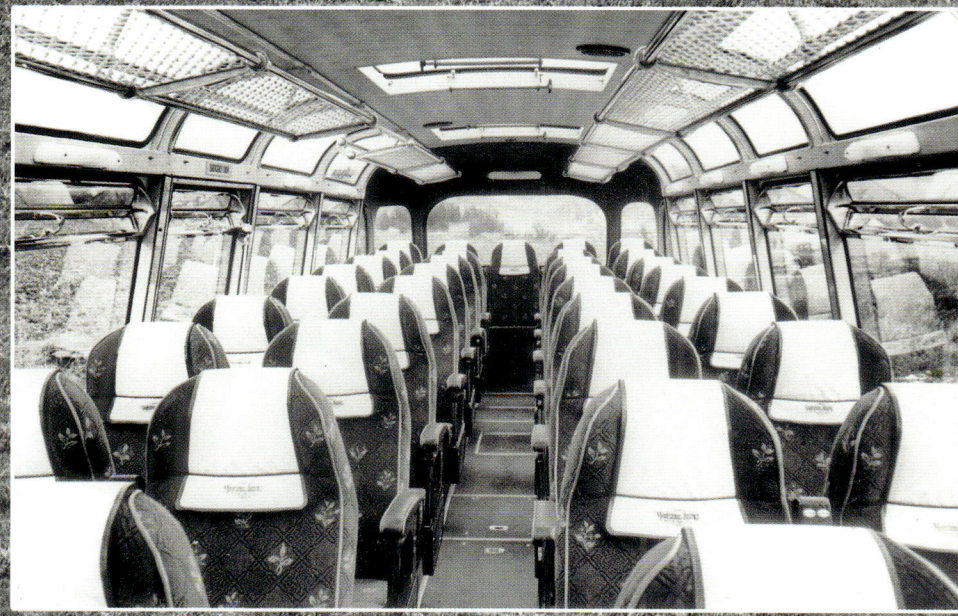

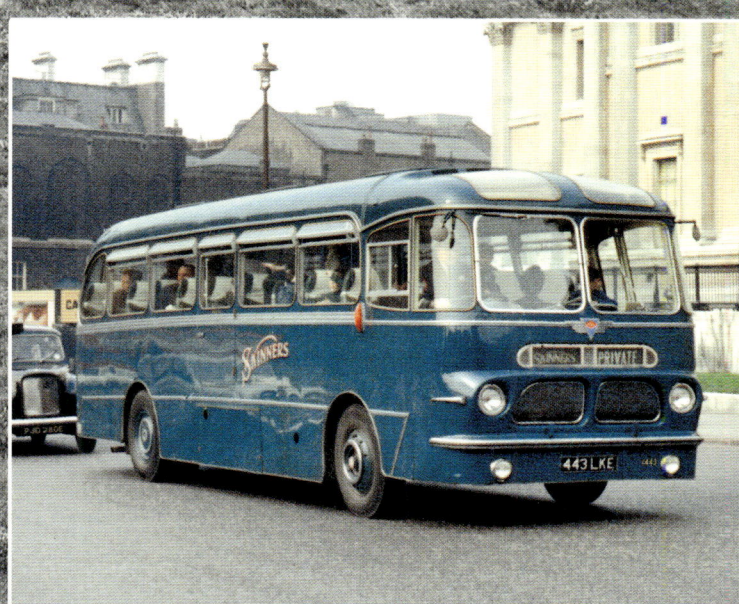

summer peaks

Until ever-rising car ownership reduced the need, the summer peak on express services required all available coaches and more. During the start of the school holidays London's Victoria Coach Station was a very busy place for Maidstone & District with many coaches leaving for the Kent and Sussex holiday resorts. For example, Warner's Holiday camp on the Isle of Sheppey had several duplicates booked for the journey, as did the Coombe Haven holiday park at Hastings.

To cover this demand, ordinary single-deck buses with thinner, harder, low-back seats were used for duplicates, not the most comfortable for these journeys. In 1959 the company took delivery of bus shell AEC Reliances with quasi-coach seats, referred to as dual-purpose, but in many ways they were not ideal for coach work, nor bus work. These would be used as reliefs for express services and some days it has been known that up to 100 vehicles were needed just to cover the holiday camp traffic for the Isle of Sheppey. There's more on the dual-purpose phenomenon further on.

Maidstone & District would hire in from independent operators including Lewis and Cliff's coaches from South London, as well as operators more local to the company, like Pilchers of Chatham, Horlocks of Northfleet, AC Coaches, Moody's of Gravesend and Warrens of Ticehurst.

An example of the intensity of the Isle of Sheppey operations can be seen by taking a single day in July 1961, when the required vehicles were:

E6	London - Medway Towns - Sheerness	8
E19	London - Dartford - Leysdown	10
E23	Leyton - Medway Towns - Leysdown	7
E14	Leyton - Medway Towns - Sheerness	2
plus	services to the holiday camps	38

Included in the total were nine buses with either bus or dual-purpose seating. At some weekends this would increase to nearly 20, coming from any depot that could spare the resources.

Above is the sole Harrington Wayfarer AEC Reliance coach in Scout livery, C444, referred to on the previous page, here in Hastings' notoriously steep Wellington Square.
M&D AND EAST KENT BUS CLUB

The picture on the right, although taken in early National Bus Company years in 1972, shows the organised mayhem that was for years a common sight at London's Victoria Coach Station in the peak summer periods. Six Maidstone & Ditrict coaches and dual-purpose vehicles were among East Kent and Southdown vehicles, at least two of them on relief journeys.

Nearest to us was a Duple Commander III bodied Leyland Leopard, in the centre Harrington Wayfarer IV bodied AEC Reliance 4433 (originally CO433), and behind it two coach liveried - but essentially bus shell with dual-purpose seats - Willowbrook BET-style bodied Leyland Leopards.

Under the awning were two other M&D vehicles, a Harrington Grenadier bodied AEC Reliance with its cantilevered bootlid up and another dual-purpse single decker alongside.
THOMAS MOORE

On the right, S335, a 1961 Weymann bodied AEC Reliance dual-purpose bus, was poking out of the entrance to Southdown's Eastbourne garage, having come in along the coast on a journey on bus route 99 from Hastings, while a lady in a headscarf was sheltering from the rain in the adjacent doorway.

S335 only carried the mainly cream coach livery from May 1962 until May 1969.
DAVID TOY COLLECTION

In 1968, now renumbered 3327, another dual-purpose Weymann bodied AEC Reliance delivered new as S327 in 1961, had just arrived at Wigmore on the service from Gillingham. The destination blind had already been set for its return journey.
MIKE HODGES

dual purpose ... coach or bus?

The concept of a dual-purpose vehicle, suitable for use as a bus or a coach, had been around for some time, but it was during the 1950s it came into more prominence generally in the UK. Maidstone & District in particular, as we mentioned on the previous pages, was having to put spare buses not needed so much at weekends into front-line express coach service at busy holiday weekends. So having vehicles that were perfectly servicable as buses during the week that could then be acceptable as coaches at weekends must have seemed a good idea, especially then, as high speed running was not permissable by law anyway.

Maidstone & District's first dual-purpose buses were SO265-284, AEC Reliances with the earliest, modern for its time (but very box-like compared with the later curved-screen style versions) BET-style bodywork by Park Royal. These were followed by 20 more to an almost identical design with bodies built by Weymann in 1960, and a further 30 Weymann examples in 1961.

When Maidstone & District switched to buying 36ft long single-decker buses from 1962, dual-purpose versions had a new prefix SC, neatly straddling the fence in classification between bus and coach. M&D's first AEC Reliance 36-footers had a fussy 4-piece flat windscreen, protruding destination roofbox and rounded rear roof dome, and two of the seven delivered in 1962/3 were dual-purpose SC31-32.

From 1965 deliveries of single-deck buses and dual-purpose versions had the new really handsome double-curvature windscreen and rear window style of bodywork with destination screen incorporated into a very neat peaked shape. The dual-purpose versions also incorporated a rather elegant brightwork grille and twin headlights.

Further deliveries broadly followed this same style, although by the time the Leyland Leopard was in favour with the company, 36ft long dual-purpose single deckers had five longer window bays rather than the earlier six.

In the pictture above, on a London-bound E4 express coach service working from Hastings, brand new SC75, a 1966 AEC Reliance with a Marshall body, had just pulled in for the scheduled refreshment break at the well-known Blue Boys Inn at Kippings Cross on the main A21 between Lamberhurst and Pembury. Passengers were making purposeful strides towards the door, eager for refreshments or toilets, or both.

Despite being basically a bus body, the twin headlights, brightwork grille, double-curvature windscreen and peaked front dome, and carrying cream and green coach livery, made these vehicles not too bad for London express services.
RAY STENNING

M&D's first 36-footers were less attractive and even coach livery couldn't make them look appropriate for coach work. SC32 was in Maidstone's Mill Street bus station in the picture on the right.
MIKE HODGES

the Wayfarer IV rebuilds

A rather unusual exercise in Maidstone & District's dual-purpose vehicle policy occurred when the company decided to make some Harrington Wayfarer IV coaches more suitable for one-man-operation as service buses, rather than the alternative policy of making services buses better able to work as coaches when required.

The vehicles selected were the 18 AEC Reliances delivered in 1958, CO390-407, renumbered C390-407 by then. The rebuild involved a complete new original square BET-style bus front section grafted on to the existing coach body ahead of the front axle. Although not as ungainly as it sounds, it did mean it was possible to have a conventional bus destination box in the front dome and a bus-type folding entrance door.

Harrington did the rebuilds in Spring 1963 and between February and July 1965. There were minor differences between vehicles. Naturally, they gained the SC prefix.

Then in 1970 it was decided to make them only suitable for bus work and work began on changing the coach seats for bus ones. Although it was intended that all would be turned into buses, in the end only 10 were treated.

Although not one of the Harrington Wayfarer IV coaches that were rebuilt, 4442 (originally CO442) at the top shows the distinctive frontal styling of this body design.
M&D AND EAST KENT BUS CLUB

In the middle picture you can see how the lines of new bus front blended quite well with the coach structure, even if the final effect might seem a bit brutal.

One of these regularly ran on the 137 between East Grinstead and Crowborough in the mid-1960s, and here by the old East Grinstead two-level station SC395 was just leaving on one such journey, showing RELIEF on the blind. It's doubtful the route ever needed reliefs!
RAY STENNING

On the left is what had become 3352 (originally CO393) in Sevenoaks bus station on a local route, by now with low back seats and in in green and cream bus livery.
DAVID TOY COLLECTION

Passing typical South Coast seaside town Regency architecture, Harrington Wayfarer IV bodied AEC Reliance coach CO383 had a full complement of passengers enjoying a Maidstone & District day tour.
DAVID TOY COLLECTION

By the 1960s M&D was using full-colour for its excursion publicity, but it was only the cover picture (Henley-on-Thames for the 1966 programme). These were printed *en masse* as 'blanks,' with the area from which they ran and all the insides overprinted in black afterwards.

a nice day out

Day tours were particularly popular with the older generation, and there were lots to choose from. Maidstone & District's programme had expanded through the 1950s and early 1960s from sightseeing and seaside to cover such things as race meetings at Lingfield, Epsom, Goodwood and Lewes, and to events like the annual Farnborough Air Show. Always well subscribed was a combined road and River Thames tour. By 1961 the annual mileage for excursions and tours was 831,700 (3% of the company total). As a comparison, the 22 express services accounted for 2,012,500 miles (7.45%).

Tour number 46 (licence no. M100) **South Coast Tour** was a typical day out from Maidstone, and during the summer of 1966 it ran on 11 different dates costing 14/- for an adult and 7/- for a child. It would have been operated by an AEC Reliance, either a Harrington bodied 'TKM' or by a newer Wayfarer IV, and departure time was 9.10am from Mill Street bus station. The route it took is shown below. At Rye there was a stop for half an hour before continuing along the A259 coast road through Hastings and Bexhill to Eastbourne, arriving 1.15pm for a one and a half hour stay in the town.

Eastbourne was Southdown and Eastbourne Corporation country, with plenty of Southdown green Leyland Titan PD2s and the newer PD3s with Northern Counties bodies, plus blue and cream AEC Regent IIIs with Weymann or Bruce bodywork and AEC Regent Vs with East Lancs bodywork of the corporation.

After the lunch stop the coach continued on the A259 to Seaford, Newhaven and along the cliff tops (which gave stunning views over the English Channel) to arrive in Brighton at 4pm for a two hour stop. Brighton had many attractions for the short stay, but for any enthusiast there would be plenty to see with the three bus operators of the town - Brighton Corporation, Brighton Hove & District and Southdown.

At 6pm the coach would start its return journey home through Lewes on to Hawkhurst, stopping for half an hour in Goudhurst, a village with more than one pub and commanding views of the countryside all around, and then back to Maidstone for 9pm.

a holiday by M&D...
over the hills and far away

In late 1962 the company took 10 Harrington Cavalier bodied AEC Reliances, C21-30, powered by AEC's standard AH470 engine, to update the holiday tour fleet. Most were stored until the start of the 1963 tour season. The Cavalier really was a supremely elegant looking coach - finely proportioned with its sharp, flowing lines and an absolute delight to the eye. And my-oh-my, didn't this body style just ooze class!

Most thought the Cavalier looked particularly smart in Maidstone & District's cream and green livery and, with just 37 seats and side cant and front dome roof windows, it was an ideal coach for the extended tour programme. Neighbouring Southdown also used its Cavaliers for its extended tours, or coach cruises as it preferred to call them. These seated just 28 with a two-and-one seat layout.

Maidstone & District's Cavaliers were spread around most of the garages that operated the extended tours - Maidstone, Tonbridge, Tunbridge Wells, Bexhill, Hastings, Gravesend, Gillingham and Sittingbourne.

The company's offering of holiday tours in 1966 ranged from 3 days to the Lincolnshire Tulip Fields at the end of April and into early May for £13, to 11 days touring the Scottish Lochs and Highlands with 15 departures between the end of May and early September, obviously a popular choice, costing £49/10/-. These were all featured in its *Over the hills and far away* brochure shown on the right.

On the second night of the Scottish Lochs and Highlands tour, having travelled from Buxton through Knutsford and up the M6 to Southport for lunch, then on to Preston, Kendal and Windermere, the tour arrived at

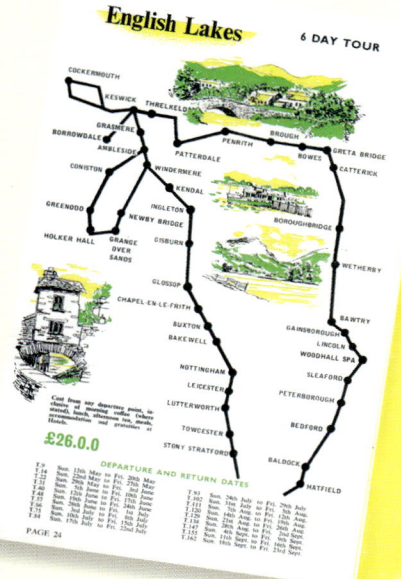
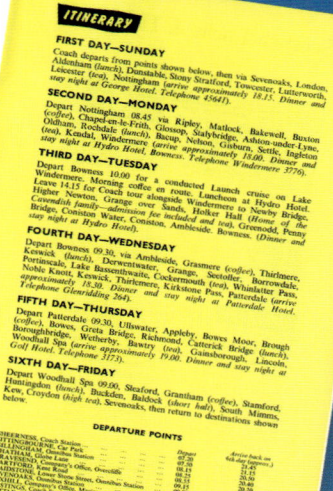
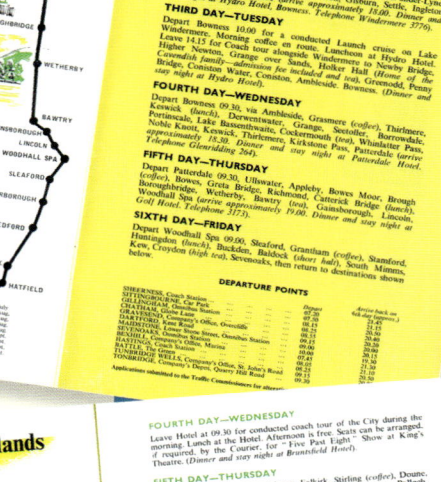

Keswick for dinner and the night, staying at Keswick Hotel. Helpfully, the brochure gave the hotel's telephone number - easy to remember; it was Keswick 20.

The Isle of Wight was another popular holiday destination and Maidstone & District operated an 8-day centred tour based in Shanklin. It ran every Saturday from 28 May until 17 September inclusive. Closer examination of the itinerary explained that patrons were to take the company's express service E7 or E18 to Portsmouth, the British Railways ferry over to Ryde and then (ancient) steam train to Shanklin Station.

They then had to make their own way between the station and the Shanklin Hotel. Excursions on the island would be provided by local coach companies on the island. This holiday cost £20/7/6 until 25 June and from 17 September, rising to £21/17/6 between 2 July and 20 August.

If you went on the 4-day tour centred on Bournemouth, you would have similarly taken the E7 express service to get there and back, but at least taxis were arranged to get you between Bournemouth Square bus and coach station and the Bourne Hall Hotel. Of the other two days, one was at leisure at the resort and the other a Hants & Dorset afternoon tour to Lulworth Cove.

Other tours run entirely by a Maidstone & District coach would be staying mainly in one location with half-day and full-day trips out, or a full touring holiday staying somewhere different most nights.

Over the 1966 season there were approximately 170 departures on these extended tours. The Cavaliers were only four years old in 1966 and were the top rank coaches for these tours. Shorter holidays used the 1957 batch of AEC Reliance C377-389. The drivers allocated to the tours were specially trained and were taken around the routes and to the hotels before the season started. They had basic training in changing bulbs and minor repairs, and the coaches carried spares, including injector pipes and filters, that could be changed if a problem arose near a BET, BTC or Scottish Bus Group bus garage.

These tours were well patronised in those days. The coaches were always well presented with the headrest covers having the company name on them. The high standards of the specially selected drivers (in their smart summer uniforms) added to the enjoyment of the passengers.

The Prospect Hotel (later renamed The Yorkshire Hotel) was a favourite with coach tour operators, and Maidstone & District used it as a stopover for two nights on its Yorkshire and Derbyshire Dales tour in 1966.

In another year in the early 1960s, Harrington Cavalier bodied AEC Reliance C24 was on a stopover there on a Scottish Highlands and Royal Deeside tour, as you can see on the opposite page.
M&D AND EAST KENT BUS CLUB

The West Country was another popular destination for Maidstone & District holiday tours, and on the right Cavalier C30 had allowed patrons to enjoy a stop off somewhere on a North Devon and West Country tour on a lovely summer's day.
M&D AND EAST KENT BUS CLUB

A couple of Harrington Wayfarer IV bodied AEC Reliances were waiting to leave London's Victoria Coach Station for destinations in Kent in the picture above.

The large boards showed whose coaches left for where, although the nearest M&D coach had strayed to underneath the boards for East Kent destinations.
RICK READING

The picture below, taken in Maidstone Mill Street bus station, shows the Bedford VAL demonstrator 883 HMJ that Maidstone & District had on loan in August 1963.
M&D AND EAST KENT BUS CLUB

express developments

The express network had also grown with additional and modified services. By the summer of 1960 the E5/6 Faversham/Sittingbourne to London had increased to 13 trips per day with extra journeys on Saturdays and Sundays. Looking at the summer 1965 timetable, the E7 from Gillingham to Bournemouth via Sevenoaks, Portsmouth and Southampton, continued to Totnes via Dorchester and Exeter. That took 13¼ hours but only ran at weekends. On this service Maidstone & District drivers only went as far as Bournemouth but the coaches continued with Royal Blue drivers. There was also an overnight journey on a Friday night/Saturday morning that went all the way to Newquay and Perranporth. The E18 took a different route from Gillingham to Bournemouth via Portsmouth and Southampton with connections to the West Country by Royal Blue, operating on a Saturday and Sunday.

Having already bought its first 36ft long buses in 1962 and 1963, in September 1963 Maidstone & District bought two Willowbrook BET-style dual-purpose buses with 49 coach type seats, SC31/32 - one of these is shown a few pages back. Maidstone was the home for SC31 and Sheerness took SC32.

But from 8-22 August 1963 M&D tried a new 36ft long coach on its express services, a Bedford twin-steer VAL14 with a Duple Vega Major 52-seat front-entrance body, 883 HMJ. The coach operated mainly out of Maidstone on the London services. It had a 6.54-litre Leyland O.400 engine producing 131bhp, coupled to a 5-speed gearbox. No orders were placed and the company would stay with AEC for its next coaches.

These, in 1964, were C33-37, more 36ft long AEC Reliance 2U3RAs with the AH590 engine and 6-speed manual gearbox, but this time carrying Harrington Grenadier 47-seat coach bodies. The Beadle/AEC Regal rebuilds of the WKM batch were being withdrawn around this time as well.

The Grenadier was a sharpened-up, slightly more modern development of the Cavalier, using longer side windows, a slightly revised lower front panel with a straight moulding in place of the Cavalier's dipped shape, and a taller screen with sharper peak over it. The Grenadier looked quite impressive at 36ft long, better than the Cavalier which always looked a little stretched at this length.

After the Grenadier was introduced, Harrington ran both models concurrently in the Hove factory and Southdown, for example, specified Grenadiers with Cavalier lower front panels while Grey Cars in Devon had Cavaliers with Grenadier lower fronts.

under the River Thames into Essex

Before 1964 if you wanted to get between Kent and Essex, by and large it meant travelling into London and changing on to an Eastern National coach service out into Essex. An alternative was on foot via the Gravesend-Tilbury ferry using connecting coach services at either side - all a bit of a chore and time consuming, although there was one ex-Westcliff service that actually crossed on the ferry, and Eastern National had a chain of booking agents in Kent.

In 1964 all that changed with the opening of the Dartford Tunnel under the Thames between Dartford in Kent and Purfleet on the north side of the river in Essex, opening up a whole lot of opportunities for coach operators to link Kent and Sussex with Essex.

Dartford Tunnel Coachways was formed by Eastern National, East Kent and Maidstone & District, masterminded by John Wilson of Eastern National. Later, Southdown joined the operation. The main network is shown on the right. Resources and receipts were pooled to make the operation efficient and easy to run.

Maidstone & District had duties on the X33 Hastings-Maidstone-M2-Dartford-Basildon-Walton-on-the-Naze, a journey time of 5 hours 41 minutes, and the X35 Tunbridge Wells-Tonbridge-Basildon (with Eastern National connections to Walton-on-the-Naze). The Saturdays only X40 Gillingham-Medway Towns-Basildon-Great Yarmouth took 6 hours 5 minutes.

At the top, C34, one of the earlier batch of Harrington Grenadier bodied AEC Reliance coaches, was parked up at Portsmouth, having arrived there on an E18 working from the Medway Towns.
M&D AND EAST KENT BUS CLUB

Basildon was the main interchange point on the Dartford Tunnel Coachways network, allowing many journey possibilities. Above, M&D dual-purpose SC44 was on its way to Clacton.
W T CANSICK

The Duple Commander III had quite a thrusting appearance, as you can see in this picture on the left of Maidstone & District's first one, 4601, here on a West Country express in Plymouth's Bretonside bus station.

In Maidstone & District's coach holiday publicity in the late 1960s, by now an A4 size brochure, the Commanders were shown depicted as touring coaches.
DAVID TOY COLLECTION

On the left below you can observe how the Commander IV was cleaned up to become a very attractive coach for the time.

The awkward kink in the lower moulding was removed, the headlights faired in, and other tricks used to emphasise the strong horizontal theme.
DAVID TOY COLLECTION

M&D's dual-purpose Leopards had the later 5-window bay version of the BET body style, as shown below by 2809 on a local bus working in Maidstone.
DAVID TOY COLLECTION

the last AECs and the first Leopards

In 1965 Maidstone & District took delivery of its last AEC Reliance coaches, 15 2U3RA models with Harrington Grenadier 47-seat coach bodies again, C58-72. These were among the last bodies built by Harrington on heavyweight chassis, as the factory closed its doors the following year. Introduction of these Grenadiers saw the withdrawal of the Harrington and Leyland bodied Leyland Royal Tigers. Between 1967 and 1968 the TKM batch of Harrington Wayfarer II bodied AEC Reliance were also withdrawn, as were the three Harrington TS3 integrals.

Loyalty to the Reliance for coaches had lasted 11 years and all had carried Harrington bodies. No further coaches were bought until 1968, when the company turned to the Leyland Leopard PSU3A/4RT with Leyland O.680 engine coupled to a pneumocyclic gearbox. The first batch, 4601-4612, carried the modern-looking and attractive Duple Commander III 45-seat body, but those delivered in 1969, 4613-4622, had the tidied up and very impressive Commander IV body with 44 seats. More followed in 1970, 4623-4628, and these also had Duple Commander IV bodies but with 48-seats. Some didn't enter service until 1971. Although the Commanders shown on this page were photographed on express or private hire duties, they were shown in Maidstone & District's holiday tour brochure as being used for those holidays.

After this, coaches conformed to National Bus Company standards and all-white Duple Dominant bodied Leopards appeared from 1973.

The map on the left shows Maidstone & District's principal express coach services for the summer of 1965. For clarity, the Dartford Tunnel services through to East Anglia are not shown, nor are special services to holiday camps.

We wanted to end the coaching section with one of the final Harrington bodied coaches delivered to Maidstone & District, 4158, seen below on a Dartford Tunnel Coachways working leaving Basildon bus station on its way to Clacton-on-Sea

This was a fine example of this coachbuilder's artistry, combining elegant flowing lines with a contemporary crispness. It does make you wonder where the company would have gone with styling, had it survived beyond 1966.

DAVID TOY COLLECTION

— regular express services to London
-- occasional express services to London
— summer express services

development of the Harrington Wayfarer

Maidstone & District favoured bodies built by coachbuilder Thomas Harrington of Hove for a large number of coaches and buses over many years. Indeed, the Wayfarer II and IV coach styles will always be closely associated with Maidstone & District, practically defining its coaching image in the late 1950s and early 1960s.

The Wayfarer body was introduced in 1950 for underfloor-engined chassis, and was the first time Harrington had used a name for one of its designs. However, as Harrington's body style for underfloor-engined chassis developed over the following decade it should be pointed out that the factory seldom used the name Wayfarer for its own subsequent designations, in publicity or on the vehicles, so the commonly used references to Mk II, III and IV are perhaps more convenient than strictly accurate. There are adverts for Harrington coachwork depicted in this book that clearly make no reference to the name.

Once it introduced a different style for lightweight front-engined chassis, Harrington was more diligent in using a name - in this case, Crusader - and, of course, continued to do so with the introduction of the Cavalier, Grenadier and its last model, the Legionnaire.

More flexible, bespoke coachbuilding methods meant that the first Wayfarer style had quite a few variations due to customer preference, and many continued to feature the trademark Harrington dorsal fin at the rear. Indeed, some Mk IVs for other customers even had this later in the decade.

Strangely, Maidstone & District never had any of these first Wayfarers but neighbouring Southdown did. In 1966 Southdown loaned some to Aldershot & District, which were left in Southdown green but acquired Aldershot & District fleetnames. In the picture below by Ray Stenning, one of these, Southdown 1689, was on an excursion to Kew Gardens. Interestingly, Southdown's Wayfarers didn't have the usual flared out skirt or flowing wheelarch shapes that most others of this style did.

Maidstone & District CO307 was bowling along White Rock approaching Hastings Pier in the big picture, on a journey to London.

This AEC Reliance had a Harrington coach body of the style that has come to be known as Wayfarer II, although not necessarily a Harrington designation. Along with the later-style Wayfarer 'IV', this was THE Maidstone & District coach of the period.
THE BUS ARCHIVE/ROBIN HANNAY

On the far right is a contemporary Harrington advert for its coachwork showing a front-engined coach with the stylish dorsal fin at the end of the roof. It was claimed to aid ventilation.

Harrington, always keen on pushing build technology, developed the integral Contender in 1952 with Commer running units, mainly in co-operation with the national airline BOAC, and it went through a number of body style changes, more-or-less mirroring the changes in the Wayfarer body, but with variations. There's a Harrington advert for the Contender Mk IV (similar to the Wayfarer Mk II) on the opposite page. Incidentally, the Contender name was always promoted by Harrington for this integral model.

Maidstone & District had a one-off, straight-waisted and lantern-screened Harrington body on a Leyland Royal Tiger chassis very similar to the BOAC integral Contenders and this carried the Commander name on its body.

There was often a degree of overlap from one version of the Wayfarer to another, and even between the Contender and the Wayfarer, so M&D's next batch of Royal Tigers in 1953 had an amalgam of the revised Mk II Wayfarer front with the Contender style of straight waist, although there was a slight dip to final short window, as shown at the bottom of this page and in the advert next to it.

As we have mentioned a few pages back, Maidstone & District did have a batch of integral Harrington-Commer Contenders and these were in the dipping waist style, although they did have the entrance door ahead of the front axle, whereas the large number of same style of Mk II Wayfarers the company bought on AEC Reliance chassis had a central door.

The Mk III Wayfarer, which Maidstone & District didn't buy, started production in 1955, although the Wayfarer II continued to be available. It combined the general look of the Wayfarer II with a number of styling features that would continue, slightly modified in most cases, on to the Mk IV. Not many Mk IIIs were built.

The final Wayfarer type, the Mk IV (referred to by the factory as just Mk IVA, never Wayfarer) appeared at the Commercial Motor Show in 1956. Maidstone & District took to this model with enthusiasm, as we have already noted. Others did, too, and there were a number of BET operators up and down the country who bought this model, as did loyal Harrington supporter Grey Green in London, and several independents. The very last Wayfarer built left the factory in late 1961 and was the final Maidstone & District one.

CO272, M&D's single Harrington Commander bodied Leyland Royal Tiger, was delivered in October 1952 to Maidstone depot and then transferred to Gillingham.

It was used on the West Country express services in its early life and featured detachable roof boards for this purpose. Above, it had stopped for a refreshment break on this service. You can make out the Commander name just rear of the lantern screen.
OMNIBUS SOCIETY

When delivered, the Royal Tigers were initially used on the company's extended tours programme. In the picture below on the left, CO290 was parked above the Atlantic Ocean while on a tour of the West Country.
OMNIBUS SOCIETY

Mystery tours often featured in most coach operators' programmes, and M&D was no exception. Above, on an afternoon mystery tour, was AEC Reliance CO386 with the final version of the Wayfarer style. This was one of the 37-seat coaches bought in 1957 ready for the 1958 touring season of extended tour duties and delivered with glass panels in the roof cant.

The sticker in the windscreen indicates this was coach no. 3, so the excursion must have benn well booked.
SOUTHDOWN ENTHUSIASTS' CLUB

CO420 in the shot below was one of the 1959 Wayfarer IV bodied AEC Reliances that had 41 seats and no glass roof panels. Here it was passing through Westerham in Kent on a private hire job in 1967.
RAY STENNING

Maidstone & District had a varied local excursion programme from the majority of its depots. At the top, at Gravesend, CO330 was waiting to take passengers out for a day tour of some Buckinghamshire scenic delights.

This AEC Reliance had the more common Wayfarer II body with the dipping waistline and centre door.
M&D AND EAST KENT BUS CLUB

Silver Star of Porton Down near Salisbury had a liking for Harrington bodywork and bought Mk II, III and IV versions. The lower of the two pictures above shows a Mk IV on the left and a Mk III on the right, clearly displaying the progress of the style.

By the time of this photograph, 1 July 1964, Silver Star had been taken over by Wilts & Dorset. Note Silver Star's individualism in the pointed dome at the front. This used to carry an illuminated star (of course!).
DAVID PENNELS

moving the engine to the back

The appearance of the rear-engined Leyland Atlantean in the Maidstone & District fleet was quite sensational in its day.

It instantly modernised the image of the double-decker bus wherever the type was used.

the Leyland Lowloader

Maidstone & District had an introduction to the rear-engined double decker in December 1954, when STF90, the prototype Leyland Lowloader, was demonstrated to the company. This new Leyland chassis had a lightly turbocharged Leyland O.350 engine positioned transversely at the rear of the rear-entrance platform. The gearbox was a Wilson preselective unit, quite different from the usual manual gearbox fitted to other buses in the M&D fleet.

The Saunders-Roe body was 7ft 6ins wide with a full front and seated 61. The larger O.600 engine, as used in the Leyland Titan PD2s in Maidstone & District's fleet, could not be fitted to the Lowloader as it was too large - legislation of the day required an 18in cut back on the rear platform as an emergency exit. This concept bus did not go into production, but when legislation changed in 1956 to allow a 30ft length and a maximum weight of 14 tons, Leyland showed the first rear-engined Atlantean at the 1956 Commercial Motor Show.

... becomes the Atlantean

This was a fully integral vehicle built by Leyland and the Metro-Cammell-Weymann group, and had 78 seats with the entrance at the front opposite the driver. The larger O.600 engine could now be used coupled to a semi-automatic gearbox, but the price was 40% higher than a conventional chassis.

This Atlantean had a drop-centre rear axle, giving the bus a low height without having the upper-deck bench seats and sunken side gangway of a lowbridge body. Brakes were air/hydraulic, and suspension was independent at the front, with conventional springs at the rear. The BET group (which Maidstone & District was part of) took interest in the integral Atlantean and it was demonstrated to several of the group's companies in the North and the Midlands. The group liked the concept but not the price, so Leyland went back to develop a new version with a separate chassis.

ideal for Hastings

Maidstone & District wanted to replace the trolleybuses at Hastings with motorbuses, and after Leyland showed the group its new revised Atlantean chassis, this was what was decided would be fit for purpose for the new vehicles for Hastings. The Leyland O.600 engine in the Atlantean was rated at 125 bhp at 1,800rpm and linked to a semi-automatic gearbox. Air brakes were fitted. This was a new standard for Maidstone & District, as the majority of previous purchases had had vacuum brakes. One of the cost savings was a straight rear axle instead of a drop-centre one. The bus also had conventional road springs.

Above is the first sight of things to come. In December 1954 Maidstone & District had Leyland's new rear-engined bus on demonstration.

The Lowloader had a Leyland O.350 engine on the rear platform with an angle drive to a preselective gearbox under the stairs. The body was built by Saunders Roe with 61 seats and here it was parked outside the company's headquarters, Knightrider House in Maidstone.
M&D AND EAST KENT BUS CLUB

Out with the old and in with the new on the left.

Showing a blind display appropriate for the end of the trolleybuses in Hastings, Weymann bodied Sunbeam W, 34, was alongside one of its replacements Atlantean DH493 at the depot.
P M PHOTOGRAPHY

On the opposite page, in a manufacturer's official photograph, DH527 was showing off the impressive appearance that Maidstone & District's Atlanteans made when new, helped by the lack of vertical distortion by using architectural photography techniques.
CLASSIC BUS COLLECTION

Above, you can clearly see the distinctive rear profile of the MCW bodied Leyland Atlantean, with the tranversely mounted engine in its bustle; also the two-piece lower deck rear window.

DH500 was delivered in May 1959 for the Hastings trolleybus replacement scheme. It was on the 151 worked out of Silverhill. Note the garage shed plate towards the nearside of the engine bustle.

M&D AND EAST KENT BUS CLUB

All the new lowbridge Leyland Atlanteans had been allocated to the Hastings area by mid-1959. Hastings-allocated DL47 was running under the trolleybus wires in Queens Road on the 76 route in this picture on the left while still very new and very shiny.

TRAVEL LENS

The wheelbase was 16ft 3ins and the unladen weight with MCW body was 8t 12cwt. M&D initially ordered 50 Atlanteans. Of these, 34 had Metro-Cammell 78-seat highbridge bodies, DH490-523. The similar bodies on DH524/5 had 60 coach-type seats. The remaining 14 had semi-lowbridge 73-seat bodies from Weymann, DL43-56. To achieve the required low height, the last seat rows on the upper deck were on a raised platform (to give enough headroom at the back downstairs where the floor was higher to go over the straight rear axle). Obviously, this meant a nearside side gangway upstairs by this section, which gave an odd look to both decks.

Two of the batch had different engines - DH493 had a larger Leyland O.680 and DH497 a Leyland O.600 Power Plus with an output of 150bhp. The standard bus bodied Atlantean cost in the region of £7,000.

on show at Earls Court

The first Maidstone & District Atlantean, DL43, was exhibited at the October 1958 Commercial Motor Show at Earls Court in London, one of four Atlanteans at the show that year. MCW bodies were quite upright and boxy - that was the fashion of the day - with the engine in a bustle at the rear and a distinctive 2-pane lower deck rear window above the bustle. DL43 was a very impressive bus in M&D's green and cream livery with the traditional cream moustache under the windscreen.

The interior had apple green window pans with a darker green seat material and lining panels, while the roof was in a cream Darvic material. The bus was delivered to the company in January 1959 and went to Hastings for driver training. The trolleybus conversion was to take place at the end of May 1959. Before that date DL43 and DH490 were seen in service on trolleybus routes. By the end of May, 94 trolleybus drivers had been retrained to drive the new diesel buses.

The odd layout of the lowbridge Atlanteans, due to not having a dropped-centre rear axle, resulted upstairs in pairs of seats across the gangway for two-thirds of the bus and towards the rear four-abreast bench seating on a raised plinth with a side gangway.

You can see this in the top picture above on the right. The lower picture shows the downstairs.
M&D AND EAST KENT BUS CLUB

This drawing (of a ficticious lowbridge Atlanrean) shows the arrangement to better effect. Note how the forwardmost bench seat was based on the raised dais rather than on legs.

Interestingly, at first it was found that there was reluctance for former trolleybus drivers to overtake another bus; the experience of trolley poles coming off was hard to forget. Both the former trolleybus drivers - in fact, all drivers - had to learn a new technique of driving the new buses with no clutch pedal. On many of the previous buses there had been the need to double declutch when changing gears; the Atlantean had a small gear control attached to the steering column. It was a very easy process to change gear, most drivers went straight into the next gear without a pause, but later Leyland recommended a pause between the gear changes to help gearbox band life and make a smoother gearchange. The set back front axle was something new on a double decker. Drivers also had control of the doors, leaving the conductor to carry on collecting fares.

into service

With the forthcoming introduction of the new Hastings fleet, work had been carried out on the Hastings network of services. The local council at Bexhill lowered the road at the Sackville railway bridge to enable low height double deckers to go underneath, whereas previously only single-deckers could go under the bridge.

The four Hastings trolleybus routes were withdrawn along with four of M&D's own routes and a further four were revised. Seven new routes were introduced within the Hastings area with the introduction of the Atlanteans. The last day of trolleybus operation was on 31 May 1959. There was a final procession watched by many of the local residents and holidaymakers.

Of the 50 Atlanteans, 24 highbridge ones were allocated to Silverhill and three to Hastings. The lowbridge ones were split between nine at Hastings and five at Bexhill. The remaining nine Atlanteans were divided between four at Gravesend, one at Tunbridge Wells and four at Maidstone.

In the Gravesend area they went on the 26 Gravesend to Faversham and the 46 to Valley Drive. During the summer Gravesend's shining new Atlanteans could be seen on weekend private hires to the Kent coast, often pausing for a refreshment halt for their passengers at the Central Hotel in Gillingham.

East Kent borrowed DH523 for two weeks in September 1959 and operated the bus in the Thanet area. The company had just taken into service 40 AEC Regent Vs with Park Royal 72-seat full-front bodies and wanted to compare the Atlantean with its new vehicles. In late 1959 DH512 was transferred to Gillingham for trials at that depot.

Luton-based Leyland Atlantean DH579 from the 1961 delivery was turning into Watling Street before descending Chatham Hill to continue its journey through Chatham and Rochester to Borstal. Its journey had started from Gillingham Strand.

There's a little more about both terminal points on page 100.
MIKE HODGES

more Atlanteans

Another 25 Atlanteans were delivered between May and July 1960, DH526-550, and were spread between Tunbridge Wells, Sittingbourne, Faversham, Gravesend, Sheerness and Gillingham. Route 26 got more Atlanteans on it, after gaining union agreement, the route being operated by Faversham, Sittingbourne, Gillingham and Gravesend depots. During the summer of 1960 DH525 went to Portsmouth Corporation to be viewed by the municipal operator, which did lead it to buy a large Atlantean fleet.

M&Ds fleet of Atlanteans was growing with a further 35 following on in late 1960 and early 1961, DH551-585, the majority of the batch going to the Medway Towns garages, but a small number went to Silverhill to release earlier examples from the first batch to the Medway towns. A new feature on DH571-585 was illuminated advert panels. The panel was illuminated by bulbs. These caused problems when they failed as the panel had to be removed to change any of the bulbs.

a few problems

By the end of 1961 Maidstone & District had 110 Leyland Atlanteans in service, but all was not well. They were giving various mechanical problems in service. Rear sub-frames were cracking, the centrifugal clutch had constant failures, and gearboxes, fan drives and propshafts were also becoming troublesome. The drivers also complained that the Atlantean was underpowered for its size. This was all affecting reliability. With the help of Leyland, modifications were carried out to bring the buses in line with the new Mk2 Atlantean specification, mentioned further on, the majority of the work being done at Postley Works.

In the Medway towns the Atlantean had become a prominent part of the fleet, with many local routes now operated by the new buses, including the 140 group of services. M&D was not complacent and between May and June 1962 the opposition was tried in the form of a Daimler Fleetline CRG6LX with a Metro-Cammell body, 246 DOC.

Gravesend had several duties on the 26 to Sittingbourne and Faversham via the Medway Towns. The route was an early convert to the Leyland Atlantean and DH551 in the picture above was parked at Gravesend after returning on the 26. Buses in this batch had offside illuminated advert panels fitted to them, which were not a success.

That's a Harrington-Commer Contender bus alongside - there's more about these on page 32.
SOUTHDOWN ENTHUSIASTS' CLUB

To compare its AEC Regent Vs with the new rear-engined generation, East Kent borrowed M&Ds DH523 for two weeks in September 1959. The bus operated in the Thanet area and below it was at Ramsgate on the 52 from Margate Harbour to Ramsgate Harbour.
M&D AND EAST KENT BUS CLUB

the two coach Atlanteans

The last two Atlanteans in the first highbridge batch, DH524/5, were different inside by having 60 coach-style seats and extra luggage pens. They also had saloon ceiling racks on both decks, and the plan was to use these two coaches on the E1 Maidstone to London express service. The bodies were built by Metro-Cammell in Birmingham but the interiors finished off by sister company Weymann at Addlestone to this different style. Seats on both saloons, trimmed in the same way as the coach fleet, were made as pairs but had individual headrests. Despite this, the exterior was still painted in standard bus livery, which was a bit of a shame really. Just think how wonderful they might have looked in coach livery!

These were the only two of Maidstone & District's Atlanteans to have air suspension on the front axle, which gave a somewhat lively ride (it was not unknown for passengers to feel ill on the top deck). The standard Leyland O.600 engine had an output of 125bhp.

Both vehicles were allocated to Maidstone on delivery in November 1959. Despite all good intentions, in just a short time it was clear there wouldn't be an agreement with staff to operate these double-deck coaches on the E1; the union could see a reduction in seasonal overtime on express duplicates if more were bought. Luggage capacity was stretched with a full load of passengers, and passengers complained of the luggage pens obstructing the forward view on the lower deck. The vehicles were also limited to express services that didn't have any low bridges along the route.

They were moved to Sheerness with the idea that they could be used on the E14 Leysdown/ Sheerness to Leyton, and did have a short stay at that depot. By June 1960 both were moved again to Tunbridge Wells, where they went on bus work, mainly the 85 between Tonbridge and Speldhurst. In September 1960 DH524 went back to Sheerness, where it did operate from time to time on the E23 during summer peak weekends the following year. The rest of the time was spent on bus work including the 36 Sheerness to Eastchurch Aerodrome.

In July 1964, DH525 was moved to Gillingham but by September was back to bus work in Tunbridge Wells. It was converted to bus specification with 78 seats in October 1966. Its sister vehicle stayed as a 'coach' but had the luggage pens removed and upseated to 64 in October 1970, eventually becoming a 78-seat bus in October 1971.

It is sad to note that these two fine coaches were never used to their full potential. They were in fact the first Atlantean coaches built, a month before Ribble's Gay Hostess fleet.

The Metro-Cammell bodies built in the West Midlands were sent to Weymann at Addlestone in Surrey for the interior to be finished as coaches. Below you can see the coach type seats, luggage pens at the front and the offside rear downstairs, and luggage racks on both decks.
M&D AND EAST KENT BUS CLUB

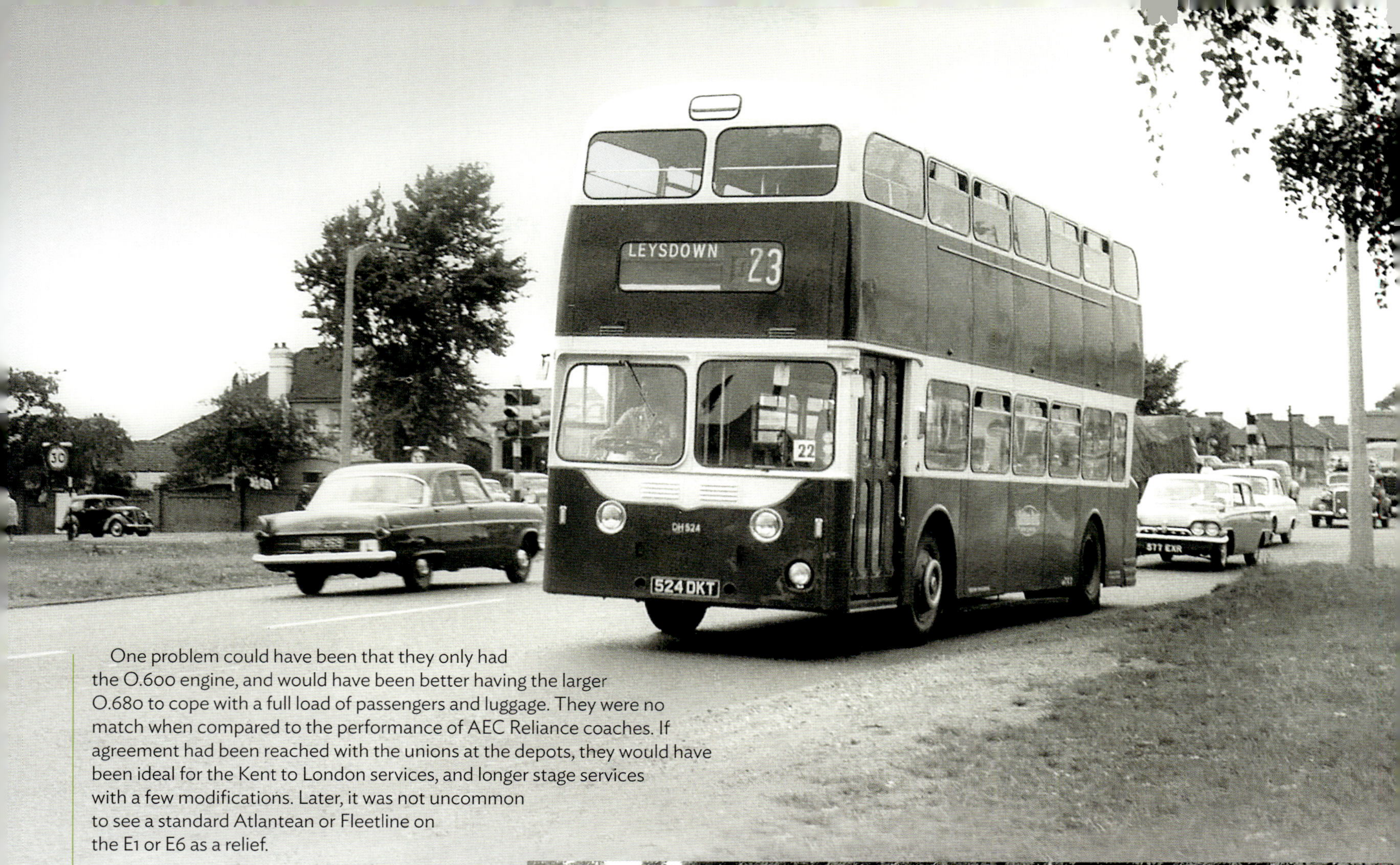

One problem could have been that they only had the O.600 engine, and would have been better having the larger O.680 to cope with a full load of passengers and luggage. They were no match when compared to the performance of AEC Reliance coaches. If agreement had been reached with the unions at the depots, they would have been ideal for the Kent to London services, and longer stage services with a few modifications. Later, it was not uncommon to see a standard Atlantean or Fleetline on the E1 or E6 as a relief.

There are very few photos of the Atlantean coaches working express service, even though for a while DH524 was used on such work from Sheerness. Above, with not many passengers and the front riding a bit high on the air suspension, DH524 was on the E23 to Leysdown from Leyton in East London. The bus was used on local Sheerness service when it wasn't doing this.

M&D AND EAST KENT BUS CLUB

The second coach Atlantean, DH525, was allocated to Tunbridge Wells depot but was rarely seen on any express duties. It spent most of its time on local bus services, particularly the 85 Tonbridge-Tunbridge Wells-Speldhurst, a route with a journey time of 56 minutes. On the right it was in pristine condition. There are two of the 'bathtub' style Standard Vanguard cars behind.

M&D AND EAST KENT BUS CLUB

The colour picture on the opposite page shows the same bus (coach) at Speldhurst.

M D WOODS

To the left, DH525 was at Maidstone on the 10 to Folkestone. It was only there for a short time, as it spent most of its working life at Tunbridge Wells, but the 10 was one of the routes that M&D thought these vehicles might be good for.

DAVID TOY COLLECTION

TONBRIDGE - SPELDHURST

For full Service between Tonbridge and Tunbridge Wells, see Summary H.

Via Tunbridge Wells — Service **85**

Mondays to Saturdays

HIGHAM WOOD EST., Hunt Road	......	......	0643	......	......	......	0720	......	0740	0753	......	......	0827	......	0910	......	1010	......	1110
CAGE FARM EST., Canterbury Cres.	......	*	......	*	0652	*	......	0730	......	......	0802	*	......	0839	......	0941	......	1041	......
Cage Green	......	0624	0647	0650	0655	0715	0724	0733	0744	0757	0805	0815	0831	0842	0914	0944	1014	1044	1114
Tonbridge, Station	......	0632	0655	0658	0703	0723	0732	0741	0752	0805	0813	0823	0839	0850	0922	0952	1022	1052	1122
Southborough Common, Fountain	......	0641	0704	0707	0712	0732	0741	0750	......	......	0822	0832	0848	0859	0931	1001	1031	1101	1131
TUNBRIDGE WELLS, War Memorial	0630	0652	0715	0718	0723	0743	0752	0801	......	......	0833	0843	0859	0910	0942	1012	1042	1112	1142
Tunbridge Wells, Central Station	0632	0654	0717	0720	0725	0745	0754	0803	......	......	0835	0845	0901	0912	0944	1014	1044	1114	1144
Langton, Greyhound	0644	0706	††	††	0737	0757‡	††	0815	......	......	0847	††	††	0924	0956	††	1056	††	1156
SPELDHURST	0652	0714	......	......	0745	......	......	0823	......	......	0855	......	......	0932	1004	......	1104	......	1204
HIGHAM WOOD EST., Hunt Road	......	1210	......	1310	......	1410	......	1510	......	1610	......	1710	......	1810	......	1910	......	2010	......
CAGE FARM EST., Canterbury Cres.	1141	......	1241	......	1341	......	1441	......	1544	......	1641	......	1741	......	1841	......	1941	......	2041
Cage Green	1144	1214	1244	1314	1344	1414	1444	1514	1547	1614	1644	1714	1744	1814	1844	1914	1944	2014	2044
Tonbridge, Station	1152	1222	1252	1322	1352	1422	1452	1522	1555	1622	1652	1722	1752	1822	1852	1922	1952	2022	2052
Southborough Common, Fountain	120[illegible]	1231	1301	1331	1401	1431	1501	1531	1604	1631	1701	1731	1801	1831	1901	1931	2001	2031	2101
TUNBRIDGE WELLS, War Memorial	1212	1242	1312	1342	1412	1442	1512	1542	1615	1642	1712	1742	1812	1842	1912	1942	2012	2042	2112
Tunbridge Wells, Central Station	1214	1244	1314	1344	1414	1444	1514	1544	1617	1644	1714	1744	1814	1844	1914	1944	2014	2044	2114
Langton, Geyhound	††	1256	1326	1356	1426	1456	††	1556	1629†	1656	1726	1756	1826	1856	[illegible]	[illegible]	[illegible]	[illegible]	[illegible]
SPELDHURST	......	1304	1334	1404	1434	1504	......	1604	1637†	1704	1734	1804	[illegible]	[illegible]	[illegible]	[illegible]	[illegible]	[illegible]	[illegible]
HIGHAM WOOD EST., Hunt Road	[illegible]																		
CAGE FARM EST.																			

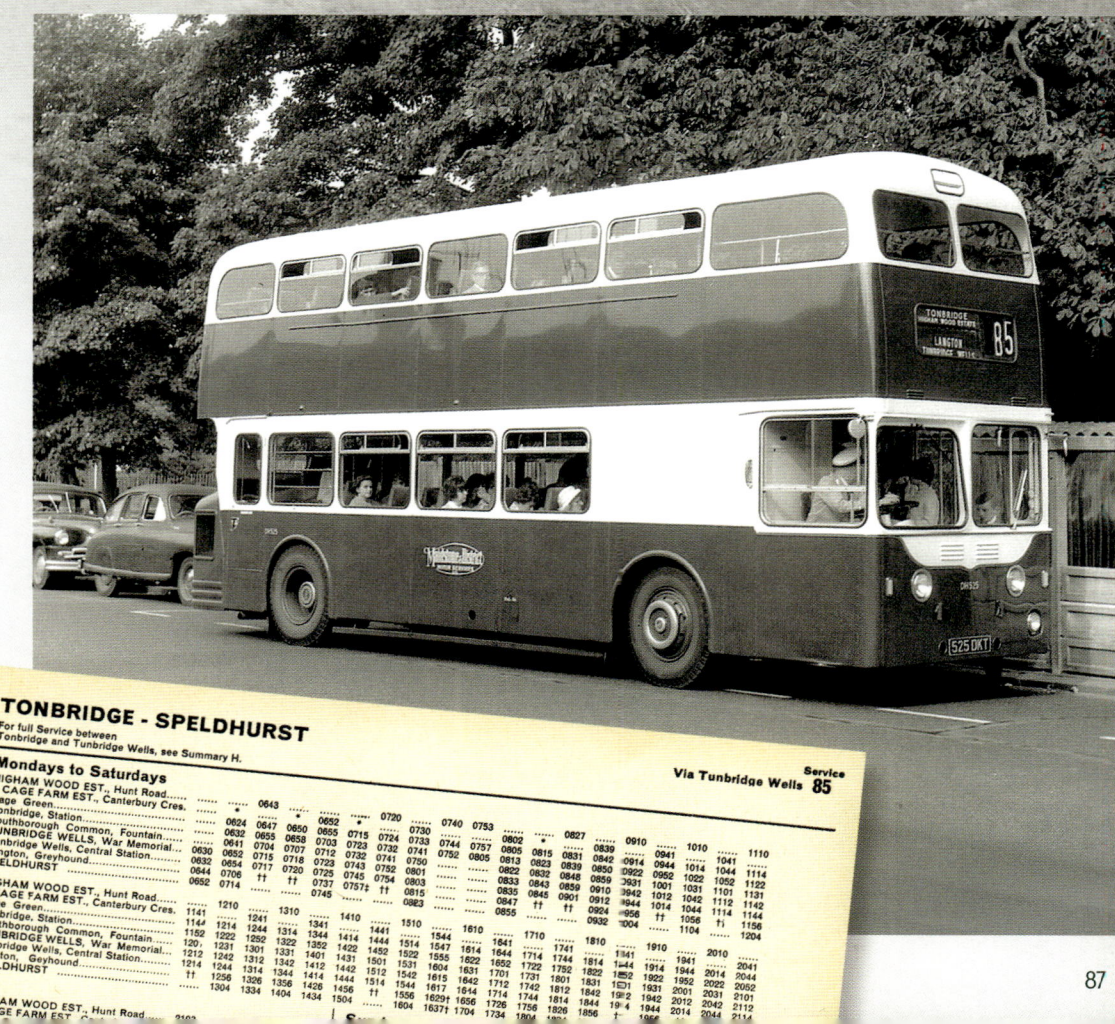

Leyland bought a Leyland Atlantean Mk2 with an Alexander body, SSD 669, from Glasgow Corporation to use as a demonstrator. Maidstone & District had the bus on demonstration in late September 1963 and the picture on the left shows it in Maidstone on route 1 on its way to Gillingham.
M&D AND EAST KENT BUS CLUB - R GIBBONS

The annual Air Display at Biggin Hill Airfield, up on the North Downs a few miles north of Westerham, brought buses and coaches from far and wide in abundance.

Maidstone & District ran excursions from towns in its area, and there were many day trips by bus from places within London Transport's operating area, both the red Central Area and the green Country Area, and in the 1960s this used to bring line after line of RTs, RFs and Routemasters.

In September 1966 an RCL Green Line 'coach' was at the right of this line up at the airfield. But of more interest here are the three Maidstone & District Leyland Atlanteans on hire to London Transport.

DH606 on the left and DH588 on the right were Mk2 Atlanteans. The adverts would suggest that at least DH588 was based at Gravesend. They were probably hired in by London Transport's Northfleet garage.
RAY STENNING

the Mk2 Atlanteans

With the experience of Atlanteans in service and feedback (and complaints) from operators, Leyland made improvements to the Atlantean chassis and introduced the Mk2 in 1963. These included a beefed-up engine producing 130bhp, a fluid flywheel in place of the lock-up clutch, the engine and gearbox now removable as separate units, improved fan, better propshaft, and a new 3-piece rear cowling. Maidstone & District ordered 47 Mk2s with Weymann 77-seat bodies, DH586-632, the last Atlantean order for M&D under BET control. A number of the batch had illuminated off-side advert panels but, as with the previous batch, they were not successful and from 1968 were removed.

Delivery of this last batch of Atlanteans started in February 1963. The Medway Towns depots had 30, split between Gillingham and Luton. The rest were dispersed in small numbers to Gravesend, Sittingbourne, Maidstone, Tunbridge Wells, Tonbridge, Silverhill and Hastings.

In September 1963 the company borrowed a Leyland Atlantean Mk2 demonstrator with an Alexander 78-seat body, SGD669, and used it on route 1 between Maidstone and Gillingham. The bus had been bought from Glasgow Corporation by Leyland to show the upgrades over the PDR/1. At the end of 1964 the 157 complete Atlanteans were allocated as follows:

Gillingham	30	Bexhill	7	Sittingbourne	9	Tunbridge Wells	13
Luton	37	Hastings	11	Sheerness	4	Tonbridge	7
Gravesend	13	Silverhill	21	Maidstone	5		

the 158th Atlantean

Before the Mk2s were delivered, an unusual demonstrator appeared late in 1962. This was a Leyland Atlantean chassis built to the Mk2 specification in October that year. The chassis was viewed by the engineering department to compare with the earlier version. The bare chassis (it had added weights on it for stability) was taken to Knightrider House by Roy Wells, who later became the engineering manager of Postley Works, and shown to senior management.

M&D's engineering department wanted to buy spare units for the Atlantean fleet, including an engine, gearbox, angle-drive, steering box and smaller units. To buy the chassis and dismantle it would be more cost-effective rather than buying individual units, as new engines and gearboxes (and other units) had a premium if sold individually. The chassis was bought from Leyland who, understandably, was not very happy with this proposal, but eventually did agree to sell.

The new chassis was taken to Postley works where Roy Wells and his team dismantled it for spares. The chassis number, 23069, came after that of DH632, the last of the Mk2s, and the sale to M&D did not actually show up on Leyland's build list; only that it had been dismantled.

a change to the Daimler Fleetline

Mention was made earlier of the Daimler Fleetline that was demonstrated to Maidstone & District between May and June 1962. This led to 35 Fleetlines being ordered for delivery in 1963. The Fleetline could have an overall lower height thanks to a drop-centre axle, meaning both saloons sticking to a conventional seating layout; Maidstone & District's lowbridge Atlanteans didn't.

The chassis of these buses was the Daimler Fleetline CRG6LX, signifying a Gardner 6LX engine. It produced 150bhp at 1,750rpm, higher than the Leyland O.600, and brought Gardner engines back into the fleet after many years of Leyland and AEC engines. Bodies were built by Northern Counties to seat 77, with one of the most noticeable differences being the side shields that eliminated the characteristic engine bustle. The design was well balanced with equal depth windows on both decks, and omission of the Northern Counties traditional 'threepenny bit' top outer corners of the upper-deck front windows. They also had smart wheel trims. Fleetnumbers were DL57-91.

The Fleetlines began to enter service in January 1964 with twelve going to Maidstone, eight to Gillingham, five to Luton, two to Tonbridge, and four each to Borough Green and Tunbridge Wells. With this large intake of double deckers, disposal of Daimler CWAs, wartime Guy Arabs and an inroad into some Bristol K6As could take place. The company found the back-up from Daimler to be far superior to that it had received from Leyland, who seemed not to have developed its service department sufficiently to cope. Daimler, a smaller company in comparison, was more flexible

After delivery, Fleetlines took over operation of lowbridge route 91 between Tunbridge Wells and East Grinstead. In this picture taken in early 1967, DL87 was pausing at the Dorset Arms in Withyham on its way to East Grinstead through Hartfield and Forest Row.
RAY STENNING

Parked at Maidstone depot when all new and shiny just after delivery was one of the final Northern Counties Daimler Fleetlines, 6128. Behind it was one of the first batch, renumbered 6078 by this time.
MIKE HODGES

A further two batches were delivered between 1966 and 1968, bringing the total of Maidstone & District's Northern Counties bodied Daimler Fleetlines to 75. The earlier full rear destination was replaced with a triple route number on these two later batches.

DL92-111 were delivered in 1966 and the final batch in 1968, but these had fleetnumbers in the new non-prefix series 6112-6131. They were the last double-deckers to be delivered in the traditional M&D livery, and arrived equipped for one-man-operation with upper deck periscope and illuminated signs at the front and by the entrance door.

Maidstone & District's Daimler Fleetlines were not entirely trouble free. M&D was soon to find that there was a weakness in the transmission, in the coupling between the engine and gearbox. The gearboxes and transfer boxes had a short life.

Maidstone & District's Daimler Fleetlines were withdrawn from service after a 12- to 15-year life, being fully depreciated by then. However, many of the company's PDR Leyland Atlanteans stayed with the company longer, some getting transferred to other NBC companies and giving a service life of over 20 years.

Daimler Fleetline DL64 was delivered in December 1963 and allocated to Gillingham depot. Below, parked at the depot, you can see the GL shed plate on the nearside rear above the rear lights.

The side shields at the rear of the Northern Counties bodies did rather make cleaning the top of the engine cover and the rear widow difficult. Note the full size rear destination display, not repeated on the later batches.
JULIAN BOWDEN

a day at the Seaside

Maidstone & District had frequent bus services running to a number of seaside resorts, including Brighton, Eastbourne, Bexhill and Hastings along the Sussex coast. But of course in the summer months it ran countless excursions from all over its patch to the many seaside towns in the South East easily reachable by coach, and advertised them extensively.

On the right is a page from M&D's coach excursion programme for 1961 from the Wealden towns and villages of Hawkhurst, Sandhurst, Cranbrook, Sissinghurst and Goudhurst.

Below is the very first of the fine 37-seat Leyland bodied Leyland Royal Tiger coaches, CO273, that came into the fleet in 1952. We're not sure which coastal resort this coach was at, but it had parked right alongside a very inviting shingle beach on a hot summer's day with a sparkling sea looking most inviting and a deep azure sky overhead. Although, oddly, a fair number of passengers, mainly elderly ladies, were content to stay on the coach. Perhaps it had only just arrived or was about to depart.

In its day, that Leyland coach body was a pretty impressive and handsome style.

around the patch

Although the trend at the end of the 20th century was to have large out-of-town depots on industrial sites with less under-cover storage for buses, that wasn't the case in earlier times. A network the size of Maidstone & District's meant the company had depots spread all over its territory, some big and some small, from Edenbridge in the west to Ashford and Faversham in the east, and from Gravesend and Sheerness in the north to Bexhill and Hastings in the south, and many were close to the centre of towns. Of course, there were outstations too, dotted around the patch.

In this section we travel around the various M&D depots, looking at their routes and operations, and the vehicles either run from there or that passed through. We're also taking a few diversions on the way, to look at other aspects of the towns and areas served, touching on history, architecture, railways, folklore, anecdotes and stories, and anything else that helps to give us a richer understanding of and deeper insight into the true character of this fascinating bus company in its heyday.

In this picture, Leyland Atlantean 5544, operating out of the Medway Towns, was heading past beautiful spring blossoms as it was heading south from Cliffe on the Isle of Grain towards Strood.
MIKE HODGES

Maidstone	page 94
Gillingham	page 101
Luton (Chatham)	page 106
Hastings	page 114
Silverhill	page 116
Bexhill	page 122
Tunbridge Wells	page 124
Tonbridge	page 131
Hawkhurst	page 132
Edenbridge	page 134
Rye	page 139
Tenterden	page 140
Ashford	page 142
Borough Green	page 144
Isle of Sheppey	page 146
Gravesend	page 150
Faversham	page 161
Sittingbourne	page 162

As well as depots, the company owned several houses used by senior depot staff. In Nelson Road in Gillingham, for example, several terraced houses were owned as well as others in adjacent Grenville Road.

At Sittingbourne a flat was also owned by M&D and there were other premises at Tunbridge Wells.

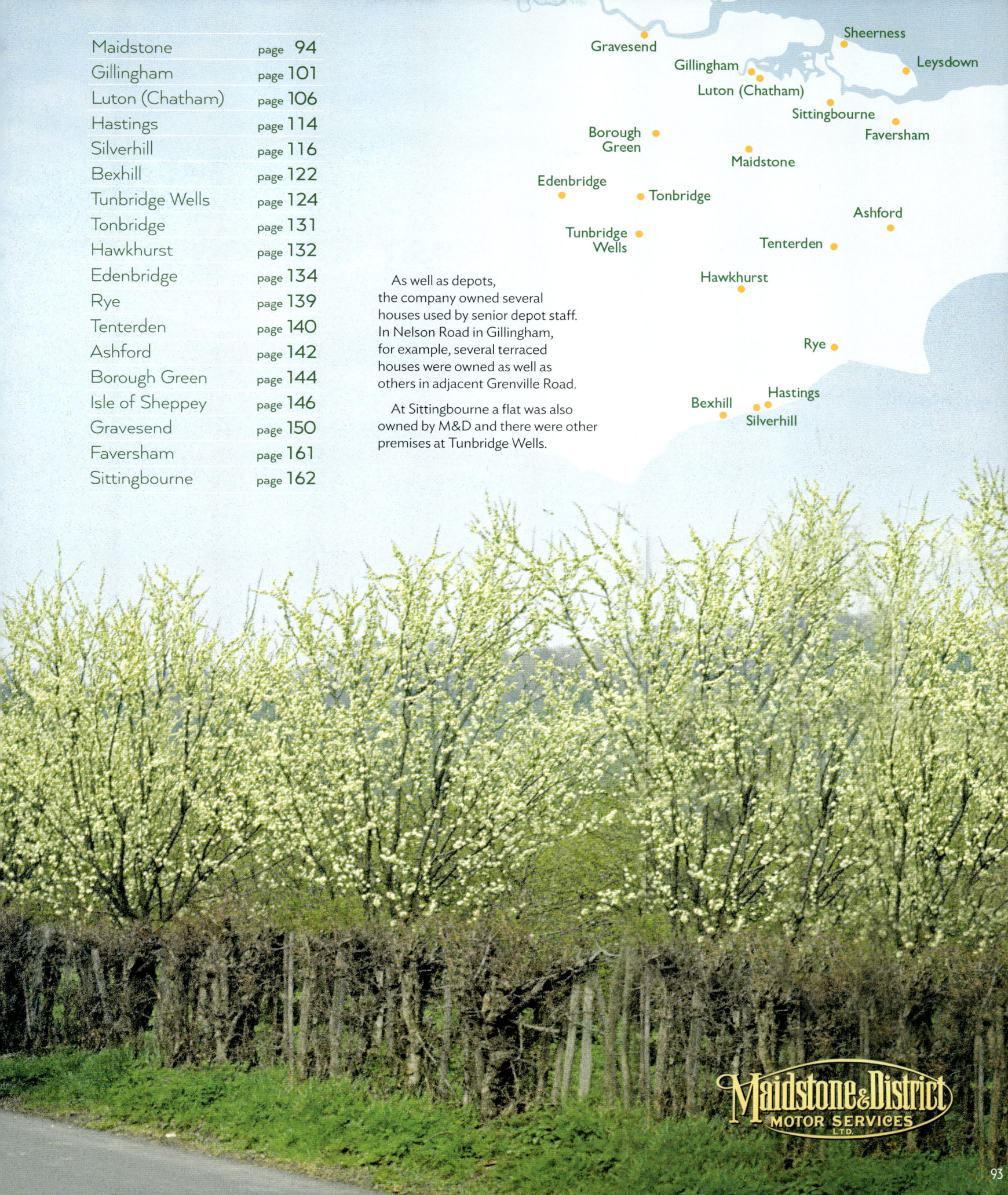

Eastcourt Estate, Hawthorne Avenue	1
Eastcourt Estate, Beechings Green	1A
Eastcourt Estate, Beechings Way	1B

GILLINGHAM - MAIDSTONE

For full Service between Huntsmans Corner and Eastcourt Estate, see Summary A.

Mondays to Saturdays—Continued

Service No.	1	1A	1 NS	1	1 NS	1B	1	1A	1	1A	1	Then at these minutes past each hour 1B	1	1A	1	1A	1		1B
MAIDSTONE, Lower Stone Street Bus Station	0831	0841	0846	0851	0856	0901	0911	0921	0931	0941	0951	01	11	21	31	41	51	until	1701
County Hall	0835	0845	0850	0855	0900	0905	0915	0925	0935	0945	0955	05	15	25	35	45	55		1705
Running Horse Turning	0839	0849	0854	0859	0904	0909	0919	0929	0939	0949	0959	09	19	29	39	49	59		1709
Lower Bell	0845	0855	0900	0905	0910	0915	0925	0935	0945	0955	1005	15	25	35	45	55	05		1715
Upper Bell	0849	0859	0904	0909	0914	0919	0929	0939	0949	0959	1009	19	29	39	49	59	09		1719
Buckmore Park	0852	0902	0907	0912	0917	0922	0932	0942	0952	1002	1012	22	32	42	52	02	12		1722
Fort Horsted	0856	0906	0911	0916	0921	0926	0936	0946	0956	1006	1016	26	36	46	56	06	16		1726
CHATHAM, Military Road	0906	0916	0921	0926	0931	0936	0946	0956	1006	1016	1026	36	46	56	06	16	26		1736
St. Mark's Church	0913	0923	0928	0933	0938	0943	0953	1003	1013	1023	1033	43	53	03	13	23	33		1743
GILLINGHAM, Gillingham Road	0917	0927	0932	0937	0942	0947	0957	1007	1017	1027	1037	47	57	07	17	27	37		1747
Beatty Avenue	0922	0932	......	0942	......	0952	1002	1012	1022	1032	1042	52	02	12	22	32	42		1752
EASTCOURT ESTATE, Beechings Green	......	0941	......	......	......	......	......	1021	......	1041	......	...	...	21	...	41	...		......
EASTCOURT ESTATE, Beechings Way	......	......	......	......	......	1001	......	......	......	......	......	01	...	...	...	...	...		1801
EASTCOURT ESTATE, Hawthorne Avenue	0931	......	......	0951	......	......	1011	......	1031	......	1051	...	11	...	31	...	51		......

Service No.	1	1A	1B	1	1	1A	1	1 NS	1	1B	1 NS	1	1	1A	1	1B	1	1A
MAIDSTONE, Lower Stone Street Bus Station	1711	1721	1731	1741	1751	1801	1811	......	1821	1831	......	1841	1851	1901	1916	1931	1946	2001
County Hall	1715	1725	1735	1745	1755	1805	1815	......	1825	1835	......	1845	1855	1905	1920	1935	1950	2005
Running Horse Turning	1719	1729	1739	1749	1759	1809	1819	......	1829	1839	......	1849	1859	1909	1924	1939	1954	2009
Lower Bell	1725	1735	1745	1755	1805	1815	1825	......	1835	1845	......	1855	1905	1915	1930	1945	2000	2015
Upper Bell	1729	1739	1749	1759	1809	1819	1829	......	1839	1849	......	1859	1909	1919	1934	1949	2004	2019
Buckmore Park	1732	1742	1752	1802	1812	1822	1832	......	1842	1852	......	1902	1912	1922	1937	1952	2007	2022
Fort Horsted	1736	1746	1756	1806	1816	1826	1836	††1845	1846	1856	††1901	1906	1916	1926	1941	1956	2011	2026
CHATHAM, Military Road	1746	1756	1806	1816	1826	1836	1846	1855	1856	1906	1911	1916	1926	1936	1951	2006	2021	2036
St. Mark's Church	1753	1803	1813	1823	1833	1843	1853	1902	1903	1913	1918	1923	1933	1943	1958	2013	2028	2043
GILLINGHAM, Gillingham Road	1757	1807	1817	1827	1837	1847	1857	1906	1907	1917	1922	1927	1937	1947	2002	2017	2032	2047
Beatty Avenue	1802	1812	1822	1832	1842	1852	......	......	1912	1922	......	......	1942	1952	2007	2022	2037	2052
EASTCOURT ESTATE, Beechings Green	......	1821	......	......	......	1901	......	......	......	......	......	......	......	2001	......	......	......	2101
EASTCOURT ESTATE, Beechings Way	......	......	1831	......	......	......	......	......	......	1931	......	......	......	......	......	2031	......	......
EASTCOURT ESTATE, Hawthorne Avenue	1811	......	......	1841	1851	......	......	......	1921	......	......	......	1951	......	2016	......	2046	......

CONTINUED ON NEXT PAGE.

CODE ON PAGE 49.

43

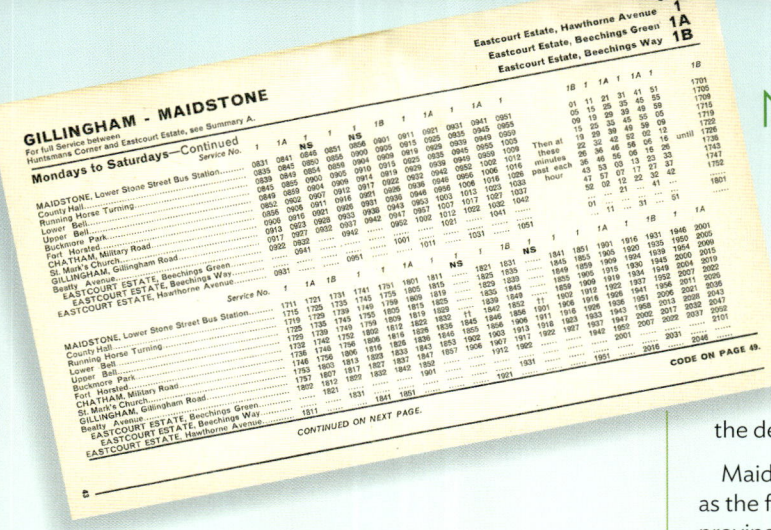

Maidstone M

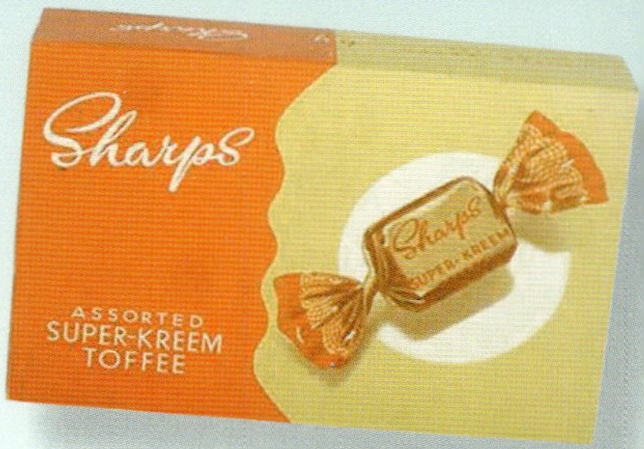

Maidstone is the county town of Kent. It began as nothing more than a Saxon village but by the 13th century had more-or-less grown into a town and continued to grow over the following centuries. Being on the River Medway meant it was ideal for transporting fruit and vegetables from Kent by water into London. It became an important market town for a large part of the county, with weekly markets and a large annual fair. These would attract people from many outlying towns and villages and helped the development of bus services in the area.

Maidstone & District had two bus stations in Maidstone. The one in Mill Street, regarded as the first bus station in the country, opened in 1922 but as the years went by this was proving to be inadequate, so Lower Stone Street bus station was opened in 1951.

Maidstone's population had grown to 56,000 by the early 1950s. The town was not a hugely industrialised place, but there were some major employers within and near the town. For example, the Rootes Group had taken over Tilling-Stevens commercial vehicle manufacturer (including buses) in 1950 and the factory continued to make the famous 2-stroke horizontally-opposed 3-cylinder (6 pistons) TS3 diesel engine there. The factory closed in the 1970s.

Paper production was important. Tovil Paper Mills was on the outskirts of the town with the larger Reed Paper Group at Aylesford only a few miles away, a very large employer for the area. The cement industry was represented by the Rugby and Portland companies, with their plants a little downstream along the Medway Valley. Sharps had a toffee factory in Maidstone (it used to advertise in the timetable books) and Foster Clark, who used to make such foods as custard powders, jellies, desiccated soups and lemonade powder, also had a factory here. Style & Winch was the well-known Kentish Brewery on the banks of the River Medway near the town centre.

On this page, on its way into Maidstone on route 1, DH584 was passing the Running Horse. This Leyland Atlantean was delivered in 1961 with a Metro-Cammell 77-seat body. In the distance you can see the chalk hillside where this Atlantean would make the long climb up to Blue Bell Hill on the return to Gillingham.

Route 1 and its variations ran on a 10-minute frequency between Maidstone and Gillingham in the early 1960s, continuing on to different parts of Eastcourt Estate.

OMNICOLOUR

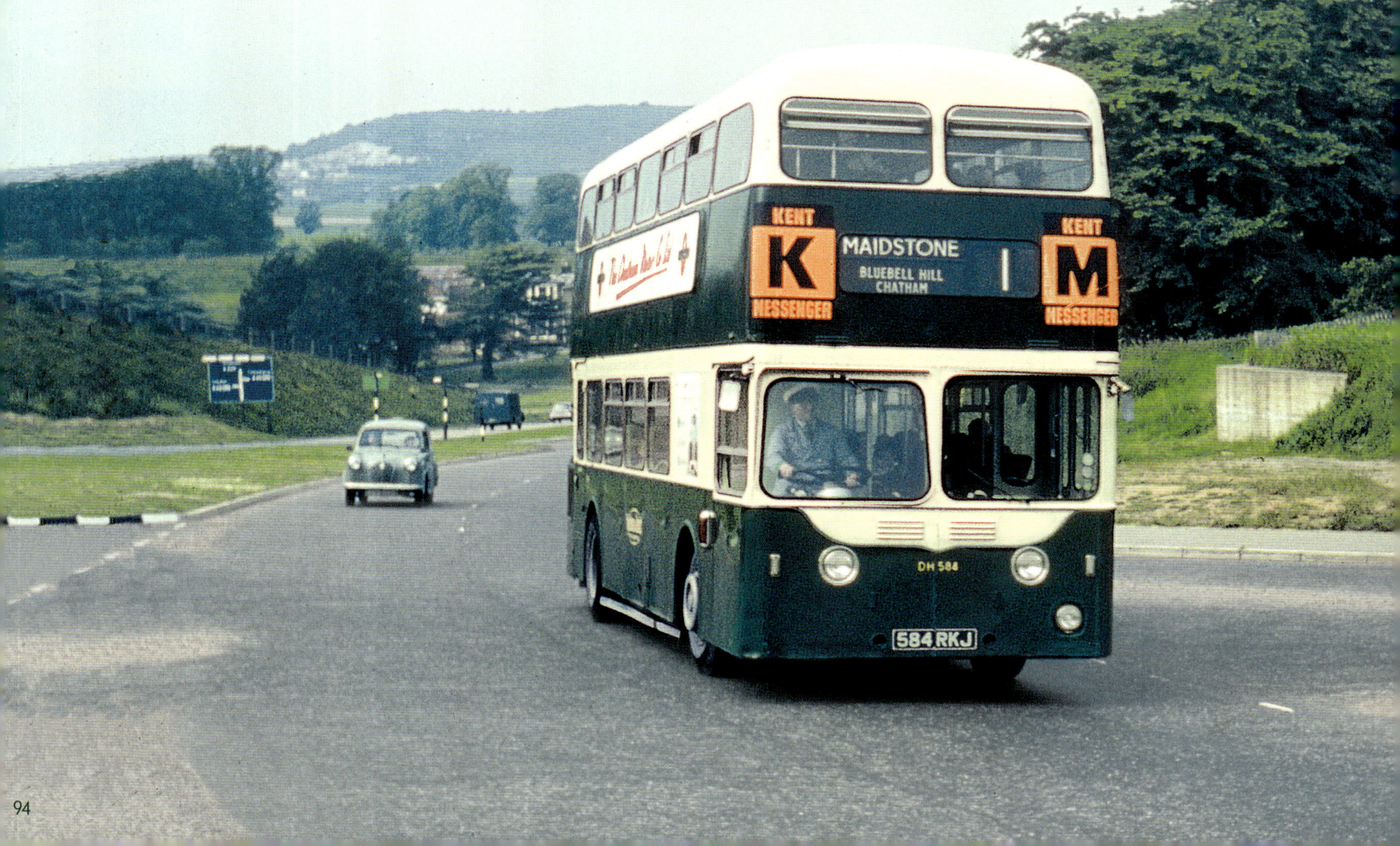

Town services in Maidstone were run by the Corporation with a small trolleybus network as well as diesel buses. The picture on the right was taken at the top of the High Street opposite the Queen's Monument and shows trolleybus no. 58 on the way to Loose.

This Sunbeam W4 was delivered in 1944 with a Park Royal utility body but in 1960 was rebodied by Roe with this 62-seat body.
OMNICOLOUR

After a previous purchase of Leyland Titan PD2s, Maidstone Corporation then turned to Leyland Atlanteans with Massey bodies. A new livery was also introduced, replacing the golden ochre and ivory with Fiesta blue and primrose cream. At the bottom on the right was no. 34 delivered in December 1965 and converted to one-man operation in December 1968.
DAVID TOY

Municipal public transport began in Maidstone on 14 July 1904, when Maidstone Corporation Tramways began a service to Barming, followed by routes to Loose and Tovil. The Barming trams were replaced by trolleybuses in 1928, the Loose trams in 1930. By the 1950s the diesel-engined buses in the fleet were a mixture of Park Royal, Duple and Weymann boded Guy Arabs, Daimler CVG6s with Brush and Northern Coachbuilders bodies, and more recent Leyland Titan PD2/20 with Massey bodies. The Sunbeam and Karrier trolleybuses left in the fleet were replaced by Massey bodied Leyland Atlanteans in a new pale blue and primrose livery in 1967.

After becoming Maidstone Borough Council Transport in 1974 following local government reorganisation, on 9 August 1981 its services were integrated with local ones of Maidstone & District under the banner of Maidstone Area Bus Services. There were route changes and route swapping, and Corporation buses now were to be seen outside the borough in nearby villages to the south of the town. This reorganisation also saw closure of M&D's Maidstone depot in Knightrider Street.

This arrangement finished and the routes were carved up between the two operators with deregulation on 26 October 1986. Maidstone Borough Council's bus services became the council-owned, 'arm's-length' company, Maidstone Borough Transport (Holdings) Limited, trading as Boro'line with a new yellow and blue livery.

Boro'line expanded into tendered bus operation in London, perhaps a little too vigorously because in 1989 it posted a loss of £1.25 million.

On 17 February 1992 the London operation was sold to Kentish Bus and two days later Boro'line was placed into administration. Then on 29 May 1992 Boro'line ceased operations. The vehicles and the Armstrong Road offices and depot were sold to Maidstone & District by the administrators.

Maidstone used to suffer shockingly bad traffic congestion, which was painfully heavy in the summer months. A by-pass was actually planned before the Second World War, but it wasn't until 1961 that Maidstone was by-passed with the opening of that section of the M20.

In 1951 Knightrider Street in Maidstone had an allocation of 106 buses and coaches, although this would always increase in the summer to cover the extra express, tours and private hire work. The double-deck fleet then was a mixture of highbridge Daimler CWA6s, Bristol K6As and the then new all-Leyland Titan PD2/12s, plus lowbridge Bristol K6As, Leyland Titan PD2/12s and elderly Titan TD4s. Single-deck buses were a mixture of AEC Regals, Leyland Tigers and new Bristol LL5Gs. Coaches allocated to Maidstone were AEC Regals, Dodge 84s, Beadle/AEC semi-chassisless types and Leyland Tigers.

In the 1950s the main service between Maidstone and Chatham and Gillingham was the 1, supplemented with the half-hourly 7 and the hourly 33 from Tunbridge Wells. The 7 came via Hadlow and Tonbridge, the 33 via Paddock Wood and Pembury. This pattern provided a combined frequency of ten minutes between Chatham and Maidstone. These services were normally operated by Bristol K6As, although later the Leyland Titan PD2/12s would also be seen. Later the 7 and 33 were cut back to run only between Tunbridge Wells and Maidstone, although a 10-minute frequency between Maidstone and the Medway Towns was still provided.

Once the Atlanteans started coming into the fleet, they soon appeared on the 1. All direct services from Maidstone to the Medway Towns had to climb the long hill from the Lower to the Upper Bell on the A229, known as Blue Bell Hill, and this was a test for any bus with a good load. Today it is a dual carriageway, but in the 1950s it was a narrow climbing road with no passing places. The 2-hourly route 5 from Gillingham used to go this way to Maidstone, and it interworked with the 57 from Gravesend, both continuing to Hastings via Cranbrook, Hawkhurst and Battle every hour. This was a very scenic 2¾ hours journey on the top deck of a bus. Later the 5 was cut back from Gillingham with only the 57s continuing north from the county town.

Above was Harrington Wayfarer IV bodied AEC Reliance coach C426 parked in Palace Avenue with the blinds set for the summer-only E8 from Gillingham and Chatham through Maidstone, Cranbrook and Hawkhurst to Eastbourne. The Rootes factory is behind.
JEREMY WILLIAMS COLLECTION

The 139 ran roughly hourly to Coxheath, a village just over 2 miles south of the town. Below, Northern Counties bodied Daimler Fleetline 6115, one the final batch delivered in Spring 1968, was showing its illuminated one-man operation sign on the front, although it was not fully ready for OMO until the August and the 139 didn't become a one-man route until 1971.
JEREMY WILLIAMS COLLECTION

In 1966 M&D took a second batch of Daimler Fleetlines with Northern Counties bodies to the same specification as the first batch, except for a rear triple route number screen in place of a full destination.

On the right was Fleetline DL94 leaving Maidstone on route 20 to Gillingham via West Malling and the villages along the west bank of the River Medway.

OMNICOLOUR

Between November 1953 and April 1954 Maidstone & District had on loan the 1952 Beadle-Commer integral 37-seat coach shown above.

It was in Palace Avenue with the Rootes factory behind, where the Commer TS3 engine, as fitted to this coach, was made. This coach was given temporary fleetnumber C0500. Note the left trafficator still slightly out.

M&D AND EAST KENT BUS CLUB

20 of the BET-style bodied 36ft AEC Reliances that came in 1965 were dual-purpose with 49-seat bodies built by Weymann. They became quite common on the E1 from Maidstone to London, which ran roughly every 2 hours.

SC45 was passing the 14th-century Tithe Barn immediately south of Mill Street Bus Station, departure point for the E1. Coming up behind was a Maidstone Corporation Massey bodied Leyland Titan PD2.

M&D AND EAST KENT BUS CLUB

You could also get to Hastings on the 12. This went via Headcorn, Tenterden and Northiam. In the 1950s it operated mostly hourly during the day but during the 1960s the frequency was reduced to 2-hourly. Sheerness on the Isle of Sheppey was reached by the 41 from Maidstone, Sittingbourne and Faversham by the 3, and Sevenoaks by the 9.

As well as the 'main road' services to the Medway Towns, the 29 gave a half-hourly link downstream along the Medway valley through the villages of Aylesford, Eccles, Burham and Wouldham - there's more about this route on page 190. There was also the hourly 20 which headed west from Maidstone to West Malling then struck northwards along the west bank of the Medway. This was operated by lowbridge vehicles, pre-war Leyland TDs in the 1950s and later Bristol K6As with, on the odd occasion, a Leyland Titan PD2/12.

There were two joint services with East Kent out of Maidstone, the 10 to Folkestone via Lenham, Charing, Ashford and Hythe, and the 67 to Canterbury via Lenham, Charing, Chilham and Chartham. There's more about these on pages 164 and 165.

Maidstone as county town of course was also a hub, with both regular and, in some cases, irregular services from a number of villages all around.

Route 44 had one journey each way on a Tuesday from Frittenden for villagers to get to Maidstone on market day. On this route at the top of the opposite page was SO302, one of the 1960 delivery of AEC Reliance buses with Weymann dual-purpose bodies of the earlier, rather square BET style. This bus was allocated from new to Maidstone depot.
DAVID TOY COLLECTION

To update the lowbridge fleet 21 Bristol K6As with Weymann 53-seat lowbridge bodies were delivered in 1949 and 1950, the last Bristol Ks to enter the fleet. The lowbridge layout was not liked by passengers or conductors, and the driver's cab was cramped compared to the highbridge version. All these lowbridge examples went in 1963/4, replaced by new Daimler Fleetlines.

On layover, with the crew in deep discussion, DL22, the last of the batch, was at Ashford Road Yeoman at the terminus of route 109 at the bottom of the opposite page. The 109 was an unusual route in that it went across Maidstone to West Malling. The majority of the company's local services started and finished in the town.

West Malling was served by no fewer than six bus routes, five of them from Maidstone and the 39 from the Medway Towns.
OMNICOLOUR

There's more about the lovely village of Aylesford on page 190, but below on route 29 on its way towards Maidstone was Guy Arab DH473 with a lightweight Weymann Orion body.

Eight Guy Arab IVs had been ordered for Chatham & District but due to the merger of Chatham & District into Maidstone & District in 1955 they were delivered in M&D green and cream.
OMNICOLOUR

The Medway Towns

What has become known as the Medway Towns is the conglomeration of Gillingham, Chatham, Rochester and Strood, and made up the largest urban area of Maidstone & District's operations. The area has always had important military and naval associations. It was in King Henry VIII's time that the Royal Navy opened a dockyard here, and it was at Chatham that Nelson's warship HMS Victory was built. Chatham Dockyard was the largest employer in the area with, at one point, 10,000 people working there, and on the same site was the Royal Navy Barracks, HMS Pembroke. In the 1950s you could still see big gun cruisers at the annual Navy Days, which always drew big crowds, and Chatham Dockyard was still building O-class submarines.

As well as the Navy there were several other military establishments. The Royal School of Military Engineering was at Brompton, between Chatham and Gillingham, and a Royal Naval Armaments Depot at Chattenden; this had its own military railway. The Royal Marines had barracks not far from Military Road. On the bank of the River Medway at Rochester was Acorn ship repair yard and nearby the Mac Lynch scrapyard where Second World War submarines could be seen being dismantled.

A new oil refinery had been built on the Isle of Grain and this needed contract buses for its staff. Other employers were CAV with a factory in Rochester, Holborn-Eaton at Strood, and there were other industries developing at Rochester airport. Not far away were the large Reed paper mills at Aylesford which employed staff from a wide area, including the Medway Towns.

The city of Rochester is famous for its Norman castle standing opposite the cathedral, a pertinent reminder of the struggles between king and church in medieval times. Rochester is also famous for its associations with the Victorian novelist Charles Dickens, who set several of his novels in the area.

Before the M2 opened in 1962, the main trunk road between London and Dover was the A2, which passed through all of the Medway Towns and during the summer would become very busy with coaches on day trips to Kent coast resorts. The main bottlenecks were through Rochester, particularly the bridge over the River Medway and at the bottom of Star Hill, which would lead to long traffic delays.

The Medway Towns was not an easy operating area with hills that would test any bus. Chatham Hill was the most demanding, being very long on a continuous gradient, while Star Hill was shorter but very steep. There was also the long climb from Chatham Station along the Maidstone Road to Fort Horsted.

Although seen all across Maidstone & District's territory, Leyland Atlanteans became very common in the Medway Towns.

DH566 on this page, with the back ends of two generations of small Ford cars in view, was caught at Gillingham Strand, the nearest thing the Medway Towns got to a seafront.

The open-air pool with a view of the power station across the Medway estuary was, nevertheless, very popular. And among dockland impediments it afforded a good view of Her Majesty's finest going to and from Chatham naval dockyard.

The bus was bound for the pleasant Rochester suburb of Borstal, where the first institution bearing that name was established in 1902. Borstal soon became the name for all such establishments throughout the country.
THE BUS ARCHIVE/ROY MARSHALL

In the early 1950s all the rebodied Guy Arabs were allocated to Gillingham, and after the demise of a separate Chatham & District 13 were transferred to Chatham.

Above, Weymann bodied DH21 had just turned into Chatham Military Road on a short working of the 19 to Wainscott, it normally running from Gillingham to Hoo or Grain.
SOUTHDOWN ENTHUSIASTS' CLUB

Away from the bus routes it would have originally run on in the Medway Towns, ex-Chatham & District 920 had, in the picture on the right, become DH451 after being absorbed into the parent fleet. This Bristol K5G had its utility body replaced by this Weymann one in 1951.

Here it was on the outskirts of Gravesend on a 23 working from Chatham via Cobham, a less frequent route than the main road services between the Medway Towns and Gravesend.
SOUTHDOWN ENTHUSIASTS' CLUB

Maidstone & District had two depots in the Medway towns: Nelson Road, Gillingham and Luton Road, Chatham. Before September 1955, when M&D's subsidiary Chatham & District was merged with its parent company, Luton was the home of the subsidiary, and this is described in more detail further on. In October 1951 there were 143 buses and coaches based at Gillingham, although this would increase by another 15-20 coaches in the summer, and 54 at Luton.

Gillingham GL

Gillingham depot in Nelson Road replaced an earlier one at Fox Street in 1921, but was rebuilt during the war after it had been bombed on the night of 27 August 1940, when 51 buses were destroyed along with much of the building. There's more about that on the next page. There was a bus station in front of the rebuilt depot with running sheds at the rear; also a large booking and enquiry office. Through services, except for expresses, used an island on Nelson Road adjacent to the bus station.

By 1955 Gillingham had become the stronghold for the early Guy Arabs re-bodied by Weymann, but the majority of the double-deck fleet were Bristol K6As with varying styles of bodies. There were also still four pre-war highbridge Leyland Titan TD7s and two lowbridge TD4cs plus a solitary lowbridge Bristol K6A. Single deck buses here were AEC Regals, Bristol L6As and Beadle/AEC semi-chassisless types. Gillingham was an important depot in the company's coaching operations and had AEC Regals, Beadle-Leylands, Leyland Royal Tigers, AEC Reliance and Leyland Tiger TS7s.

Between 1948 and 1949 the company took 32 AEC Regal IIIs with Harrington bodies into the fleet.

These coaches were seen all over the company's area, and here on the left CO109, a Sheerness coach, was at Gillingham bus station waiting for its passengers on the E19 to Leyton in East London.
G MEAD

Until the 7 and 33 routes were cut back to Maidstone in 1960 and the 5 in 1962, Gillingham had a hand in their operation. The 26 and 40 were two longer distance routes that passed though the bus station and these are shown on pages 154-9. The 26 went from Faversham and Sittingbourne - some journeys only from Sittingbourne - to Gravesend. Coming into Gillingham from the Faversham end, the 26 passed through Newington and Rainham, then turned off to descend Canterbury Street and Nelson Road to reach Gillingham Bus Station. It then went on to the centre of Gillingham, through Chatham and had to fight its way through the rest of the Medway Towns traffic and emerge at Strood before proceeding to Gravesend.

This route was timed to take 1 hour 53 minutes from end to end, but this could be longer if the traffic was badly congested within the towns. At the summer peak it was not unknown for the 26 and the 40 to be an hour late at their final destinations. In 1955 the 26 had a half-hourly service from Faversham with a 10-minute frequency from Sittingbourne, which by 1965 had been reduced to 15 minutes. The 40 ran hourly from Sheerness through the Medway Towns to Gravesend, joining the 26 at Key Street to the west of Sittingbourne.

All through the 1950s and 1960s services still struggled in Rochester and Strood because of traffic congestion, especially at peak times during the day and in the summer months. In 1962, when the M2 motorway opened, the traffic flow did improve. It was not really until the second bridge over the Medway at Rochester was built in 1970, together with other road improvements, that the traffic flow improved to an acceptable level.

During the later 1950s Gillingham's double-deck allocation stayed with Guy Arabs and Bristol K6As and a small number of Leyland Titan PD2s, plus lowbridge Bristol K6As. The need for single-deck buses was met with Beadle/AEC semi-chassisless types, Bristol LL5Gs and new AEC Reliances. Gillingham's first Leyland Atlantean turned up in late 1959, followed by more through the 1960s.

when bombs fell on Gillingham

Gillingham suffered one of its worst air raids during the Battle of Britain at around midnight on Tuesday 27 August 1940, when German bombers attacked the town. As well as Gillingham bus depot, the main fire station, the Co-op, a newsagent, a sub Post Office and a butcher's shop were all hit and many houses set on fire. Twenty people were killed, including three Maidstone & District staff. During the raid an incendiary bomb fell on a theatre, and apparently the audience inside, unaware of the raid, were asked politely to leave.

Staff, servicemen and civilians all tried to save the buses but were hampered by the heat and because their steering wheels were locked in accordance with anti-invasion regulations and only two of the staff had keys. Rescued buses were parked around local streets and had to be searched for next morning. All the same, a service of sorts was provided from early the next morning. A more or less normal service was provided on the Thursday with a motley collection of buses lent from all over South East England.

The map above shows Maidstone & District's bus network in the Medway Towns in 1965.

Gillingham depot had three Bristol LL5Gs with standard ECW rear-entrance bodies. On the left on the Saturdays-only route 112 to Cooling was SO60 leaving the stop in Military Road in Chatham. This service had five journeys each way and took nearly 50 minutes.

G MEAD

The 8 was a local Medway Towns route from Chatham through Gillingham to Rainham which then turned south to Wigmore. It ran every half hour with alternate buses continuing to the village of Bredhurst, terminating at the Bell, as was Atlantean 5568 disgorging its remaining passengers in this picture. The Bell dates back to 1500 and was extended in both the 17th and 19th centuries.

There has been a settlement here since Neolithic times. St Peter's church, south of the village, is a typical downland flint church dating from the 13th century. At the Reformation in the 16th century the church treasures were hidden and, apart from the Bredhurst Paten discovered and restored in 1907, have never been found. This late 12th or early 13th century communion plate, made of copper and originally gilded, is one of only four known to exist. The other three were all found in the graves of bishops or archbishops. This one is now in the Victoria & Albert Museum.

MIKE HODGES

Mention is made later on of the transfer of route 19 from Luton depot to Gillingham after Chatham & District was fully absorbed into Maidstone & District.

Daimler Fleetline DL86 had arrived at Hoo for its return to Gillingham Green before the conductor had managed to change the destination on the blind. This was one of the Northern Counties bodied Daimler Fleetline CRG6LX low height double deckers of 1964.
M&D AND EAST KENT BUS CLUB

The upper picture of the two below shows tram no. 30 of the second batch to be delivered, descending towards Military Road in Chatham on its way to Gillingham Victoria Bridge from Chatham Cemetery via Brompton.

The lower picture shows tram 15 from the first batch outside St Mary's church in Dock Road, not long after the system first opened.
M&D AND EAST KENT BUS CLUB

Luton C ... and the Chatham & District story

The depot in Luton Road was built in 1902 as a tramway depot and taken over by Maidstone & District in October 1930, when the Chatham & District Traction Company officially began bus operation in the Medway Towns. Maidstone & District acquired a majority interest in what had previously been the Chatham & District Light Railways Co., when British Thomson-Houston Co. Ltd sold its interests in that company to M&D in 1927. But we must go back to the end of the 19th century to learn how this all came about.

Then, a growing population in the Medway Towns needed a good public transport system. There had been a few horse buses, but by the end of the 1890s, Chatham & District Light Railway Company was formed - financed by the British Thomson-Houston Co. Ltd - and on 17 June 1902 started operating a 3ft 6in gauge tramway system. The original routes were:

Chatham Station to Brompton
Chatham Cemetery to Gillingham (Victoria Bridge)
Luton to HM Dockyard
Chatham Town Hall to Shalders Arms (via Chatham Hill & Canterbury Street)

There had been an extension to the Strand Bathing Pool but as it wasn't well used the line was removed in 1905.

The tramway system was run with 25 cars built by Milnes, numbered 1-25. These had a 4-wheel 6ft wheelbase truck with two 25hp motors. Bodies were 28ft long and 6ft 3ins wide, and the lower deck had four bays with reversed stairs to the open top deck. A further 10 trams were ordered from Brush and delivered during 1903 (26-35), but these had three bays in the lower deck and half-turn spiral staircase.

The next trams were delivered in two batches - 37-46 in 1907 and 47-48 in 1911, all built by Brush. The last new trams were supplied by UEC of Preston (49-51) and were assembled at Luton depot in 1911; they were some of the heaviest built with a weight of 13 tons. A single second-hand tram was bought from

Maidstone in 1928, although frequent de-railing meant this last tram was not very successful, even though the defect was eventually rectified. All trams were open top and they wore a grass green and cream livery.

In 1906 there was an extension to Rainham Mark and the system eventually reached Rochester, funded by Rochester Corporation under the Rochester Corporation Tramways & Improvements Act 1903. The corporation leased the system to Chatham & District Light Railway Co.

As mentioned, Maidstone & District acquired a major shareholding in the tramway in 1927. Infrastructure was in desperate need of capital injection and the trams, no longer in the best of condition, were overdue for replacement. To improve flexibility there was a desire to move to motorbus operation but it needed an Act of Parliament for this to happen. This was sought and royal assent was given on 10 May 1929, with a new name of Chatham & District Traction Company and a start date for buses on 1 October 1930.

By August 1930 Maidstone & District had the majority share holding (it paid in excess of £3,200 for this privilege) and so the company became an M&D subsidiary. However, there were still problems. The Corporation of Rochester owned the tramway in the town and had leased the network back to the Chatham Tram Company until 1945. The 1929 act cancelled this agreement but the act stipulated that M&D had to pay compensation to the council for 12 years. The act also stated that Chatham & District buses had sole right over the replacement of the tram routes and the councils of Gillingham, Chatham and Rochester had the right to buy back the company in 1959. This would have been the reason why the company was kept as a subsidiary. The act also stated that Chatham & District could operate routes within 12 miles of Chatham Town Hall.

For its own fleet, Maidstone & District was then buying Leyland Titan TD1 double deckers, so it was no surprise these were bought for Chatham & District to start the new services. Carrying Leyland 48-seat bodies, 43 were bought in 1930/1 and delivered in the new distinctive livery of apple green, ginger brown and cream.

To replace the tram system in the Medway Towns and inaugurate the replacement motor bus network, Maidstone & District bought Leyland Titan TD1s with Leyland 48-seat bodies. Below, on the way to the Strand on route 5 was 364, delivered in 1931 and withdrawn in 1939.
OMNIBUS SOCIETY

when tragedy struck – twice!

The Chatham tram system had only been opened four months when, on the morning of 30 October 1902, there was a major accident which resulted in four fatalities.

Tram 19 was on an early morning workers' service from Gillingham Green going via the Dockyard Main Gate, grossly overloaded. The tram's licensed capacity was 50 but that morning 70 passengers were on the tram, some standing on the top deck. At the top of Westcourt Street (1 in 9½) the tram should have waited for one of the two pilots, whose job it was to ensure the rails were clean and sanded, and to ensure the motorman kept to the 3mph speed limit.

With no sign of the pilot the motorman decided to descend. It had been raining and the tracks were greasy. He lost control on the curve and, unfortunately the tram overturned, crashing into the wall of the Dockyard police headquarters. As well as four deaths, 64 people were treated in hospital for their injuries.

The enquiry found that the pilots did not start work until after the time of the accident, but the radius of the curve was only 36ft where it should have been 60ft, and the gradient more severe than the 1 in 11 shown on the company's documents; also one rail had been incorrectly set lower than the other. After the enquiry the track was removed and relayed in the parallel Middle Street. A replacement tram for no. 19 was delivered in 1903.

It would seem the tramway must have had to repair the dockyard wall more than once, for another tram lost control on 15 July 1908 while descending Middle Street. It crossed the road into the wall but, luckily, this time without anyone being seriously injured.

However, the darkest hour for the company was just before 6pm on 4 December 1951. On that foggy evening 52 Royal Marine cadets aged between 9 and 13, mostly in dark blue battledress uniforms, who were marching three abreast down Dock Road from Melville Barracks to the Royal Naval Barracks to watch a boxing tournament, were run into by Bristol K5G no. 875.

A total of 24 cadets were killed, 17 at the scene, and 7 died subsequently in hospital. 18 more were injured. It was a dark night and there was very poor street lighting. The cadets were not showing any warning lights, a number of street lights were defective and, to make the situation worse, the bus was only running on sidelights.

The driver, who had worked for the company for 40 years, was charged with dangerous driving, fined £20 and banned from driving for three years.

The vehicle concerned became something of a pariah with crews, and was only used if absolutely necessary until its withdrawal.

In 1939 Chatham & District took delivery of 37 Bristol K5Gs with Weymann 54-seat bodies. On the right, one of these, 883, was in Military Road in Chatham picking up passengers outside a military tailor's shop.
SOUTHDOWN ENTHUSIASTS' CLUB

A most unusual timing point was Jezreel's Tower, shown below. It stood off the main A2 at Rainham Road in Gillingham. The tower's story is in the text on the right.

The line-up at the back of Chatham Town Hall at the bottom of this page was photographed in August 1955. Nearest the camera was 878, a Bristol K5G with a highbridge 54-seat Weymann body. This bus was converted into a tower wagon for Hastings Tramways after the integration of Chatham & District with parent Maidstone & District.
BRUCE JENKINS

When the new operation began on 1 October 1930 these were the new motorbus routes:

1 Luton (Hen & Chicks) • Dockyard
2 Chatham Cemetery • Rainham
3 Frindsbury • Gillingham Green
4 Strood Hill • Town Hall
5 Borstal • Gillingham Strand

Two of the routes went past the Jezreels Tower on the A2 at the corner of Nelson Road. This was a well known highly prominent landmark and a timing point for buses, referred to as just Jezreels. The tower had been started by the Jezreelites, a religious sect, in 1885. It was to be their headquarters, 100ft high and funded by local tradespeople but, unsurprisingly, the tower was never finished due to a lack of funds, and was demolished in 1961. The Strand was the summer play area of Gillingham, having a sandy beach, an open paddling pool and a miniature railway on the banks of the River Medway.

Spare buses and those on layover were parked at the back of Chatham Town Hall, a practice which continued with the parent company too. As the population of the Medway Towns grew and new housing sprung up, services were changed and routes extended.

Chatham & District had four of the ill fated Bristol GO5Gs with Weymann metal-framed 48-seat highbridge bodies in January 1937 transferred from the parent company in exchange for four of the TD1s (359-62). The story of how this batch of GO5Gs were returned to Bristol in 1938 and their bodies transferred to replacement Bristol K5Gs using the same fleet numbers is told on page 22.

The GO5Gs had Gardner 5LW engines with Bristol 4-speed gearboxes in the middle of the chassis and an underslung worm and pinion differential. This gave a higher floor line and increased the overall height of the bus. Due to the type of rear engine mounting the chassis could, at times, have a vibration problem. The K5Gs, however, had a unit construction for its Gardner engine and gearbox, giving a more acceptable lower floor line. The original GO5G chassis had new bodies and went into the Bath Tramways fleet.

A further 37 Bristol K5Gs with Weymann 54-seat bodies, 870-906, were delivered to Chatham & District in 1939 to replace the earlier Leyland TitanTD1s.

With the outbreak of the Second World War, Chatham & District soon had an important part to play, especially with its services to the Dockyard. The Dockyard and aircraft factories were all strategic air raid targets, and the area suffered much damage to houses and business, and loss of life. David Toy remembers his mother telling him she had to lie on the floor of a bus in Military Road during a low level surprise raid. Unlike other towns where bus services were reduced (some Brighton buses, for example, were seconded to other towns), the Chatham fleet stayed at home due to the high demand for transport and the Maidstone & District losses at Gillingham mentioned a few pages back.

Of the first utility bodied Bristol K5Gs allocated by the Ministry of War Supply to Maidstone & District in 1942, five were transferred to Chatham & District immediately and never operated with the parent company. These were 907-911. Then in 1944 Chatham & District was allocated three Guy Arab IIs with Weymann 56-seat utility bodies, 912-4. Although the Guys had Gardner 5LW engines, they were non-standard to the Chatham fleet and only stayed until the following year when they were exchanged with Maidstone & District for three of the 1942 Bristol K5Gs with Bristol utility bodies, these becoming 915-17.

Another three K5Gs were transferred into the Chatham fleet, also in 1945 - 918 with a Strachans utility body and 919/20 with Bristol bodies (ex-M&D DH12-14). The story of the utilities and their post-war rebodying by Weymann in the 1950s is all told on page 16.

Below is Luton depot in wartime, with two utility bodied Guy Arabs and a single Bristol K5G outside. Note the wartime white edges to the mudguards and how the name above the entrance has been erased on the photo for security reasons.
M&D AND EAST KENT BUS CLUB

The Bristol utility bodied Bristol K5G at the top carried several fleet numbers in its time. It was new to Maidstone & District in 1942 as DH16 but transferred to Chatham & District in 1945 where it became 917. In 1951 the chassis was re-bodied by Weymann, but when it became part of the parent M&D fleet again in 1955 it was renumbered DH448.
DAVID TOY COLLECTION

Chatham & District 911 in the lower picture above was delivered to Maidstone & District in 1942 with a Park Royal utility body, re-bodied by Weymann in 1951. Here the bus was on route 2 to Magpie Hall Road, photographed in Military Road in Chatham.
M&D AND EAST KENT BUS CLUB

On the far left are some proud-looking Chatham & District staff.
M&D AND EAST KENT BUS CLUB

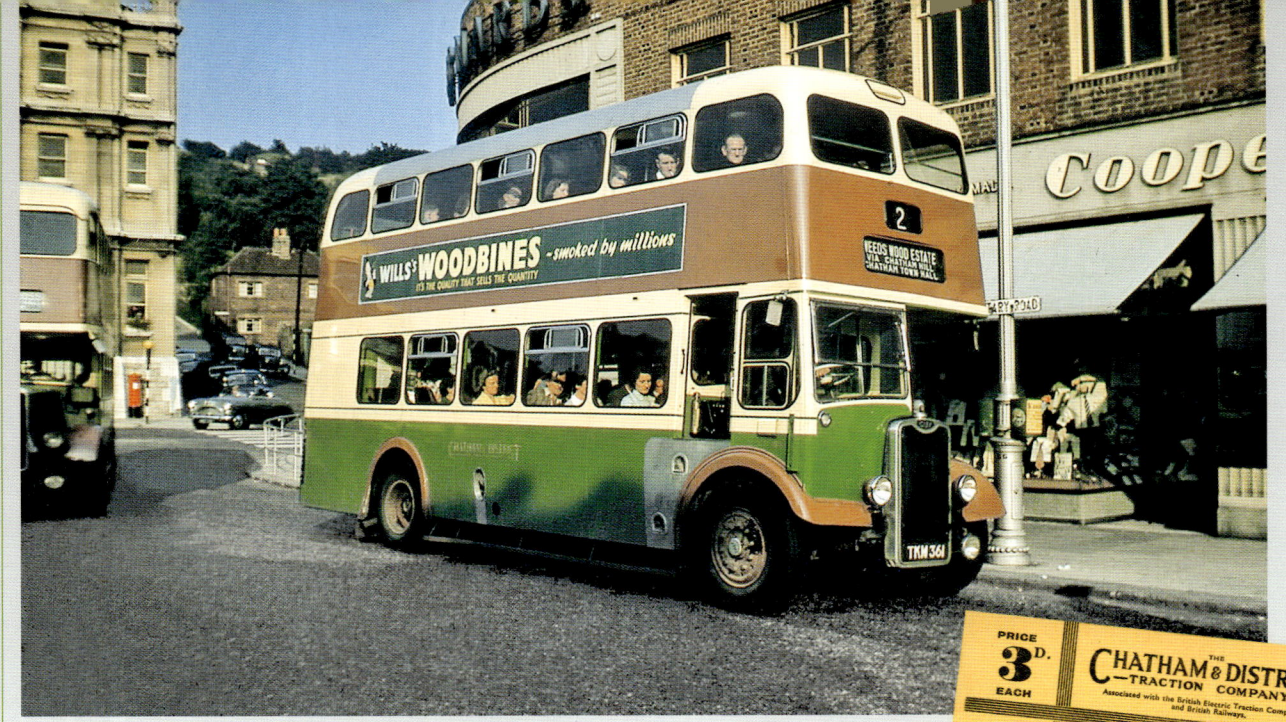

Weymann Orion bodied Guy Arab 936 was showing off the unusual Chatham & District livery in Military Road in Chatham in this picture on the right.

Although this was the very last bus new to the subsidiary company, eight more were on order but were delivered straight to Maidstone & District. One is shown on page 99.

BRUCE JENKINS

Chatham & District 920 was at the terminal of route 2 in the picture below, Webster Road in Rainham.

This bus was a 1942 Bristol K5G which received this new 56-seat Weymann body in 1951.

While still carrying its original Bristol utility body, it had been transferred from Maidstone & District in 1946. The full story of the wartime rebodies starts on page 16.

M&D AND EAST KENT BUS CLUB

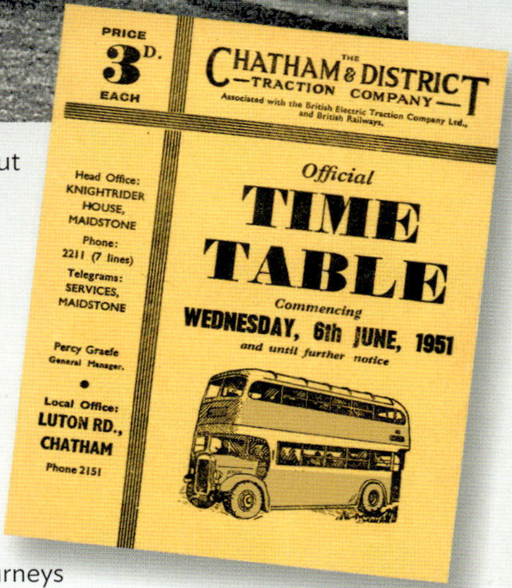
PRICE 3D. EACH

CHATHAM & DISTRICT TRACTION COMPANY

Associated with the British Electric Traction Company Ltd., and British Railways.

Head Office: KNIGHTRIDER HOUSE, MAIDSTONE

Phone: 2211 (7 lines)

Telegrams: SERVICES, MAIDSTONE

Percy Graefe, General Manager.

Local Office: LUTON RD., CHATHAM

Phone 2151

Official

TIME TABLE

Commencing WEDNESDAY, 6th JUNE, 1951

and until further notice

The Medway towns began to grow with new housing estates being built throughout the area, so by mid 1951 the Chatham & District route network was:

1 **Chatham Dockyard • Luton Burma Way**
2 **Chatham (Magpie Hall Road) • Rainham (Webster Road)**
3 **Frindsbury • Gillingham Green**
3A **Strood (Brompton Farm Road) • Gillingham Green**
4 **Luton (Wagon-at-Hale) • Strood (Salters Cross)**
5 **Borstal • Gillingham Strand**
5A **Cookham Wood • Gillingham Strand**

There were extra workmen's services to Chatham Dockyard in the mornings from Borstal, Chatham, Frindsbury, Gillingham, Luton, Rochester and Strood and return journeys in the late afternoon and evening. The maximum fare on route 5, as an example, for a complete journey was 6d, with special workman's fares mainly to the dockyard that ranged from 1d to 2½d.

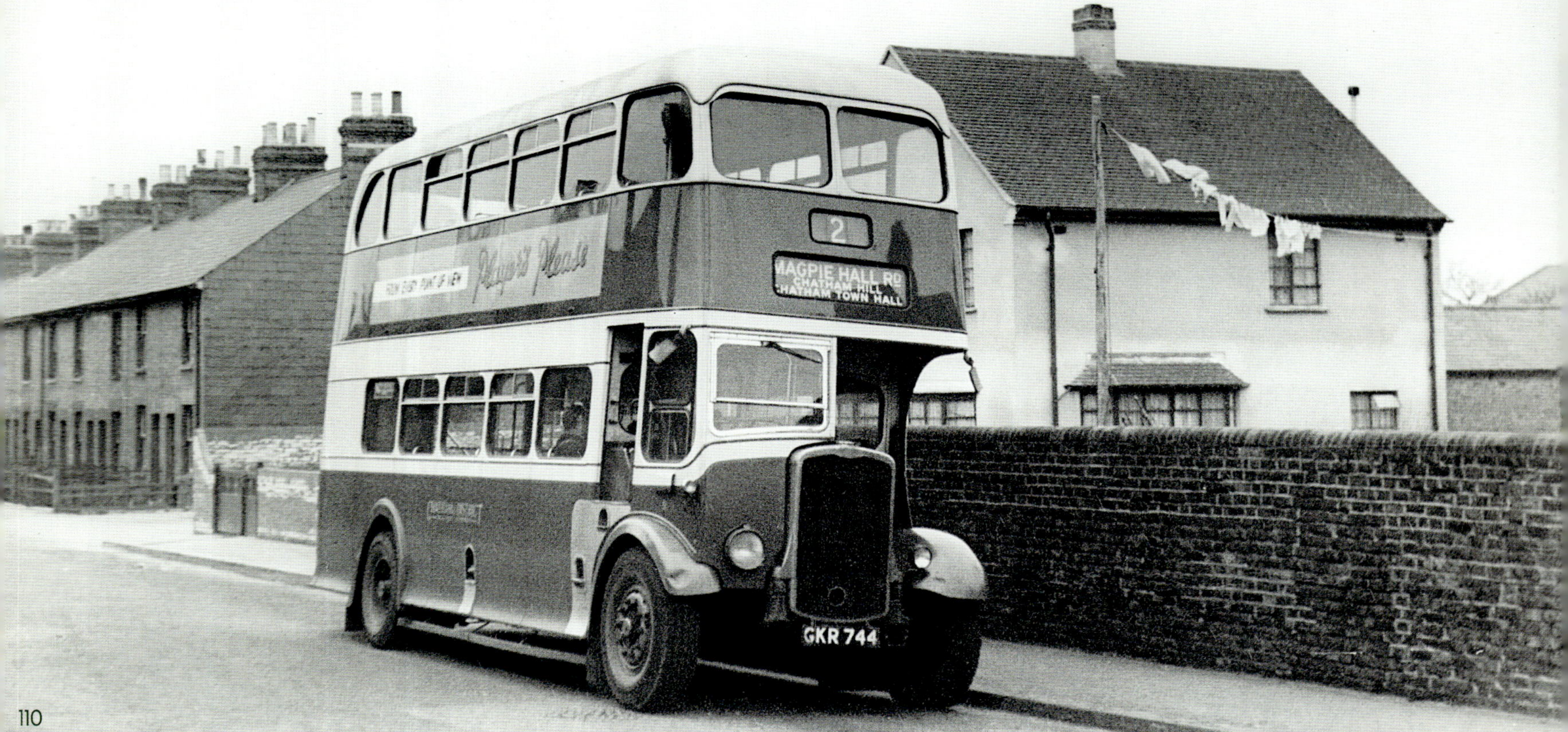

DH467, a 60-seat Weymann Orion bodied Guy Arab IV that had been new to Chatham & District in 1954, was photographed in Gillingham bus station in the picture below. These buses had the Gardner 6LW engine, which made ascending the Medway Towns' hills a little easier.
REMEMBER WHEN

Looking very presentable on the right was the passenger shelter in Dock Road in Chatham, near a collection of bus stops.
JOHN WATTS

With Bristol chassis no longer available on the open market (as part of the British Transport Commission Group, Bristol was only allowed to sell to other state-owned companies), Chatham & District turned to the Guy Arab IV and took delivery of eight with Weymann 58-seat bodies in 1953, 921-928. Bodies were the 5-bay, all-metal lightweight Orion style and looked good with the Arab radiator up front; the radiator surround was polished with the Guy feathers-in-our-cap emblem on the filler. Engines in these buses were the Gardner 6LW with an output of 112bhp, and this extra power would help them put in a good performance over the hills that characterised the Medway Towns. The exhaust brake helped, too. They had white steering wheels to remind drivers they were in charge of an 8ft-wide bus.

Instead of the more usual moquette on the seats, these had leathercloth. Another new feature was a bell cord linked to buzzer in place of the more usual bell pushes. A further eight came the following year to the same specification, 929-936. The Guy Arabs were very popular with Chatham crews.

In July 1953 the Maidstone & District chairman's report stated that over the past two years the number of passengers had fallen by 12.5 million from its three companies. This loss was due to several factors, including rising television ownership in homes, fare increases, the economic climate, and increasing car and motorcycle ownership. Nevertheless, revenue was still buoyant, but he pointed out that difficult times could lay ahead.

Having two companies operating within the Medway area had not led to the most efficient bus network, so looking to the future it would be beneficial if Chatham & District was merged into its parent company. Under the 1929 Parliamentary Act Chatham & District could operate buses until 1959, when the three Medway councils could raise a bill to buy the operation.

So the decision was made to merge Chatham & District into Maidstone & District but this would require an Act of Parliament, because Chatham & District could not be dissolved under the Companies Act. Maidstone & District applied for a Parliamentary Bill to combine the two companies and this was approved on Wednesday 30 March 1955. The changeover was to be on 1 October 1955 and all Chatham & District buses would have Maidstone & District fleetnames applied the night before. These would now be in M&D's series with the DH prefix. Route numbers were to be revised in the short term as T1-3/3A/4/5/5A. The brown livery disappeared over the coming months as vehicles were repainted into M&D green and cream.

With snow still on the ground in the picture on the left, DH272, one of 42 Bristol K6As delivered in 1949 with Weymann 56-seat bodies, was on its way to West Malling in Dock Road in Chatham. This bus was withdrawn in 1963.

The 39 used to run north from West Malling up the west side of the Medway Valley through Snodland and Cuxton, through the Medway Towns to Upchurch and Lower Halstow.

It was supplemented by the 20 that had come from Maidstone to West Malling (one of several routes - see page 98), that didn't go beyond Gillingham.

By 1965 it was only the 20 that went this way, mostly hourly throughout and half-hourly between West Malling and Gillingham.
M&D AND EAST KENT BUS CLUB

Eight more Guy Arabs with Weymann bodies were on order and these were now to be delivered in M&D livery as DH468-475. The Guy Arabs were well received by the crews for the Medway Towns operation and in the early 1960s were used in place of the Leyland Atlanteans for Sunday services, owing to their better fuel consumption. These were the last Guys for the company, the next double-deck order going to AEC, perhaps from the influence of the new General Manager who had come from South Wales which had a large AEC fleet.

In September 1956 many Chatham & District routes were revised and combined into the M&D numbering system. Revised routes were numbered 140-147. Several vehicles were transferred to Luton depot to remove some of the 1939 Bristol K5Gs. From Gillingham came 13 Guy Arabs and 7 Bristol K6As, while Hastings sent five and Maidstone two Bristol K6As.
Three of Luton's Guy Arab IVs went to Gillingham.
Luton's total allocation gradually increased from 54 to 65.

It was a very rainy day when Marshall bodied Daimler Fleetline 3825 was photographed below left. These 2-door rear-engined single deckers had a step just behind the exit door and another at the rear for the five seats that sat on top of the engine. Instead of the more usual M&D moquette these had leathercloth, which did seem from a bygone age.

This bus was sold to Alder Valley in 1974, moving on to Northern General in 1976, who sold it to a dealer in 1981.
JULIAN BOWDEN

To improve the efficiency of the 112 and 113 routes north out on to the Isle of Grain, Gillingham depot had two Albion Nimbuses allocated to it for a while.

On the right SO319 was entering Gillingham bus station on the 113. With the passenger door open, you can easily see the rather steep steps inside the entrance.

JOHN SHEARMAN

A Halifax Corporation Willowbrook bodied Daimler Fleetline single decker, its 107, was in the Medway Towns when Maidstone & District had it on loan for a week in June 1968.

The 144 was a regular haunt for it, for which it had a special 'lazy' blind display. In the picture below the bus was returning to Chatham, having just left Bligh Way terminus.

MIKE HODGES

...mpstead and Cliffe.

...Church	0946	......	1426	1751	......	2329
GILLINGHAM, Bus Station	0951	......	1431	1756	......	2332
	0958	......	1436	1801	......	2337
	1002	......	1443	1808	......	2342
			1447	1812	......	2349
						2353

This Service is operated with Pay As You Enter vehicles.

GILLINGHAM - LOWER HIGHAM

Via New Road and Rochester — Service **113**

Mondays to Fridays

GILLINGHAM, Bus Station	0727	......	......	......	......	......	......	......	......
St. Mark's Church	0731	......	......	......	......	......	......	......	......
Chatham, Military Road	0738	0928	1058	1228	1358	1528	1658	1838	1958
Rochester, Star Hill	0743	0933	1103	1233	1403	1533	1703	1843	2003
Strood, St. Nicholas Church	0748	0938	1108	1238	1408	1538	1708	1848	2008
Falstaff	0755	0945	1115	1245	1415	1545	1715	1855	2015
LOWER HIGHAM, Chequers	0802	0952	1122	1252	1422	1552	1722	1902	2022
LOWER HIGHAM, Chequers	0819	0954	1124	1254	1424	1554	1730	1909	2024
Falstaff	0826	1001	1131	1301	1431	1601	1737	1916	2031
Strood, St. Nicholas Church	0833	1008	1138	1308	1438	1608	1744	1923	2038
Rochester, Star Hill	0838	1013	1143	1313	1443	1613	1749	1928	2043
Chatham, Globe Lane	0843	1018	1148	1318	1448	1618	1754	1933	2048
Chatham, Military Road	......	......	......	......	......	......	......	......	......
St. Mark's Church	......	......	......	......	......	......	......	......	......
GILLINGHAM, Bus Station	......	......	......	......	......	......	......	......	......

Saturdays

GILLINGHAM, Bus Station	0727	......	......	......	......	......	......	......	......	......	......
St. Mark's Church	0731	......	......	......	......	......	......	......	......	......	......
Chatham, Military Road	0738	0928	1058	......	1358	1400	1528	1658	1838	1958	2128
Rochester, Star Hill	0743	0933	1103	......	1403	1405	1533	1703	1843	2003	2133
Strood, St. Nicholas Church	0748	0938	1108	1238	1408	1410	1538	1708	1848	2008	2138
Falstaff	0755	0945	1115	1245	1415	1417	1545	1715	1855	2015	2145
LOWER HIGHAM, Chequers	0802	0952	1122	1252	1422	......	1552	1722	1902	2022	2152
LOWER HIGHAM, Chequers	0809	0954	1124	1314	......	1424	1554	1724	1909	2024	2154
Falstaff	0816	1001	1131	1321	1419	1431	1601	1731	1916	2031	2201
Strood, St. Nicholas Church	0823	1008	1138	1328	1426	1438	1608	1738	1923	2038	2208
Rochester, Star Hill	0828	1013	......	......	1431	1443	1613	1743	1928	2043	2213
Chatham, Globe Lane	0833	1018	......	......	1436	1448	1618	1748	1933	2048	......
Chatham, Military Road	......	......	......	......	......	......	......	......	......	......	2218
St. Mark's Church	......	......	......	......	......	......	......	......	......	......	2225
GILLINGHAM, Bus Station	......	......	......	......	......	......	......	......	......	......	2229

This Service is operated with Pay As You Enter vehicles.

277

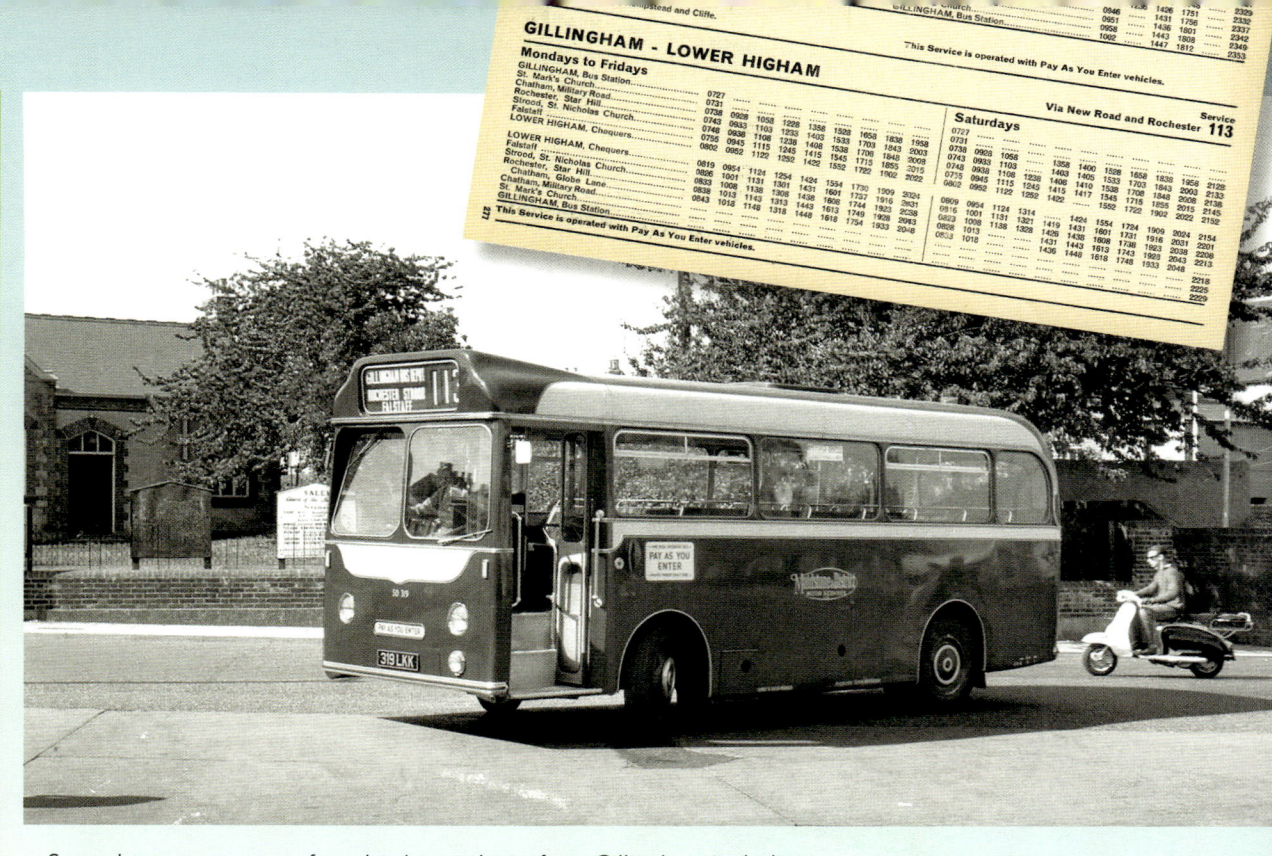

Several routes were transferred to Luton depot from Gillingham including the 19 to Grain, 29 to Maidstone, 23 to Gravesend, 32 Walderslade to Temple Farm Estate, 38A to Bredhurst, 66 Davis Estate to Brompton Farm Road, and 70 to Upnor.

Chatham & District is all now just memories, but one of Chatham & District's Bristol K5Gs, 874, has been preserved.

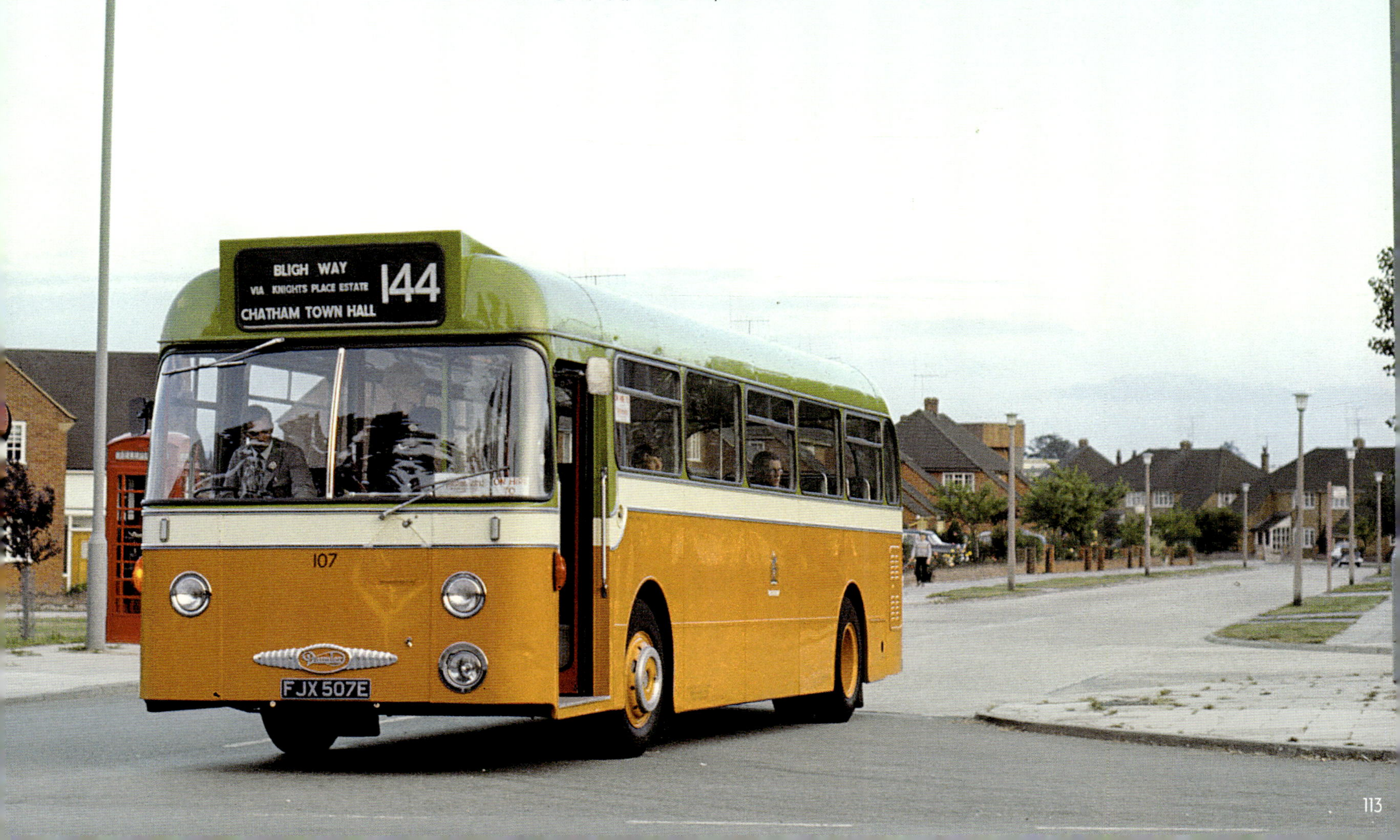

Hastings H

During the 1950s and 1960s Hastings, one of the five original Cinque Ports, was a popular seaside destination for day trips and annual holidays. Visitors would find the usual mix of amusement arcades, cafés and restaurants along the sea front, a busy town, fine pier and the charm of the Old Town with lots of passages and narrow streets (twittens) to explore. One of the oldest buildings in the Old Town, built around 1450, is the Court House at the southern end of The Bourne.

Fishing had always been important to the town's economy. Before the Second World War there were some 150 boats providing work for 400-500 families, and although in the 1950s fishing had declined in importance, visitors could still watch boats being launched from the beach and return later with their catch. This part of the beach in front of the old town is known as the Stade, which is a Saxon term for landing place.

The Stade is famous for the tall wooden towers in which fishermen used to hang their nets to dry. Interestingly, at the time of writing in 2019, Hastings still has the largest beach-launched fishing fleet in Europe. On the outskirts of the town quite a bit of light industry grew up in the post-war period. Hastings was and still is notorious for a fair number of steep hills that buses had to contend with to get out of the town.

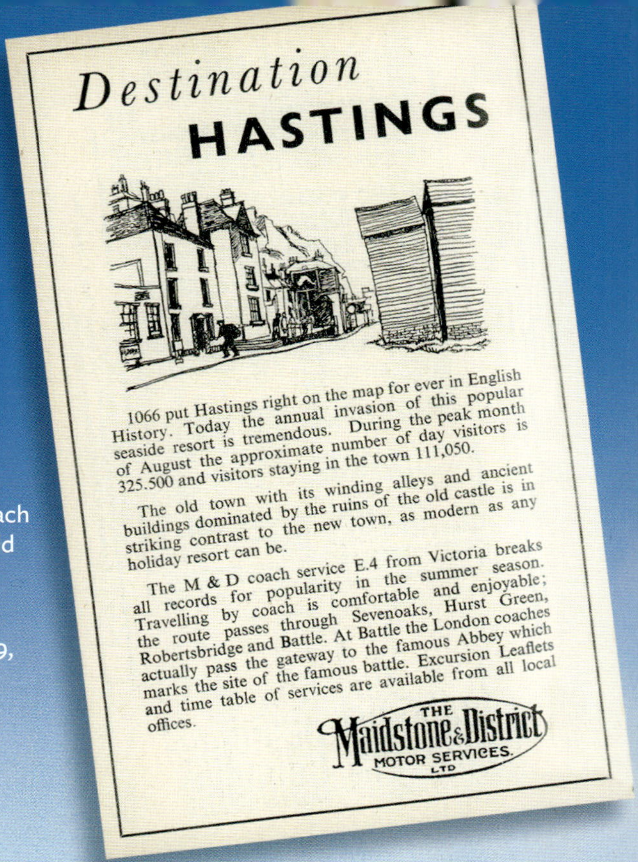

Destination
HASTINGS

1066 put Hastings right on the map for ever in English History. Today the annual invasion of this popular seaside resort is tremendous. During the peak month of August the approximate number of day visitors is 325.500 and visitors staying in the town 111,050.

The old town with its winding alleys and ancient buildings dominated by the ruins of the old castle is in striking contrast to the new town, as modern as any holiday resort can be.

The M & D coach service E.4 from Victoria breaks all records for popularity in the summer season. Travelling by coach is comfortable and enjoyable; the route passes through Sevenoaks, Hurst Green, Robertsbridge and Battle. At Battle the London coaches actually pass the gateway to the famous Abbey which marks the site of the famous battle. Excursion Leaflets and time table of services are available from all local offices.

THE Maidstone & District MOTOR SERVICES LTD

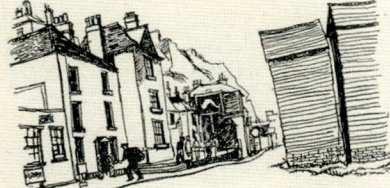

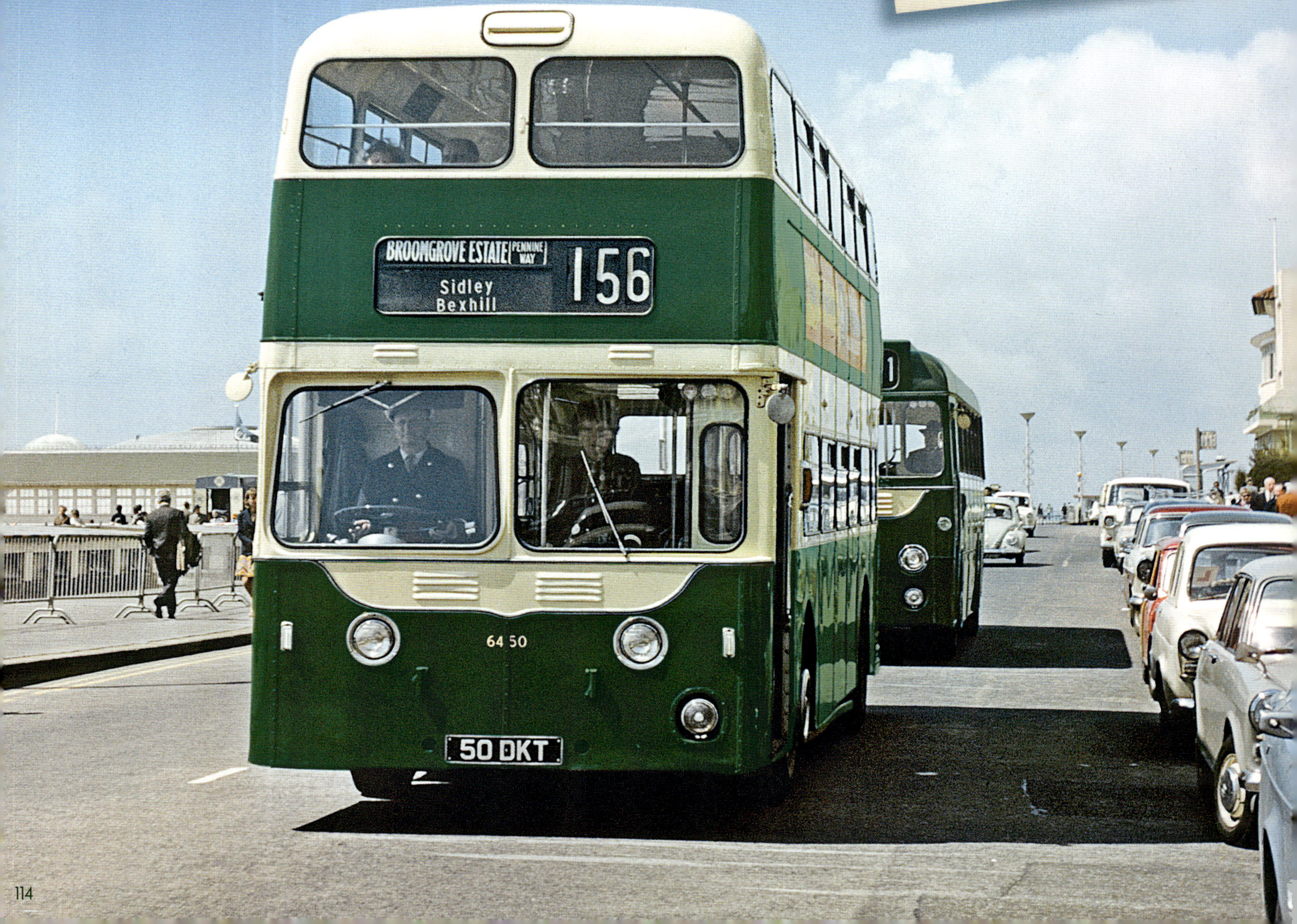

The lowbridge Atlanteans of 1959 were particularly associated with Hastings, and on the opposite page 6450 (renumbered from DL50) was bowling along White Rock on the half-hourly 156 from Bexhill with a narrow Harrington bodied AEC Reliance in quick pursuit behind.

To the left of the bus you can see Hastings Pier, built in 1872. This had a chequered career from the end of the 20th century, including a disastrous fire in 2010, but a rejuvenated pier for the 21st century opened in 2016.

THE BUS ARCHIVE/ROBIN HANNAY

The 84 connected Hastings with Hawkurst via Bodiam every 2 hours and continued to Tunbridge Wells. The 5 and 57 combined offered a more frequent link to Hawkhurst but via Battle. These then continued to Maidstone with the 5 ending up in Gillingham and the 57 in Gravesend.

At the top of this page Weymann Orion bodied Leyland Titan DH439 was passing Hastings Pier on its way out of the town on the 84.

JEREMY WILLIAMS COLLECTION

Through the 1950s M&D had two operations in Hastings: its bus and coach services and the subsidiary company Hastings Tramways, which operated a fleet of trolleybuses from the Silverhill depot. Hastings Tramways originally had a second depot at Bulverhythe but the premises were no longer operational in the 1950s, the depot instead being used to store withdrawn and de-licensed vehicles for M&D during the winter months. It was also used for the deep cleaning of coaches.

The main terminus for bus services in Hastings was on the hill at Wellington Square, where the parked buses had to have their rear wheels chocked as a safety precaution, owing to the severity of the slope. There are several pictures of that throughout this book.

The bus depot was in Brook Street, a large depot that in October 1951 had an allocation of 77 buses and coaches. The backbone of the double deck fleet then comprised Bristol K6As and two Leyland TitanTD5s. Single deck buses were AEC Regals from the 1946/47 batch and Bristol L6As. Coaches were relatively new AEC Regals, Beadle-AEC semi-chassisless and rebodied 1936 Leyland TigerTS7s. For the longer bus routes out of Hastings new Leyland bodied Leyland Titan PD2/12s ousted several Bristol K6As, which were transferred to other depots. New AEC Reliance coaches soon replaced older types in the mid-1950s.

As well as a network of local bus services, Hastings was the terminus for several longer routes. The 5 came all the way from Gillingham and Maidstone, joined by the 57 from Gravesend which had a common routeing from Maidstone Road at Rochester. Route 12 also came from Maidstone but via Tenterden on an hourly summer frequency (in the winter it was 2-hourly except on Saturdays). Eastbourne was reached by either the 15 via Hailsham and Polegate, which took 1 hour 50 minutes on a half-hourly frequency, or the 99 via Pevensey which would take 1 hour 10 minutes, again on half-hourly frequency. Tunbridge Wells was reached by the 84 via Bodiam, Hawkhurst and Wadhurst, taking 2 hours 19 minutes. However, the main route to Tunbridge Wells from Hastings was the 152 via Battle and Heathfield, which dovetailed with the 180 to Brighton providing an hourly service to Heathfield. Route 30 to Rye ran on a half-hourly frequency via Westfield and Brede taking an hour, and was an alternative to East Kent's more direct 113 that went via Winchelsea.

Hastings has many steep hills, the climb up Castle Hill being particularly notorious. This is where 3691 was in the picture below, working hard up Wellington Road on its way to Fairlight Glen on the 134, a route with a 20-minute frequency.

These 7ft 6in wide Harrington bodied AEC Reliances were bought especially for these hilly routes in Hastings, and are described on page 40.

THE BUS ARCHIVE/ROBIN HANNAY

As well as running local town services, Hastings depot had contract services to Ore Place for the Royal Army Service Corps Record Office, which included lunchtime runs, while British Gypsum at Mountfield had three buses each day. There was also a contract for the Birds Eye factory at Eastbourne from Hastings, normally operated by single deckers. And to cater for hop pickers during the 1950s there were relief workings on the 12 and 84 in the evenings and on Saturdays, as well as contract buses mornings and evenings.

Express services and excursions left from the coach station next to the county cricket ground.

Silverhill SV

Hastings Tramways was founded as a statutory company in 1900 and Silverhill depot in Beaufort Road in St Leonards was built in 1905. The first tram route began that year, the Ore-Silverhill-Hollington circular; then later, in August, a second route was opened from Ore to Market Cross in the Old Town. In 1906 the system was extended to the sea front via London Road, and a second depot opened at Bulverhythe together with a new service from St Leonards to Bexhill and later to Cooden. In January 1907 the two systems were joined.

Due to local objections to 'unsightly' overhead along the seafront, the Dolter stud current collection system was used here, but as this was only just below ground level it didn't last long. Several horses had been killed by coming into contact with the electricity supply, so in 1913 a safer petrol electric system was fitted to these tram cars instead. Eventually in 1921 a conventional overhead was used everywhere on the system. These were the tram routes in 1926:

1	Silverhill - St Leonards - Hastings - Ore		6/7	Cooden - Bexhill - Hastings - Ore - St Helens
2	Ore - Old Town			
3/5	Bexhill - Hastings - Ore		8/9	Hastings - Ore - St Helens - Silverhill - Hastings circular
4	Hollington - Silverhill - Memorial			

By the mid-1920s the company was looking into replacing the trams with trolleybuses and in April 1928 this finally happened. The Guy BTX was the chosen chassis type. Nos. 1-8 had Dodson 57-seat open-top double-deck bodies, and 9-58 single-deck 32-seat bodies by Ransomes Sims & Jeffries. The new fleetname of Hastings & District was introduced to go with the maroon livery.

In accordance with expansion by Maidstone & District in the 1930s, the company made an offer to the council to take over the trolleybus system. This was accepted and on 11 November 1935 M&D was in charge. Although the livery was changed to Maidstone & District's green and cream, the name reverted to Hastings Tramways. There was a plan to replace the system with motorbuses, as by the late-1930s the fleet was becoming outdated, but the start of the Second World War put paid to that.

Tram route 2 only ran from Ore down Harold Road to the top of the Old Town.

In trolleybus days the 9 and 11 went the same way (joined by the 1 and 2 down Old London Road) and continued into the centre of Hastings down the extremely narrow High Street.

Weymann bodied Sunbeam W trolleybus no. 38 in the picture above was making its way from St Helens and Ore down the High Street towards the Fishmarket and Memorial, before then heading along the seafront to St Leonards and up through Silverhill to Hollington.

The 11 ran up to every 6 minutes.

M&D AND EAST KENT BUS CLUB

Hastings had highbridge Atlanteans as well as lowbridge ones. In the big picture here, taken in Robertson Street, a highbridge Atlantean was in the distance, soon to arrive at Hastings Memorial, while lowbridge DL55 in the foreground was heading for the western extremity of Bexhill at Cooden Beach on a trolleybus replacement route.

THE BUS ARCHIVE/ROY MARSHALL

Trolleybuses, trolleybus wires and buses galore can be seen in the 1930s postcard on the right showing the town's Memorial Clock Tower.

So, to update the fleet, M&D bought 20 AEC 661T chassis with English Electric equipment and 54-seat bodies by Weymann (1-10) and Park Royal (11-20). The order was originally for 48 but was reduced to 20 due to the start of war. Items from the cancelled order were bought from AEC as spares by Hastings & District, and this helped to keep the new AECs working during the war years, as suppliers like AEC had to turn to the manufacture of war products.

It wasn't until after the war that it was possible to buy new trolleybuses. These were Sunbeam Ws and the first 10 delivered in 1946 (21-30) had BTH equipment with 85hp motors and Park Royal 56-seat bodies. The next 15 (31-45) were delivered over two years in 1947 and 1948, and these had 95hp motors and Weymann 56-seat bodies.

The council had a parliamentary option to buy back the system and this was debated every five years, but the interest waned and in 1957 M&D applied to Parliament to liquidate the Hastings & District Company. This was agreed and in October 1957 the trolleybus system of five routes across the town became part of M&D, and subsequently the familiar M&D scroll fleetname was applied to the vehicles. This made Maidstone & District the last BET company to operate trolleybuses. But two years later, on 30 May 1959, the last trolleybuses ran and a shiny new fleet of Leyland Atlanteans took over the next day.

Hastings trolleybus network

This shows the maximum extent of the system. Towards the end of trolleybuses in Hastings only the 2,6, 8 and 11 were operated.

In the top picture trolleybus no. 21 was on its way past Memorial, crossing from Wellington Place into Robertson Street on a short working of the 11 only as far as Silverhill, where the depot was.

This was the first of the post-war Sunbeam Ws with Park Royal bodywork.

It was being followed by DH219, one of the Saunders bodied Bristol K6As of 1948 on the 27 between Ore, Fishmarket, Memorial and Hastings Station. This ran every 20 minutes.

M&D AND EAST KENT BUS CLUB

On the left is trolleybus 8, one of the Weymann bodied AECs that entered service in June 1940, again on the high-frequency route 11 not long before this silent mode of transport went from the Hastings area.

Note the East Kent Weymann bodied AEC Reliance in the background. This was on the 113 route to Rye via Winchelsea mentioned a couple of pages back.

DAVID TOY COLLECTION

In the 1950s route 134 to Fairlight Glen used to run every 15 minutes, two an hour starting at Parker Road and two an hour starting from Hastings Station. The 1965 M&D timetable book reveals this had reduced to every 20 minutes with all starting from the station.

At the top of this page S328, a Weymann bodied dual-purpose seated AEC Reliance of 1961, was waiting to leave its stop at Hastings Station for the 14-minute journey to Fairlight Glen. Note the local advert on the external cove panels for a local TV and radio shop.
JEREMY WILLIAMS COLLECTION

SO36 was one of 16 ECW bodied Bristol L6As delivered in 1949 and 1950, caught on the right on the circular 155 route at Memorial. This bus was withdrawn from service in 1961.
R L WILSON

Maidstone & District had acquired the local Scout coach business in 1951 and Skinners in 1953. There's more about this in the coaching pages. In this picture on the left, taken in Warrior Square in St Leonards in the early 1960s, Skinners and Scout coaches were touting for business.

C122 was an AEC Regal 1V with impressive Gurney Nutting centre-entrance coachwork, a real rarity in this part of the world, and only a year old when Maidstone & District acquired Skinners.

The Scout coach, C444, was, however, one of a batch of 20 M&D Harrington Wayfarer bodied AEC Reliances delivered in 1960, two of which perpetuated the Skinners name and livery and this one the Scout identity - see also pages 53, 58, 63 and 64.
M&D AND EAST KENT BUS CLUB

At the top of this page characterful TO1 was doing brisk trade in early post-war days, well-loaded for a breezy summer ride along the seafront.

After getting to St Leonards, passengers would enjoy an inland ride past posh houses and through wooded dells to Alexandra Park, before dropping back into the town centre, then climbing the very steep hill up beyond Hastings Castle.

The last bit of the tour took them down through narrow streets and by medieval buildings in the Old Town to arrive back at the Fishmarket.

Behind the phone box in this picture is one of the characteristic tall wooden towers used by fishermen for drying their nets.

M&D AND EAST KENT BUS CLUB

Round the Town Tour

A familiar tourist attraction in Hastings for years was Maidstone & District's Round the Town Tour run with de-roofed elderly single-deckers on fine days throughout the summer. It was always a grand way to see the sights of the town and, like the tall wooden net towers, was part of the charm of this seaside town.

In 1951 four Dennis Aces from 1934 - 751, 753, 754 and 759 - had their roofs chopped off and were converted for use on the tour, getting renumbered to TO1-4 at the same time.

These were replaced in 1958 with three of the Beadle bodied AEC Regal buses delivered in 1946/47, SO9, 16 and 26, which became in open-top form OR1-3 and dutifully carried on doing the tour into National Bus Company days.

For many years this delightful jaunt cost 1/6d for adults and 9d for children, but by the time of the lower picture this had gone up to 2/-.

This bus had originally been SO26, then OR3 on conversion to open top and after 1968 8003. Later on, in NBC days, it became 4003.

It must have been a sweltering day as the driver had left his windsreen wide open.

DAVID TOY COLLECTION

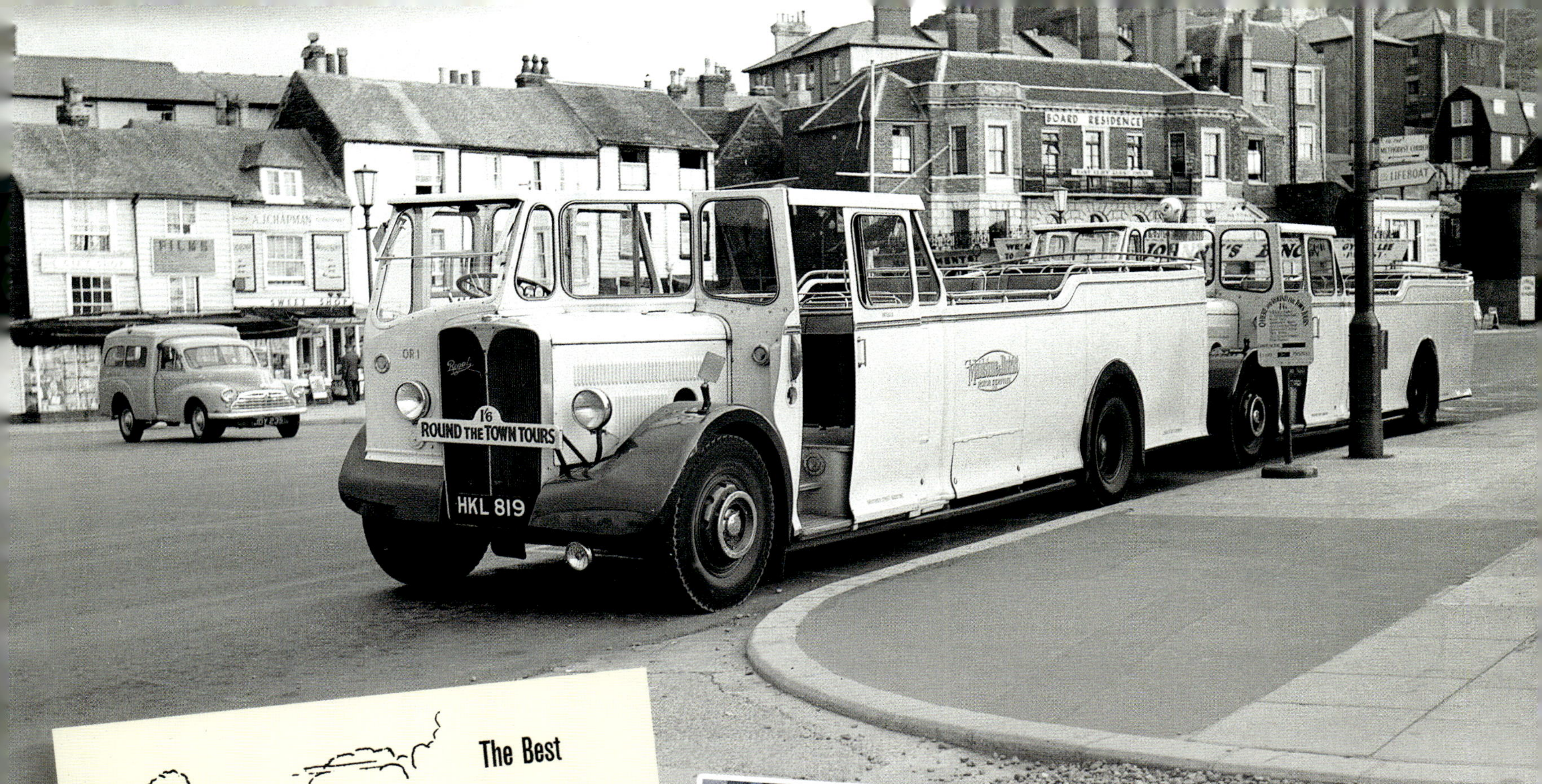

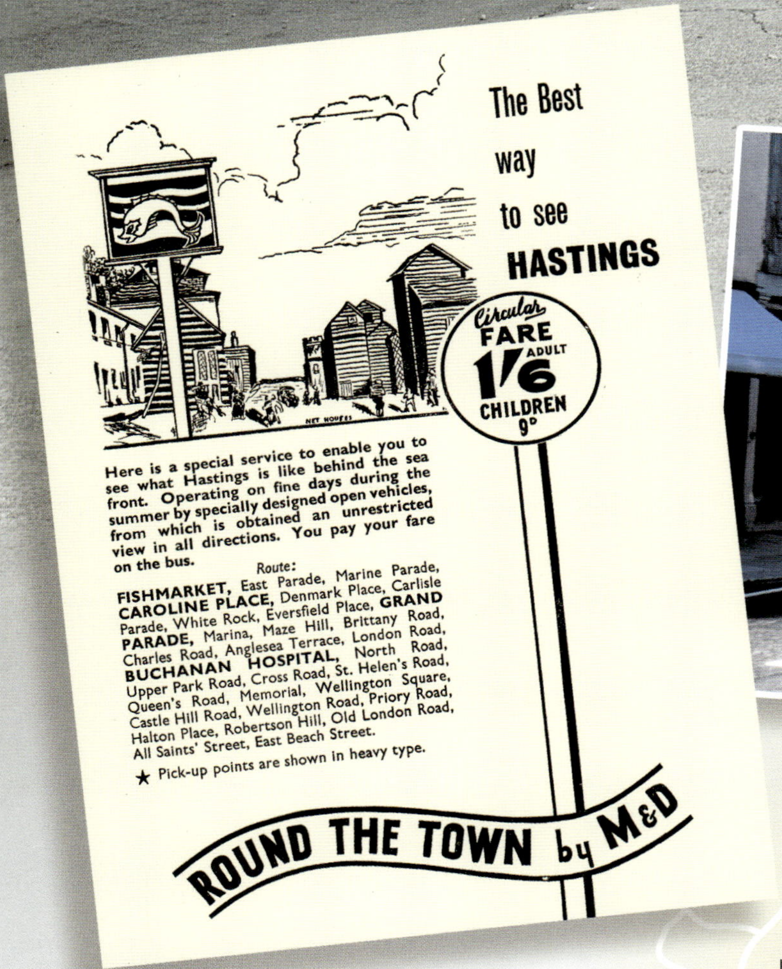

The Best way to see HASTINGS

Circular FARE 1/6 ADULT CHILDREN 9d

Here is a special service to enable you to see what Hastings is like behind the sea front. Operating on fine days during the summer by specially designed open vehicles, from which is obtained an unrestricted view in all directions. You pay your fare on the bus.

Route:

FISHMARKET, East Parade, Marine Parade, **CAROLINE PLACE,** Denmark Place, Carlisle Parade, White Rock, Eversfield Place, **GRAND PARADE,** Marina, Maze Hill, Brittany Road, Charles Road, Anglesea Terrace, London Road, **BUCHANAN HOSPITAL,** North Road, Upper Park Road, Cross Road, St. Helen's Road, Queen's Road, Memorial, Wellington Square, Castle Hill Road, Wellington Road, Priory Road, Halton Place, Robertson Hill, Old London Road, All Saints' Street, East Beach Street.

★ Pick-up points are shown in heavy type.

ROUND THE TOWN by M&D

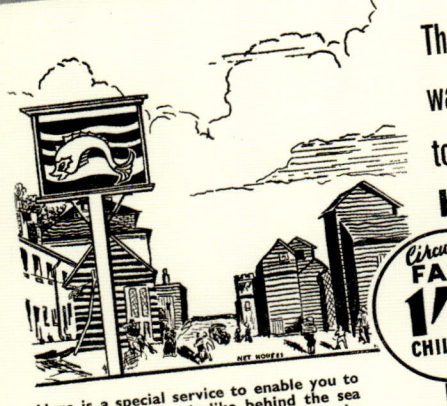

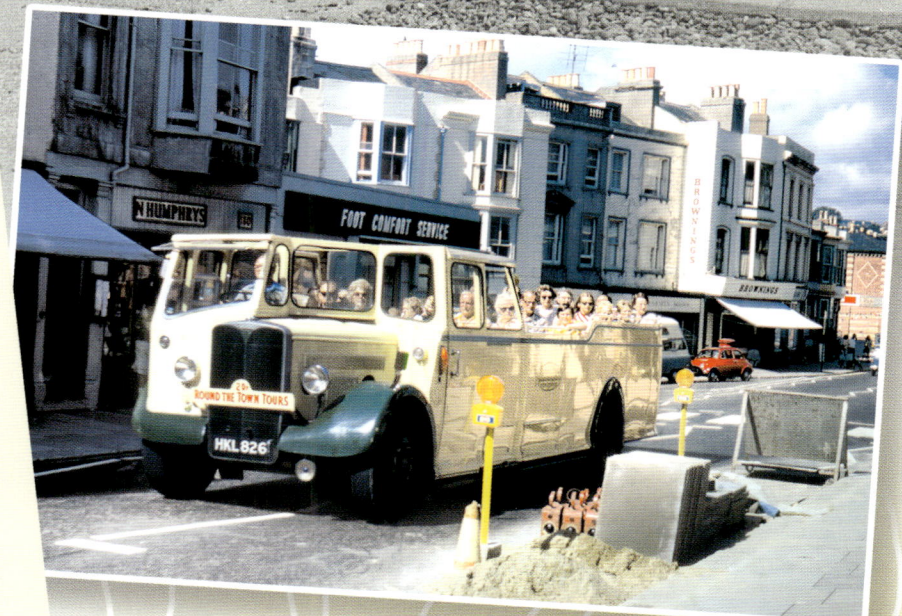

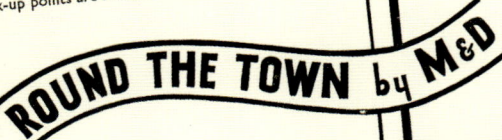

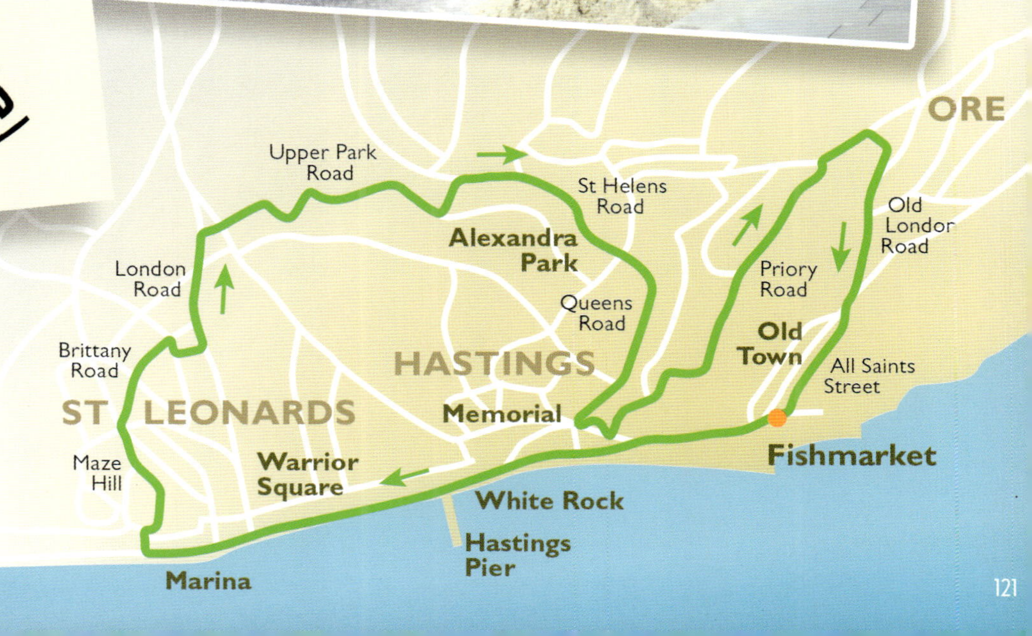

At the top of this page two of the open-top Regals led by OR1 were waiting by the Fishmarket for business, which looked decidedly slack that day.

JEREMY WILLIAMS COLLECTION

The other picture shows a nicely loaded 8002 in post-decimalisation times when the fare had risen to 20p in new money.

JEREMY WILLIAMS COLLECTION

Two lowbridge Atlanteans were passing each other on the 159 route outside Bexhill depot.
M&D AND EAST KENT BUS CLUB

Having just gone under the main coastal Hastings railway line, lowbridge Atlantean DL51, below, was approaching Bulverhythe between St Leonards and Bexhill on the half-hourly 156 to Ellerslie Lane north of Bexhill town centre.
M&D AND EAST KENT BUS CLUB

Bexhill BX

Hastings' westerly neighbour a few miles along the coast is Bexhill, a quieter resort with a character all its own and the architecturally outstanding De La Warr Pavilion on the seafront. This *Moderne* style building was designed by the architects Erich Mendelsohn and Serge Chermayeff and built in 1935.

Maidstone & District's bus depot was in Terminus Road, and in 1951 had 20 vehicles allocated, including Bristol K6A double deckers, AEC Regal and Bristol L6A single-deck buses and AEC Regal coaches.

During the summer months in the early 1950s Leyland Titan TD5 open topper OT1 was based at Bexhill, although later on it was changed for OT6. The other five were at Hastings, although it is recorded that one was allocated to Rye, at least in 1952. By 1958 all six were at Hastings, although OT6 was sent to the Isle of Sheppey for an open-top service there. There's a picture of it on Sheppey on page 149.

All six of the 1939 open-top Leyland TD5s were allocated to Hastings and Bexhill in the 1950s until one went to Sheerness in 1959. The first of them, OT1, was on Hastings sea front on the 75 to Crowhurst in the picture above, with the conductor taking fares on the top deck.
M&D AND EAST KENT BUS CLUB

In the colour shot on the right OT1 was on Bexhill local route 160 to Sidley. These open toppers were all withdrawn in 1964/5.
M&D AND EAST KENT BUS CLUB

The open toppers here on the Sussex coast were often to be seen on the 75 route between St Helens, Memorial and Wishing Tree, continuing on to Crowhurst every 2 hours.

Until the beginning of 1948 Maidstone & District also had an operational depot at Battle, later used to store mainly coaches during the winter months.

the Thumper years

An important railway line threading through the south west of Maidstone & District's territory was the Hastings line south from Tonbridge. This was completed by the South Eastern Railway in 1852, built through wooded hilly terrain and needing eight tunnels.

The South Eastern was anxious to build this as economically as possible, as it was not strong financially and in competition with the London Brighton & South Coast Railway to reach Hastings.

But the contractors skimped on the tunnel linings, rectified later with extra rings of internal brickwork, which reduced the width by 18 inches and led to narrower trains being required.

By the mid-1950s it was necessary to replace the narrow coaching stock from the early 1930s - classified Restriction 0 as it could be used anywhere on the Southern Railway - with new stock. These narrow slab-sided carriages were intended to be still steam-hauled but a decision was made in 1956 to dieselise the line, so these were built instead as 6-car multiple units with a diesel engine powering an on-board generator driving electric motors in the bogies. The first seven units were built on short underframes, the rest to standard length.

There had been a number of plans to electrify the line since the 1930s and this finally happened in 1986, with the track being singled in the tunnels to allow full-width stock to be used. Modern signalling made this an easy solution now.

But for the best part of 30 years these hills and valleys used to echo to the sound of the aptly nicknamed *Thumpers* barking and growling noisily as they accomplished the steep gradients and curves that characterise the line in this lovely part of Kent and East Sussex.

Hastings diesel-electric unit 1018 was one of the nine that were originally classified 6L, illustrated on the left in its original all-green livery.

There were also seven similar 6B units that had one second class trailer replaced by a buffet car. The other seven Hastings diesels were the initial shorter 6S units.

Because the English Electric 4-cylinder diesel engine and generator had to be mounted in a central position laterally in the driving car at each end, it was impossible to provide through gangways between units.

The first diesel timetable provided a daytime 12-car hourly service from Charing Cross with the train splitting at Tunbridge Wells. The front 6-car unit with the buffet car went fast to Crowhurst then on to Hastings, with the rear 6-car unit following as an all-stations stopper.

One interesting feature of the line is that many stations have their up and down platforms staggered instead of facing each other.

RAY STENNING

Tunbridge Wells TW

Tunbridge Wells, a major town in the west of Maidstone & District's operating territory, is not far from the Kent/Sussex border. In 1831 there were just 5,929 inhabitants but within 10 years this had risen to 8,302. Tunbridge Wells became the fastest growing town in Kent, increasingly popular with people seeking the enjoyment of retirement. The cost of living was cheaper than in London but it was still possible to get up to London easily on stagecoaches, a reliable service from the town taking five hours. But after the railways reached here in the middle of the 19th century Tunbridge Wells grew even more, becoming an important residential and now commuter town.

However, visitors had been coming to Tunbridge Wells to *"take the waters"* ever since an iron-rich chalybeate spring was discovered here by Lord North in 1606. In 1629 the first royal visitor to 'The Wells' was Queen Henrietta Maria, wife of King Charles I, who stayed for six weeks, but as there was no accommodation available at that time, the Royal entourage camped on the Common.

After this the town grew in popularity and gained a reputation as the place to see and be seen, a favourite destination for fashionable society who needed accommodation and wanted places of entertainment such as coffee houses, gaming-rooms and an assembly room for dances and balls. In 1684 Margaret, the widow of Viscount Purbeck, whose love of fashion and dancing had gained her the nickname of **The Princess of Babylon**, provided land on Mount Sion for the earliest lodging houses and the ground at the northern end of the Pantiles, where the Church of King Charles the Martyr was built.

Designed by architect John Briggs and finished in 1902, The Tunbridge Wells Opera House originally had a capacity of 1,100. It became a cinema in 1931 but during the Second World War a bomb got caught in the proscenium arch above the stage and set fire to the inside of the building. It was renovated and reopened in 1949. Later it became a bingo hall and, thankfully, in 1966 the building was granted Grade II listed status.

The interior was in Edwardian Baroque and Neo-Georgian styles. The dome on the roof originally had a nude statue of Mercury on the top, although this was removed in the 1920s, either because it was unstable or possibly condidered sinful by *'Disgusted of Tunbridge Wells'*!

In the 1960s Leyland Atlanteans were widely used on busy town services, like DH518 outside the Opera House in the picture above.

RICK READING

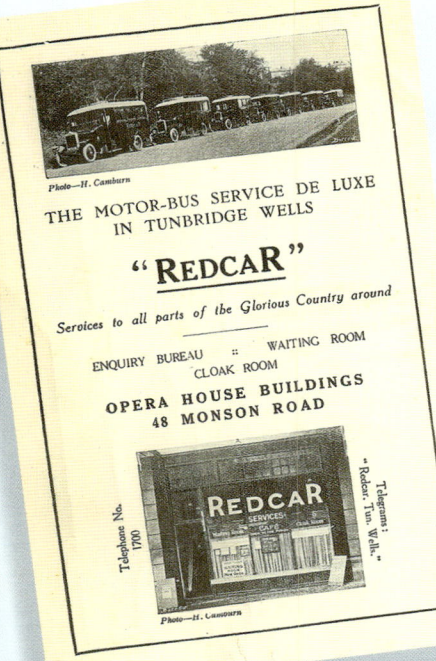

And so the town began to spread. Sir Christopher Wren sent his chief plasterer Henry Doogood to create the magnificent ceiling of the church, and it was here that later the young Princess Victoria attended church services with her mother, the Duchess of Kent.

It was probably Beau Nash we have to thank for really putting Tunbridge Wells on the map. Beau Nash was born Richard Nash in 1674 in Swansea, and was a celebrated dandy and leader of fashion in 18th-century Britain, best remembered as the self-appointed Master of Ceremonies at that other spa town of Bath. He played a leading role in making Bath the most fashionable resort in 18th-century England. After he arrived in Tunbridge Wells in 1735 - he'd had his sights on the town for some while - fashionable society blossomed here, too. As well as organising entertainments, Nash established strict rules for correct behaviour. And to ensure visitors paid subscriptions for services provided, he introduced Sarah Porter, **Queen of the Touters**, who eagerly pursued defaulters. Under Nash, Tunbridge Wells attained the height of its fame as a fashionable resort, patronised by royalty, nobility and the most famous names in the country.

In 1909 King Edward VII officially recognised the popularity of Tunbridge Wells with royal and aristocratic visitors over the centuries - including his mother, Queen Victoria - by granting the town its Royal prefix.

In bus history Royal Tunbridge Wells was the scene of intense - one might almost say, ferocious - bus warfare between rivals Autocar and Redcar in the 1920s. Autocar had been controlled by East Surrey since 1928 but in July 1933 Maidstone & District took it over as a full subsidiary. East Surrey's other bus interests got absorbed by the London Passenger Transport Board at the same time. However, M&D kept Autocar as a separate company until it also took over Autocar's rival Redcar (in which M&D had a large financial interest) in 1935. The lower bus garage in St Johns Road, with its entrance from Woodbury Park Road, came with Autocar, and the upper garage and offices fronting St Johns Road were built in 1937 after demolishing some houses that had stood there. It was extended again in 1950. Arriva, as successor to Maidstone & District, finally closed St Johns Road garage in October 2017.

The garage in Upper Grosvenor Road taken over with Redcar in 1935 was leased to the Post Office around 1937 but reverted to M&D as a vehicle store in 1967.

Tunbridge Wells had the second largest vehicle allocation within the company - in October 1951 there were 118 buses and coaches based at the depot - and still held that status into the 1960s. It had a higher proportion of single-deck buses compared to the other large depots.

Outside its home garage of Tunbridge Wells in the picture below was DL31, a 55-seat lowbridge Leyland bodied Leyland Titan PD2/12 delivered in 1951, here on the 91 to East Grinstead.

The Southdown coach parked on the garage forecourt was 1162, one of its Leyland Leopards with Weymann Castilian coachwork, a style unique to Southdown.
SOUTHDOWN ENTHUSIASTS' CLUB

Below is a shot of 1934 Harrington bodied Dennis Ace 757 in original condition parked outside the Woodbury Park Road entrance to Tunbridge Wells depot.
M&D AND EAST KENT BUS CLUB

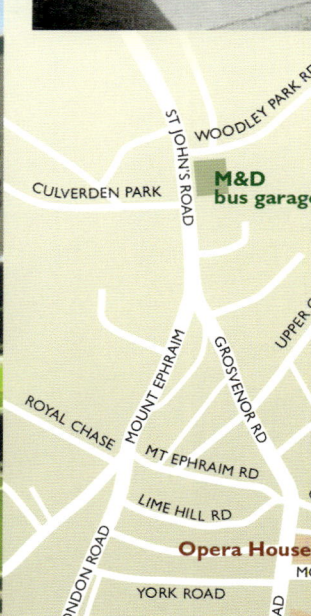

In the early 1950s the double-deck fleet was mainly Bristol K6As, with AEC Regent IIIs and Leyland Titan PD2/12s for the longer routes. Before one-man operation took hold, the single-decker bus fleet was made up of Leyland Tiger TS8s with Harrington or ECW bodies and AEC Regals with Beadle bodies. Coaches at that time were AEC Regals, semi-chassisless Beadle/AECs, all-Leyland Royal Tigers and AEC Reliances with Harrington bodies.

As a major regional centre, Tunbridge Wells drew people in from the many surrounding villages, and there was a good network of bus services into Tunbridge Wells and to and from other towns. There's a map showing bus routes to and from Tonbridge and Tunbridge Wells on the adjacent page. Before 1955 these were all crew operated, other than the three routes acquired from Ashline in Tonbridge in September 1948 - 130 to Sevenoaks Weald, 131 to Underriver and 132 to Lower Haysden. These three routes were run with 20-seat Dennis Falcons TS1-4, new in 1950. The seating of these was increased to 25 when legislation changed in 1955.

Tunbridge Wells was more or less the halfway point for the company's longest bus route, the 122 jointly operated with Southdown, and this took roughly two hours each way to Gravesend or Brighton (see page 156). Although the 152 to Hastings was only every 2 hours, there was an hourly service in summer thanks to the Heathfield Pool arrangement (see page 166). On alternate hours you could catch an Eastbourne bound 191 and get a connection in Heathfield to a 180 that had travelled from Brighton.

Maidstone based DH34, one of the 1944 Daimler CWA6 buses whose post-war rebodying story starts on page 16, was displaying its new 1951 Weymann body in the picture on the left. It had just climbed up Mount Pleasant Road and was on the hourly 33 to Maidstone.
MICHAEL DRYHURST

— hourly or better
— hourly Heathfield Pool routes
— less frequent

routes out of Tonbridge & Tunbridge Wells
summer 1965

Mention is made of the Dennis bodied Dennis Falcons bought for use at Tunbridge Wells depot on the former Ashline routes in the Tonbridge area in 1950.

However, TS4 at the bottom of the page on the left was on the former Sargent's of East Grinstead route between Edenbridge and Crowborough at Crowbough Cross.

There's more about these routes on page 136. Note the Harrington-Commer Contender bus facing the other way.
MAIDSTONE & DISTRICT AND EAST KENT BUS CLUB

Tonbridge & Tunbridge Wells

town routes	out-of-town routes
77	7
81	33
82	78
83	79
89	80
96	84
100	85
123	86
129	87
132	89
138	90
158	91
	93
	94
	96
	97
	101
	107
	119
	122
	150
	152
	191

127

Maidstone & District bought 22 AEC Regent Vs in 1956, all with Park Royal bodywork whose rear entrances featured platform doors. Eight of them were lowbridge. On the right was one of the lowbridge versions, DL35, at the top of Mount Pleasant Road where it crosses Crescent Road.

It was on route 101, a half-hourly link from Tunbridge Wells, through Tonbridge and on to the attractive village of Leigh.

M&D AND EAST KENT BUS CLUB

In 1947 six AEC Regent IIIs were bought with the larger 9.6-litre AEC engine, preselector gearbox and air brakes, a complete change from the Bristols otherwise being bought in large numbers. They carried Weymann bodies built in 1942 that had come off 1934 AEC Regents that had been acquired from Tilling and had been rebodied then.

They were all allocated to Tunbridge Wells depot and on the right was DH248 on a rather wet day just yards ahead of where the picture above was taken, but this one on local route 98 from Ramslye Estate. Note the imposing, almost pompous-looking Austin A135 Princess on the right.

M&D AND EAST KENT BUS CLUB

There was a good town bus network in Tunbridge Wells and the buses always seemed busy in the 1950s and 1960s. Some routes, like the 81 to Rusthall ran up to every 10 minutes.

Within Tunbridge Wells's allocation of single-deck buses was SO68, the one-off Saunders-Roe integral seating 43 delivered in 1953.

When the Albion Nimbus demonstrator was with Maidstone & District it was trialled on Tunbridge Wells local 89 between Tunbridge Wells West Station, the town and Molyneux Park (see page 36).

So when the company's Harrington bodied Nimbus buses arrived in 1960, one was regularly seen working the same route.

On the right SO317 was turning out of Vale Road by Tunbridge Wells Central Station, about to head up Mount Pleasant Road through the town and on to Molyneux Park.

From the late 1950s all through the 1960s and beyond, this part of the town would echo to the characterisic bark and growl of Southern Region diesel-electric multiple units (aptly known as Thumpers) as they accelerated out of the station into the tunnels either end of the platforms.
MICHAEL DRYHURST

This had a horizontal Gardner 5LW engine with a power output of 94bhp at 1,700rpm and a 4-speed manual gearbox. It had conventional road springs, vacuum brakes and a lattice underframe, and its design was influenced by the company. The bus was heavy to drive and not liked by many of the drivers. No more were ordered and the bus spent most of its life at Tunbridge Wells. Problems accrued when parts were required and the bus took longer for COF preparation in Postley Works because of being non-standard. It's shown on pages 32-33 and 181.

There were two routes between Tunbridge Wells and Penshurst. This pretty village is well-known because of Penshurst Place, the ancestral home of the Sidney family and birthplace of the Elizabethan poet and courtier, Sir Philip Sidney.

The 93 went via Bidborough and the 150 approached the village from Langton and Fordcombe, both hourly, although the 93 continued to Edenbridge.

On the right in the village, in July 1960, Harrington Wayfarer IV bodied AEC Reliance coach C8 had been sent over from Gravesend to deputise for a bus on the 93. The conductor was obviously enjoying the balmy summer air through the open door.
DAVID TOY COLLECTION

The 82 Tunbridge Wells local ran between the Central Station and Hawkenbury Cemetery every 15 minutes

Above, handsome all-Leyland Titan PD2, DH407, was running down High Street just south of Tunbridge Wells Central Station to return up London Road and Vale Road to regain the route.

RAY STENNING

Another Tunbridge Wells local was the 83 running between the West Station, Central Station and north east to Ravenswood Avenue, up to every 15 minutes.

On the left directly opposite the West Station building (behind the photographer) was DH259, one of no less than 42 Weymann bodied Bristol K6As that came in 1948 and 1949, awaiting its next turn.

Tunbridge Wells West was an imposing building opened in 1866 by the London, Brighton & South Coast Railway. In the late 1950s on a normal weekday 136 trains called there; between 6am and midnight, on average one passenger train departed or arrived every eight minutes. The station closed in 1985 but the main building remains.

M&D AND EAST KENT BUS CLUB

On the left is another of the eight 1956 lowbridge Park Royal bodied AEC Regent Vs, 6737 (formerly DL37), parked on the forecourt of Tonbridge depot. Odd that the blind was showing 152, as that route to Hastings started from Tunbridge Wells, not Tonbridge.
JEREMY WILLIAMS COLLECTION

Below at the depot is an interesting study in BET-style single-deck design.

The AEC Reliance on the far right displays the first style for 36ft long single-deckers with the flat glass two-piece twin matching screens and a protruding destination box set in a rounded dome.

The other two are slightly later Leyland Panthers, the middle one with Willowbrook body and the one on the left bodied by Strachans.

It's interesting that although the Panthers both have the same double-curvature windscreens, the Willowbrook roof dips satisfactorily to keep just a narrow strip between screen and desination recess, whereas the Strachans keeps a straight roofline, resulting in a deeper strip above the screen, thus giving the appearance of a too shallow windscreen being fitted.
RAY STENNING

Tonbridge TB

Several routes connected Tonbridge with Tunbridge Wells, many of them longer distance ones like the 122 from Gravesend and the 7 from Maidstone, and this resulted in buses between the towns often running just a few minutes apart. On the first and last runs of the day there was often dead mileage to and from the depot in Tunbridge Wells. So in January 1961 a new depot was opened in Tonbridge with an allocation of 30 vehicles. The transfer of some routes to run out of Tonbridge instead of Tunbridge Wells made for a more efficient operation.

Hawkhurst HK

Hawkhurst is a delightful Wealden Kentish village not far from the border with Sussex. It's where two major roads cross, the A229 and the A268. The name Hawkhurst is derived from Old English **Heafoc Hyrst**, meaning a wooded hill frequented by hawks. Hurst (Hyrst) in a place name refers to a wood or wooded area, and there are many places with hurst in their name in this part of the world.

The village was involved in the Wealden iron industry until the Industrial Revolution of the late 18th century. William Penn, founder of the state of Pennsylvania, owned ironworks at Hawkhurst in the 17th century. A notorious point in the village's history was the Hawkhust Gang, smugglers who terrorised the Kent and Sussex coast between 1735 and 1749, smuggling brandy, silk and tobacco.

Hawkhurst was surrounded by hop gardens, and hop growing was always a big part of the local economy. Until the early 1960s Hawkhurst used to be the terminus of a lovely branch railway line from Paddock Wood, and a feature of this line was the hop-pickers' specials during the late summer and early autumn.

For many years, hop-picking was done by Londoners flooding into Kent at the end of every summer to pick the hops used in brewing. From the 1920s to the 1950s some 200,000 East Enders - mainly women and children - made the annual pilgrimage to the Kentish hop gardens, filling the hoppers' specials trains from London. This was so popular that it was known as the 'Londoner's holiday', and for many East Enders it was the nearest to a holiday they ever got. Most farmers would invite the same families each year and whole streets would decamp en masse and set themselves up in rows of 'hop huts' in the same configuration as in their London terraces. Menfolk, if not already there, would often join them at weekends.

Increasing affluence as the 1950s rolled in to the 1960s, the demise of hops for brewing and the mechanisation of the process, plus the fact that most of the stations were inconveniently sited for the communities they served, and a move to transport schoolchildren by bus rather than train, all made it inevitable that the line didn't have a future, and so in June 1961 it closed.

Maidstone & District's new Hawkhurst depot was combined with a bus station on a site near the eastern edge of the village and used to play an important role in the services to Hastings and Brighton, to Ashford and East Grinstead and, later, in the Heathfield Pool, which is described elsewhere in this book. It was opened on 7 June 1950 with a capacity of 24 vehicles, replacing the original depot in Winchester Road on the northern side of the village built in 1921.

The bus station was an island layout with office accommodation and waiting area in the centre. The depot also provided crew changes for the longer services. This is where the apple green buses of Southdown Motor Services could be seen on the joint service to Brighton.

In 1951 the depot had an allocation of 11 vehicles, but this increased to 17 by 1964. The 1951 allocation was

3 x   Weymann bodied Bristol K6As
6 x   all-Leyland PD2/12s - 5 highbridge, 1 lowbridge.
1 x   Harrington bodied Leyland Tiger TS7 bus
1 x   Harrington re-bodied Leyland Tiger TS7 coach

By 1958 the Bristol K6As had increased to six and the Leyland PD2/12s reduced by one. Later in the 1960s the double deckers were all Leyland Titan PD2/12s and the single-deck buses and coaches were AEC Reliances, plus a solitary Albion Nimbus.

Hawkhust was the crossroads of four of M&D's longer routes.

5   Gillingham & Maidstone (later only from Maidstone) to Hastings
57   Gravesend & Maidstone to Hastings
80/84   Tunbridge Wells to Hastings
97   Ashford to East Grinstead

The depot had several short workings on the 5 and also duties on the 84 and 97. The 80 was 2-hourly from Tunbridge Wells to Hurst Green or Hawkhurst via Pembury and Lamberhurst and operated by both Tunbridge Wells and Hawkhurst depots.

There was also the 18 joint with Southdown to Brighton operated on an hourly basis for most of the day via Burwash, Heathfield, Ringmer and Lewes which, after the Heathfield Pool was instigated, became the 18/190, and this is explained in that section starting on page 166.

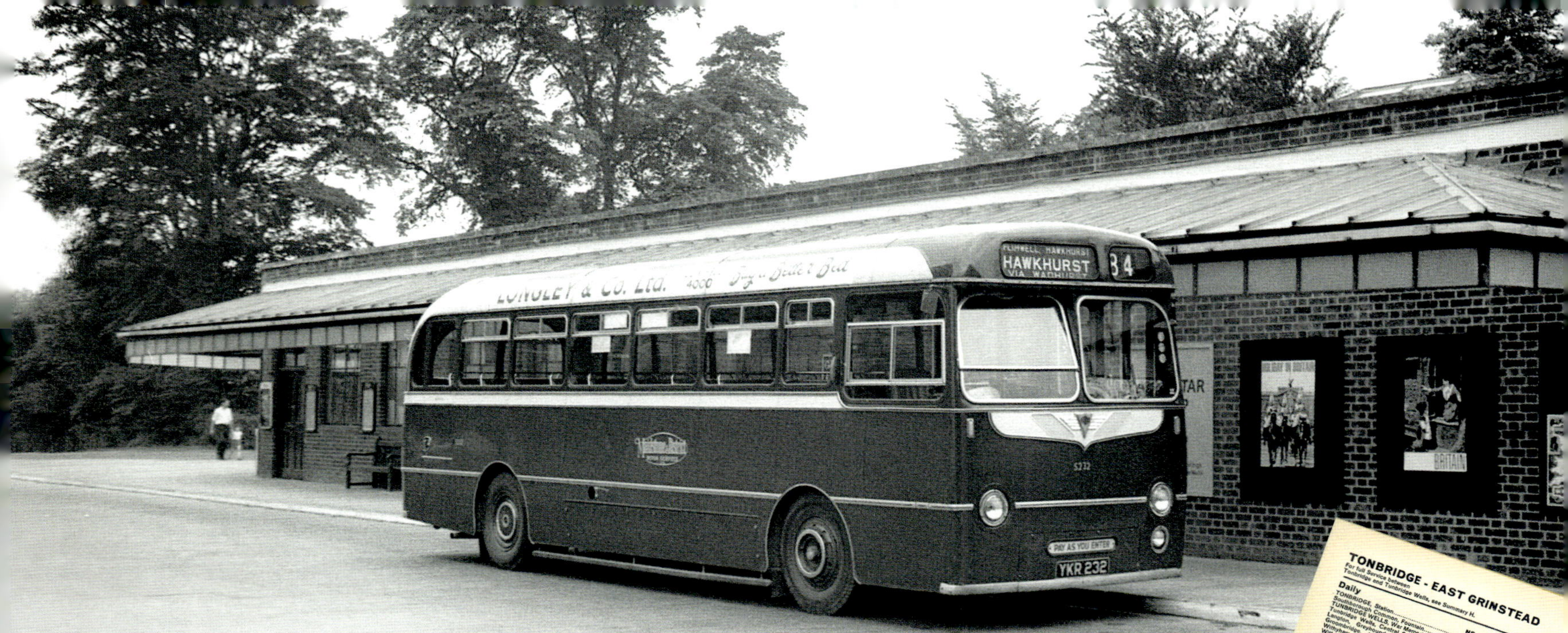

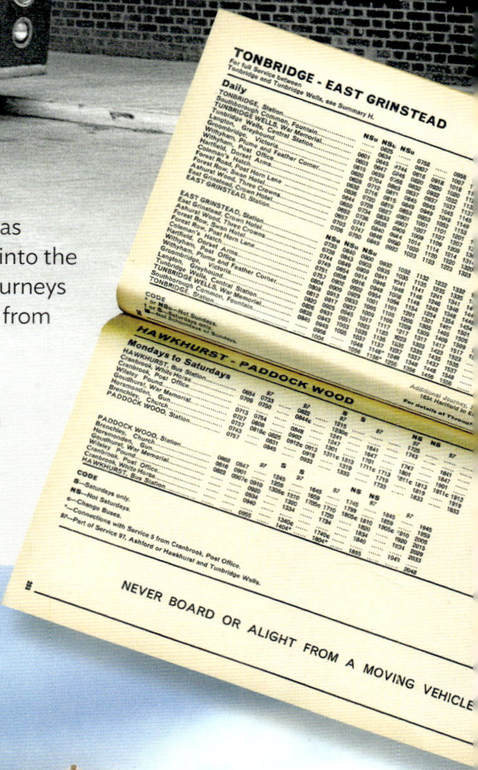
TONBRIDGE - EAST GRINSTEAD
For full Service between Tonbridge and Tunbridge Wells, see Summary H.
Daily
TONBRIDGE, Station
Southborough Common, Fountain
TUNBRIDGE WELLS, War Memorial
Tunbridge Wells, Central Station
Langton, Greyhound
Groombridge, Victoria
Withyham, Plume and Feather Corner
Withyham, Post Office
Hartfield, Dorset Arms
Coleman's Hatch
Forest Road, Post Horn Lane
Forest Row, Swan Hotel
Ashurst Wood, Three Crowns
East Grinstead, Crown Hotel
EAST GRINSTEAD, Station

EAST GRINSTEAD, Station
East Grinstead, Crown Hotel
Ashurst Wood, Three Crowns
Forest Row, Swan Hotel
Forest Row, Post Horn Lane
Coleman's Hatch
Hartfield, Dorset Arms
Withyham, Post Office
Withyham, Plume and Feather Corner
Groombridge, Victoria
Langton, Greyhound
Tunbridge Wells, Central Station
TUNBRIDGE WELLS, War Memorial
Southborough Common, Fountain
TONBRIDGE, Station

HAWKHURST - PADDOCK WOOD
Mondays to Saturdays
HAWKHURST, Bus Station
Cranbrook, White Horse
Cranbrook, Post Office
Wilsley Pound
Goudhurst, War Memorial
Horsmonden, Gun
Brenchley, Church
PADDOCK WOOD, Station

PADDOCK WOOD, Station
Brenchley, Church
Horsmonden, Gun
Goudhurst, War Memorial
Wilsley Pound
Cranbrook, Post Office
Cranbrook, White Horse
HAWKHURST, Bus Station

CODE
S—Saturdays only.
NS—Not Saturdays.
c—Change Buses.
*—Connections with Service 5 from Cranbrook, Post Office.
97—Part of Service 97, Ashford or Hawkhurst and Tunbridge Wells.

NEVER BOARD OR ALIGHT FROM A MOVING VEHICLE

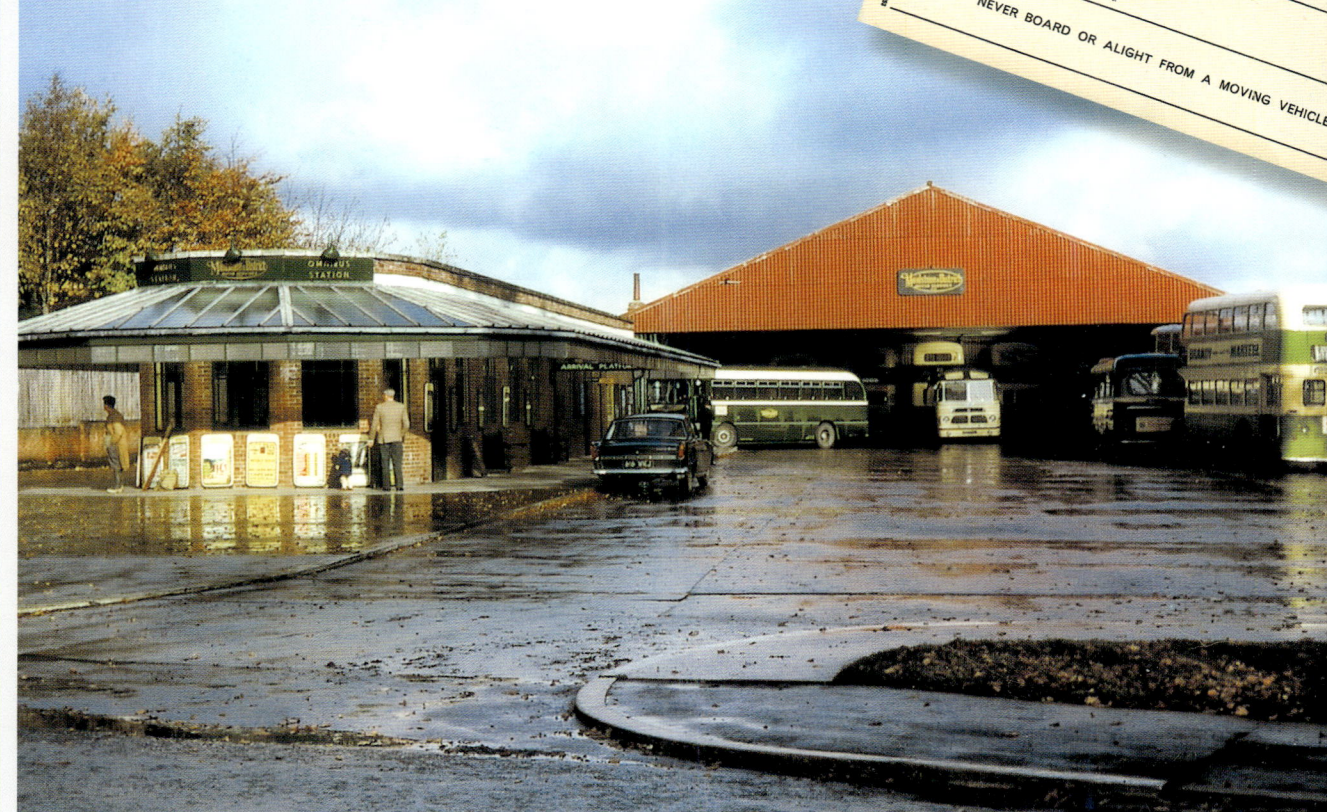

At the top of the opposite page an ex-SECR H-class 0-4-4 tank engine was with its 2-carriage push-pull train in a typical British Railways Southern Region steam branch line scene of the 1950s, here at the end of the line at Hawkhurst. Unfortunately, the station was well over a mile from the village.

LAMBERHURST

The centre of Hawkhust is where two main roads cross, as seen in the lower picture opposite. A Harrington Wayfarer IV coach was turning from the Rye Road northwards on to the A229, possibly on a London-bound journey of the E10 express service from Rye.

The lowbridge Park Royal bodied AEC Regent V was coming in on a Hawkhurst working of the 97.

M&D AND EAST KENT BUS CLUB

Hawkhurst's charming bus station/depot is on this page. Above, one of the Beadle bodied AEC Reliance buses of 1957, S232, had arrived from Tunbridge Wells, Wadhurst and Ticehurst on the hourly 84. Only some journeys continued to Hastings.

RAY STENNING

On a sun and showers blustery day on the right, autumn leaves were littering the bus station apron. Among the buses and coach, on the far right, was the solitary Albion Nimbus and a Southdown double decker.

SOUTHDOWN ENTHUSIASTS' CLUB

Route 31, operated by Rye depot, ran between Hawkhurst and Rye through lovely Sussex countryside by way of Sandhurst, Northiam, Beckley and Peasemarsh. This route was shared with John Dengate & Son of Rye (Dengate bus operations eventually came into the Maidstone & District fold in 1974 - see page 198). Maidstone & District had three journeys all the way through and it took the best part of an hour to reach Rye. The other five from Hawkhust to Rye plus the short workings from Northiam were run by Dengate.

For a while after the Hawkhurst railway line closed there was an early morning Hawkhurst to Paddock Wood route 92 journey and return in the early evening, with a few Paddock Wood to Horsmonden shorts connecting with 97s to Hawkhurst.

Hawkhust survived into the early Arriva era but finally closed in 2006, the site of the depot becoming a Tesco store and the bus station the store's car park.

Edenbridge E

Edenbridge grew up along a section of what remained of the old Roman road from London to Lewes at the point where it crossed the River Eden, a tributary of the River Medway. With the coming of the South Eastern Railway through Edenbridge as far as Tonbridge in 1842 - part of its main line from London to Dover by way of Redhill, Tonbridge and Ashford - the town expanded.

The other railway line through Edenbridge arrived in 1888, the London Brighton & South Coast line from Oxted southwards towards the junction at Ashurst with the East Grinstead to Tunbridge Wells line. Edenbridge Station on the Redhill to Tonbridge line was usually called 'Edenbridge Top' by local enthusiasts, being on what they also called the 'Edenbridge Top' line, as opposed to Edenbridge Town station on the 'lower' line from Oxted, which actually passed underneath it in a partial tunnel north west of the town.

When the South Eastern Railway's shorter main line to Tonbridge through Sevenoaks opened in 1868, the Edenbridge Top line became just a local line, although inter-regional trains, like the 'Birkenhead' from the Thanet coast through Reading and Oxford to the North West, went this way.

In the early part of the 20th century, aircraft coming into Croydon Airport used this line for navigation, and stations along it had their names written in bold white paint on the roofs.

Steam trains lasted on the line from Oxted until the early 1960s and lingered on the top line until January 1965. The Southern Region's characterful diesel-electric multiple unit trains then took over, known as Thumpers, although the top line got electrified in 1993.

Owing to its position on the River Eden floodplain, the centre of Edenbridge was prone to flooding, the most severe occurring in 1958. After this, flood defences were built. Nevertheless, 10 years later the town was once again flooded after heavy storms.

It's an attractive town with a fair few medieval buildings along with Victorian 'railway architecture' shops and dwellings, and was finally by-passed in the early years of the 21st century.

The bridge over the River Eden in Edenbridge dates from 1836, and was built of local Ashlar stone with a wide, 4-centred arch of rusticated voussoirs. It's Grade II Listed and has a bronze plaque commemorating the coronation of Edward VII.

The bus crossing the bridge in 1966 in the shot at the top of the opposite page, being followed by an Austin A110 Westminster, was S303. Delivered in 1960, this AEC Reliance carried the earliest very square BET style of body, this one built by Weymann with dual-purpose seating.

It had come into Edenbridge on the hourly top arc of the 93 from Tunbridge Wells by way of Penshurst, Bough Beech and Four Elms and would terminate in the town. Every other 93 continued back to Tunbridge Wells through Hever, Cowden and Ashurst. There's a map on the next page to explain this better.

The inset picture on the left was taken inside the small depot at Edenbridge in the mid-1960s and shows a couple of Harrington Wayfarer IV bodied AEC Reliance coaches.

Around that time one of the coach drivers working out of the depot lived in Oxted in Surrey, 6½ miles to the north west of Edenbridge. With the help of his wife's social connections, they used to get a fair number of private hire bookings in the Oxted area. If the hire involved an early start he'd take the coach home and park it in the garage of local motor dealer Spark's in Amy Road. This was right in the centre of Oxted and only 5 minutes' walk from his house. The coach was often one of the Wayfarers.

London Transport Country Area also had single-deck bus services running into Edenbridge. Routes 465 from Holland, Hurst Green, Oxted, Limpsfield, the Chart and Crockham Hill, and the 485 from Westerham and Crockham Hill, both from the north. Long-standing trunk route 434 from Crawley, East Grinstead and Dormansland (once from further away Horsham) approached the town from the south west through Marsh Green.

The 465 and 485 ran on alternate hours, from 1953 with London Transport's much-loved little GS buses. Before that, C-class Leyland Cubs were on these routes. However, in October 1962 the ubiquitous RFs took over and, just as the GSs had done, used M&D's Edenbridge depot forecourt for turning round and a short layover.

At the bottom of the opposite page was RF597 doing just that while the driver was in the depot having a cuppa and chinwag with the depot supervisor. He'd already set the blind for the return 465 journey to Holland, which meant he'd come in on a 485 from Westerham.

These routes were run out of Chelsham garage high up on the North Downs on the fringes of the finger of London suburban ribbon development that stretched south from Croydon to Warlingham.

Before the Second World War, Green Line route F used to connect Edenbridge with Croydon, London, Watford and Hemel Hempstead.

Maidstone & District's route 93 touched London Transport's operating area again, just 2½ miles north east of Edenbridge at Four Elms. This was where London Transport's 413A from Sevenoaks and Ide Hill terminated. Because of boundary agreements it didn't go any further, even though Edenbridge would have been a more useful terminus.

Above is 3755, a 36ft AEC Reliance bus from Tunbridge Wells depot turning right at Four Elms on to the B2027 towards Bough Beech, Penshurst and ultimately Tunbridge Wells. It was one of 20 Weymann curved-screen BET-style bodied buses delivered in 1965.

The 413A approached Four Elms from the road leading straight ahead in this photograph.

all pictures on these pages by RAY STENNING

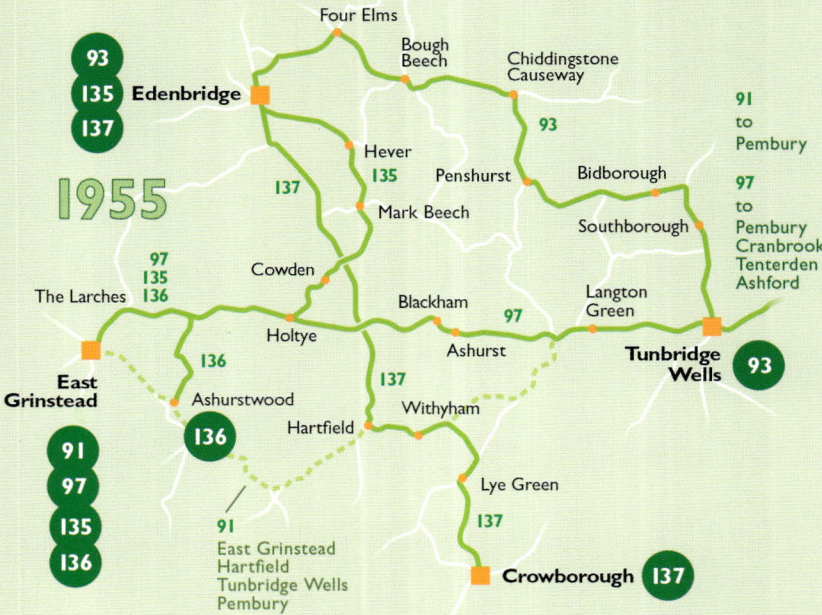

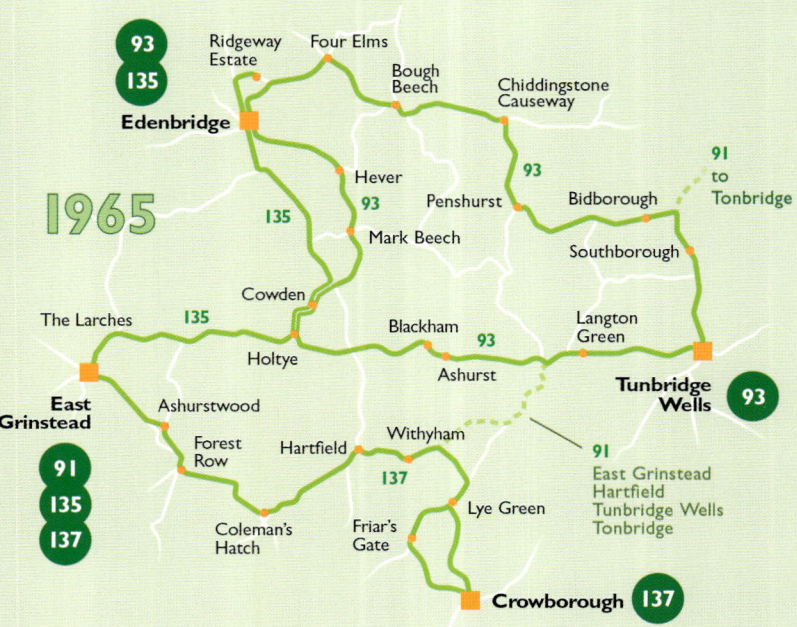

Edenbridge depot opened in January 1955 with space for seven vehicles and was the farthest west of Maidstone & District's depots, and almost of its operation. To understand how the depot came to be built, one has to understand the post-war development of bus services in the area.

Fellow BET-owned neighbouring operator Southdown had already acquired part of the business of Sargent's of East Grinstead, its East Grinstead to Brighton limited stop service in 1933, then in 1937 the local route from the edge of Ashdown Forest through West Hoathly and Saint Hill Green to East Grinstead, plus some excursion and tours licences from the town. The Ashdown Forest route became Southdown 87.

Sargent's still had the bus route from East Grinstead to Cowden and Edenbridge, and after the Second World War added an Edenbridge-Hartfield-Crowborough route and a local from East Grinstead to Ashurstwood. These began in early 1948 and although they started well, they proved financially tough-going for Sargent's. However, there was a need for these to continue running and so a bigger operator with better resources was sought.

Although in Maidstone & District's territory, M&D initially felt it was not best placed to operate these services, even though a garage at Edenbridge was being planned to replace a small outstation. So Southdown applied to take over Sargent's licences, and started running these services on 25 March 1951. No route numbers were allocated. This would have included Sargent's workers' services from East Grinstead to Crawley but these passed to London Transport instead. Southdown also acquired Sargent's excursions licences out of Edenbridge and Westerham.

Then a few months later on 30 September, Maidstone & District did take over these routes, plus the excursion licences, and that's when they were allocated numbers - 135 for the Edenbridge-East Grinstead route, 136 for the Ashurstwood route and 137 for the Edenbridge-Crowborough route. No vehicles were transferred in either takeover and Maidstone & District initially outstationed buses at Southdown's garage in East Grinstead.

After Edenbridge depot opened in 1955 improvements were made - the winter 1955 timetables for the 136 and 137 are below - but soon the services were recast to be the pattern shown in the lower map on the left.

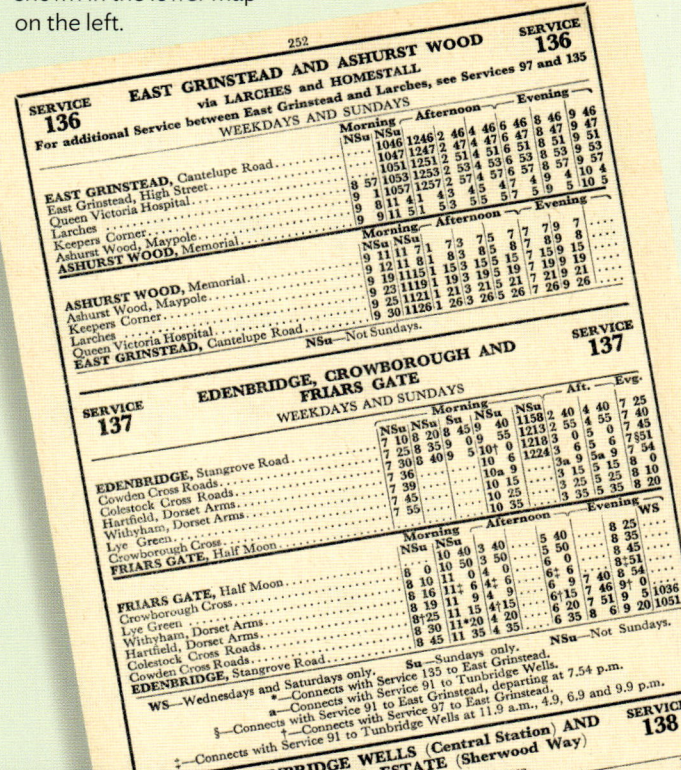

The Leyland Tiger TS8 shown on the right, originally 700 when new in 1938, carried Harrington 34-seat bodywork. However, in 1941, along with others it was requisitioned by the Admiralty for war use. It was eventually returned to Maidstone & District in March 1948 and the company then completely rebuilt the bus before returning it to service. It was renumbered SO700 in 1950 and finally withdrawn in 1954, passing to British Railways Western Region.

In this picture during the final years of its life with M&D it was on the original version of the 137 from Edenbridge to Crowborough, one of the routes taken over from Sargent's via Southdown - it's all explained on this page.

M&D AND EAST KENT BUS CLUB

In October 1955 Edenbridge depot had two Harrington bodied Leyland Royal Tiger coaches and four AEC Reliance service buses, but by the 1960s its allocation of buses and coaches were all on AEC Reliance chassis.

On the upper map on the previous page you can see how the 93 connected Edenbridge with Tunbridge Wells by way of Four Elms and Penshurst. This was hourly. When the former Sargent's routes were recast in the late 1950s, alternate 93s continued to Tunbridge Wells via Hever, Mark Beech and Cowden as shown on the lower map. Previously you could only reach Tunbridge Wells from these villages by changing at Holtye to a 97.

On the left is the route 93 timetable for summer 1965, showing the revised circular 93. It was operated by both Edenbridge and Tunbridge Wells depots.

Mention is made on the previous page of the Southdown garage in East Grinstead. This was in Cantelupe Road on the sloping site where Sargent's had had its garage. Below, two Edenbridge based vehicles - Beadle bodied Reliance bus S225 and Harrington bodied Reliance SC395 - were laying over outside the exit, while a London Transport RF on the 428 to Dormansland was passing by.

The story of the bus-fronted Harrington bodied coaches is told on pages 41 and 68.

RAY STENNING

Rye R

Around the middle of the 11th century, before England's Tudor kings introduced a standing navy, a number of South East ports were granted important legal and fiscal privileges - not to mention valuable commercial benefits and social status - in return for providing ships and men for the English Crown. Their naval service was last called upon in 1588.

The Cinque Ports were Hastings, Sandwich, Dover, Romney and Hythe, also known as the Head Ports. In the 13th century Rye and Winchelsea became Head Ports too and the formal title became **The Confederation of the Cinque Ports and the Two Ancient Towns of Rye and Winchelsea.** Rye was considered one of the finest of the ports, even though constant work had to be done to stop the gradual silting-up of the river and the harbour.

With the advent of bigger ships and larger ports, Rye's naval economy began to decline, and fishing and smuggling became more important. By the end of the 17th century smuggling was widespread throughout Kent and Sussex, with wool being the largest commodity. It got so bad that in the 18th and 19th centuries groups like the Hawkhurst Gang, who met in The Mermaid Inn in Rye, turned to murder and many went to the gallows. The Mermaid Inn was connected to The Olde Bell Inn by a secret passageway.

Rising out of the flat marshlands all around, Rye is an extremely attractive town with narrow cobbled streets twisting to the summit and many medieval buildings. The Landgate, the only survivor of four original fortified entrances to Rye, dates from 1329 and is still the only vehicular route into the ancient centre.

The railway came to Rye in 1851 on the line between Ashford and Hastings, and Station Approach is where most local bus services always terminated. Maidstone & District's Rye depot in Station Approach could hold 11 vehicles, and although built in 1939 it was then immediately requisitioned by the Army and only finally opened in 1946. East Kent also had a depot at Rye, with an allocation that varied from 20 to 30 vehicles.

During the 1950s M&D's depot had Bristol K6As for its double-deck allocation, and Leyland and AEC semi-chassisless and AEC Reliances for the coaching. As the 1960s progressed Rye became all single deck.

It operated the 31 to Hawkhurst via Northiam joint with John Dengate & Son Ltd - see page 198.

The 30 inland route to Hastings via Broad Oak was operated jointly with Hastings depot and took about an hour. East Kent operated routes to the east and the alternative route to Hastings via Winchelsea, the 113.

Outside Rye Station was the last of the Harrington bodied Albion Nimbus 30-seaters that came in 1960, S319.

It was waiting to leave on a journey to Hawkhurst, a route that was mainly operated by local bus company John Dengate & Son.

S319 was withdrawn in 1967 and broken up for scrap by Maidstone & District at Silverhill depot in 1969.

M&D AND EAST KENT BUS CLUB

In this official Maidstone & District photo below are two Harrington bodied Leylands outside the company's depot in Station Approach. KR7408 on the left was a Leyland Tiger TS2 of 1931 and CKE435 a Tiger TS7 of 1935.

MAIDSTONE & DISTRICT

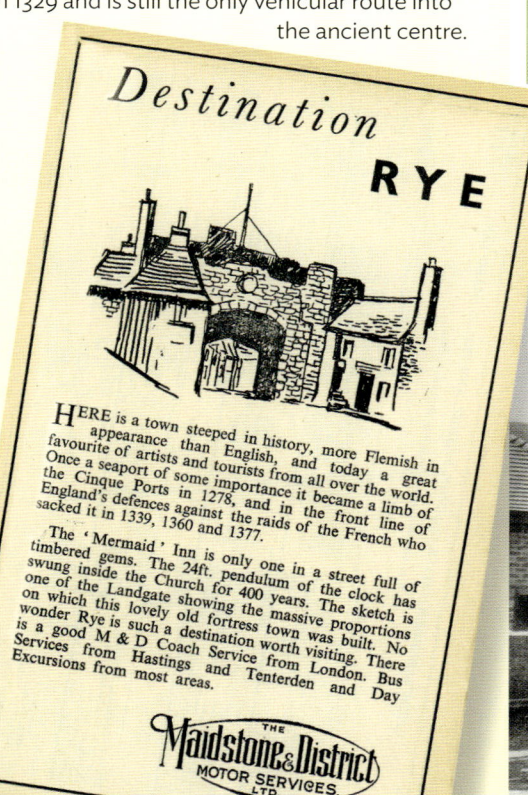

Maidstone & District's 102 route ran between Rye and Tenterden about every 2 hours, mostly via Smallhythe but the odd one or two via Rolvenden, as you can see in the 1955 timetable below.

Waiting to leave for Tenterden at Rye Station above was DL9, a fine specimen of a lowbridge Weymann bodied Bristol K6A of 1949.
M&D AND EAST KENT BUS CLUB

Several years later Tenterden was running 3288, the 1960 dual-purpose seated Weymann bodied AEC Reliance shown on the right, on the 102.

Good sheep-grazing country, the area all around was once marshland and shallow sea, the low hills in the background marking the permanent shoreline.
M&D AND EAST KENT BUS CLUB

Tenterden T

This beautiful Wealden town's name is derived from the Old English *Tenet Waraden*, meaning a den or clearing in the forest belonging to the men of Thanet. Tenterden grew considerably from the 14th century thanks to the strong local wool industry and access to the sea - much of what is now Romney Marsh was under water, and ships docked at nearby Smallhythe. Timber from the forests of the Weald was used to build ships, and in 1449 Tenterden was incorporated into the Confederation of Cinque Ports as a limb of Rye. Ships built in the town helped Rye fulfil its quota for the Crown.

The centre of the attractive town with its broad tree-lined High Street is dominated by St Mildred's church, dating from the 12th century. There are many shops and houses displaying fine 15th- and 18th-century frontages.

Maidstone & District's depot on the High Street was opened in 1927 and extended in 1934 to hold 17 vehicles. The booking office beside the garage was in a larger building known as the Tudor Rose, which was owned by the company. The rest of the ground floor was sub-let as a restaurant and the first floor was a flat occupied by a member of senior management.

In 1951 the depot had 18 vehicles. Double-deckers were Leyland Titan TD5s and new Leyland Titan PD2/12s, both low and high bridge, and also low-bridge Bristol K6As. The four coaches that were allocated to Tenterden then were a mixture of AEC Regals, while the single-deck buses were Leyland Tiger TS7s and TS8s. Later in the 1950s the TD5s were replaced with Daimler CWA6s and more Leyland PD2/12s. Later, both the bus and coach fleet were replaced with AEC Reliances.

There were two main trunk routes through Tenterden and the depot had duties on both. These were the 97 from Ashford to Tunbridge Wells and the 12 from Maidstone to Hastings. In the early 1950s the 97 continued all the way to East Grinstead, a journey time of 3½ hours end to end.

The 40-minute journey to Rye was covered by the 102 that went across the marshes through Wittersham. In 1955 on weekdays there were nine journeys in each direction.

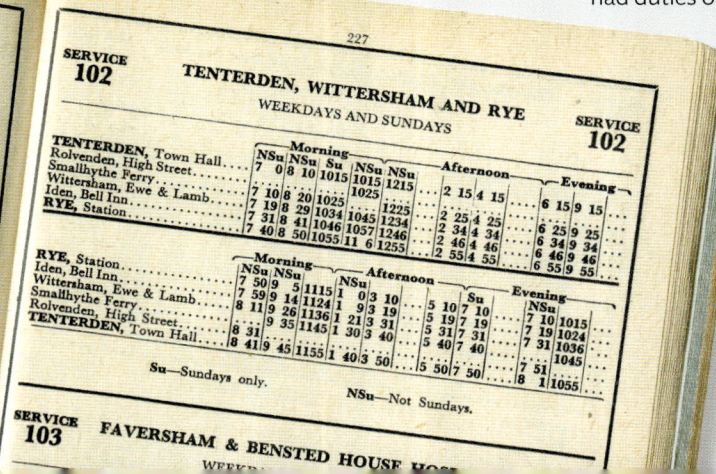

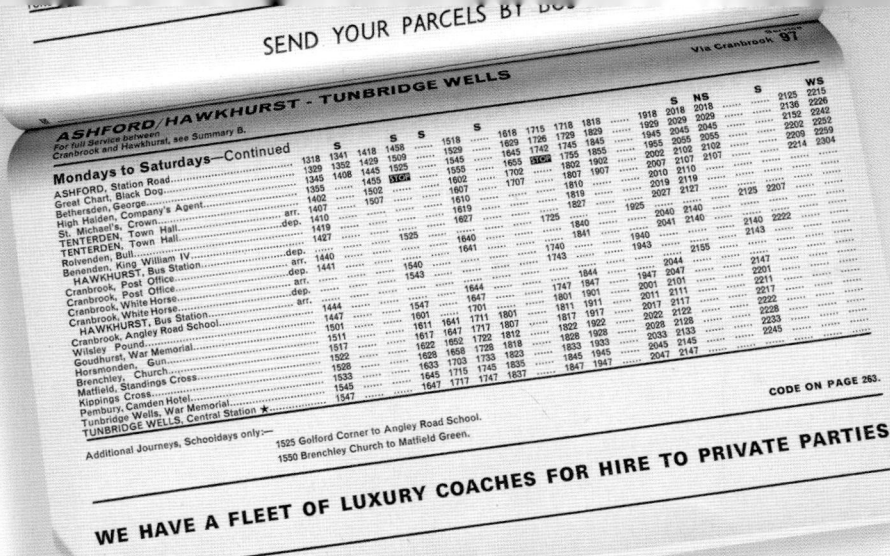

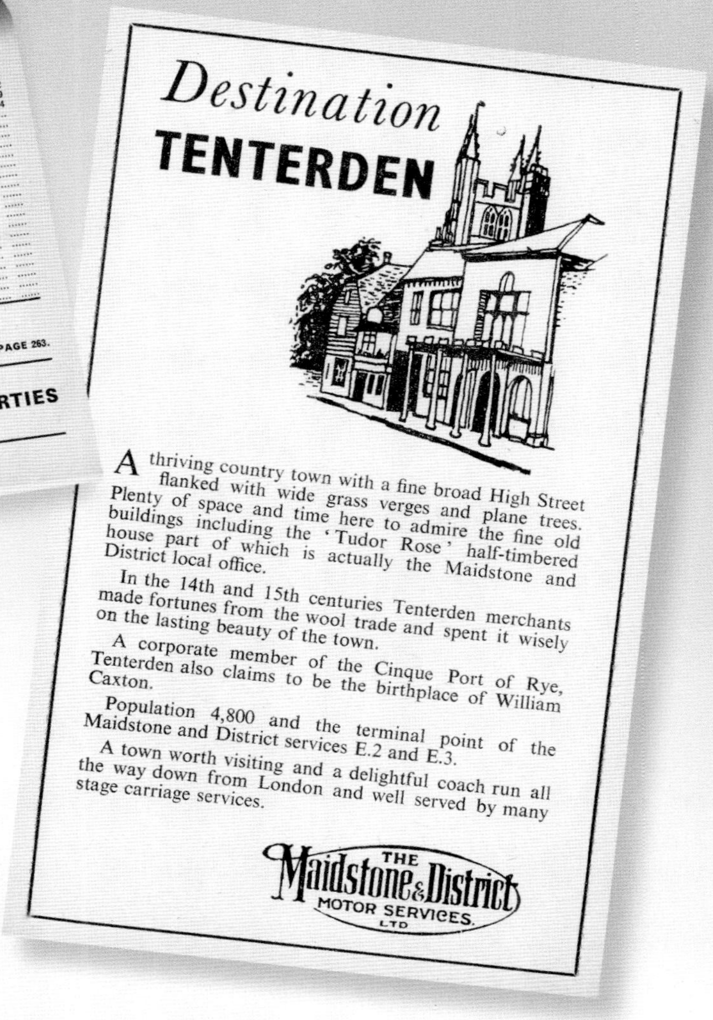

Tenterden depot was responsible for most of the journeys on the 13 to Ashford via Woodchurch. It also ran the 73 route that connected Appledore to Tenterden on Tuesdays and Saturdays, and the 115 that gave small settlements to the east of Tenterden a there-and-back shoppers' bus to Ashford, also on Tuesdays and Saturdays.

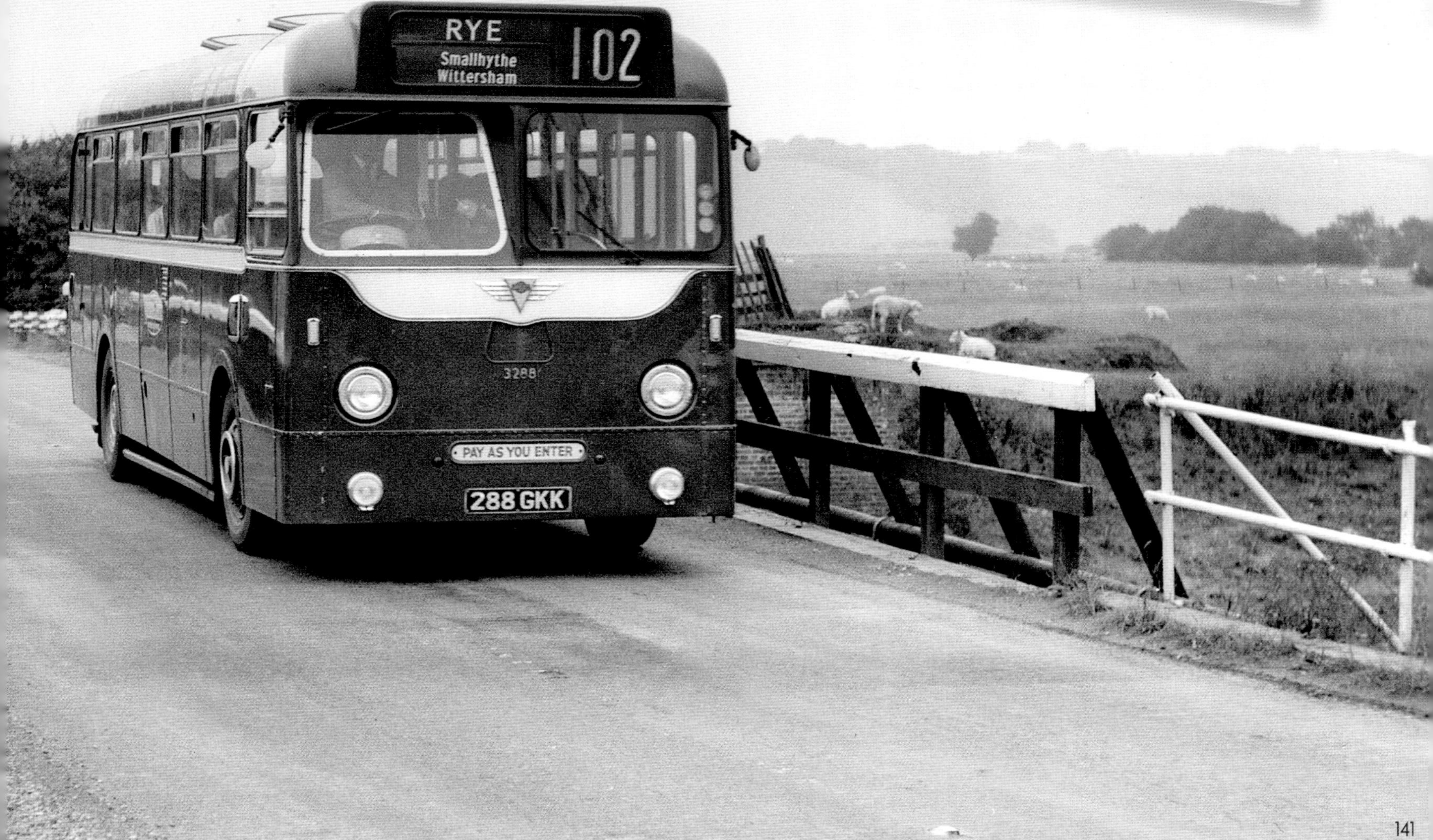

Ashford

Ashford has been a market town since the 13th century but expanded considerably with the coming of the railways, as it was an important junction where several railway lines met. The South Eastern Railway established a locomotive works there in 1847, and by 1882 it was employing over 1,000 people. There was a carriage works, too.

Maidstone & District's first depot in Ashford opened in Station Road in 1927, with space for 11 vehicles. During the Second World War it had to be evacuated for a week after the discovery of an unexploded bomb. A second depot opened in Station Road in 1954 able to house 18 vehicles. It would be almost full in the summer months but often only held 14 vehicles through the winter. There was also a booking office attached to the depot. East Kent had larger premises in the same street, able to hold 34 vehicles.

The double-deck allocation in 1951 included Daimler CWA6s, Bristol K6As, and new Leyland Titan PD2/12s. Single deckers included Leyland Tiger TS8s with ECW bodies and AEC Regal coaches. By the late 1950s the depot still had Daimler CWAs and Leyland PD2/12s, but the one lowbridge K6A there had been replaced with Park Royal AEC Regent Vs. AEC Reliances were the standard for both bus and coach single deckers.

East Kent ran the main town services, plus route 1 to Canterbury and route 2 from Hastings through Ashford to Canterbury as well. Route 10 from Maidstone to Folkestone was a joint operation between Maidstone & District and East Kent, with M&D's Maidstone and Ashford depots and East Kent's Folkestone and Ashford depots providing the vehicles. Ashford had 5 vehicle workings on the 10, split between the two companies alternating at different times to balance mileages. This is where Leyland Titan PD2/12s of Maidstone & District operated alongside East Kent Guy Arabs. Later, 30ft long Park Royal bodied AEC Regent Vs were East Kent's standard fare on the 10.

Maidstone & District's 97, operated with lowbridge double deckers, rambled across the High Weald through Tenterden, Cranbrook and Goudhurst to Tunbridge Wells, and for a number of years even further to East Grinstead, effectively the entire width of Maidstone & District's territory. Not all journeys went all the way through, as there were short workings at both ends and some journeys started from Hawkhurst instead of Ashford.

The 13 also connected Ashford and Tenterden but less frequently and by way of Shadoxhurst and Woodchurch, with some journeys continuing beyond Tenterden to Benenden Sanatorium. The Sanatorium had originally been established in 1907 to treat postal workers suffering from tuberculosis. By the 1950s, with TB cases in decline, treatment here was expanded to include chest complaints and cancer.

The 11 northwards to and from Faversham was jointly operated with M&D's Faversham depot and ran mostly hourly, with short workings from Boughton Lees and Kennington into Ashford. Routes 2 and 49 together gave Smarden and Pluckley a link into Ashford, with some journeys starting from Biddenden (route 2) and Headcorn (route 49).

There was another route between Ashford and Maidstone, this being the 12A which went along attractive minor roads through Egerton, Grafty Green and Ulcombe, but only three journeys a day reached Ashford. It was more frequent towards the Maidstone end of the route.

This snowy picture, taken on 2 April 1968 in Maidstone, demonstrates the joint working between Maidstone & District and East Kent on the Maidstone-Ashford-Folkestone route.

East Kent's 1962 Park Royal bodied AEC Regent V, YJG 823, was just leaving for the near 2-hour journey to the channel port with an M&D Northern Counties bodied Daimler Fleetline on local route 139 to Coxheath on the left.

MIKE HODGES

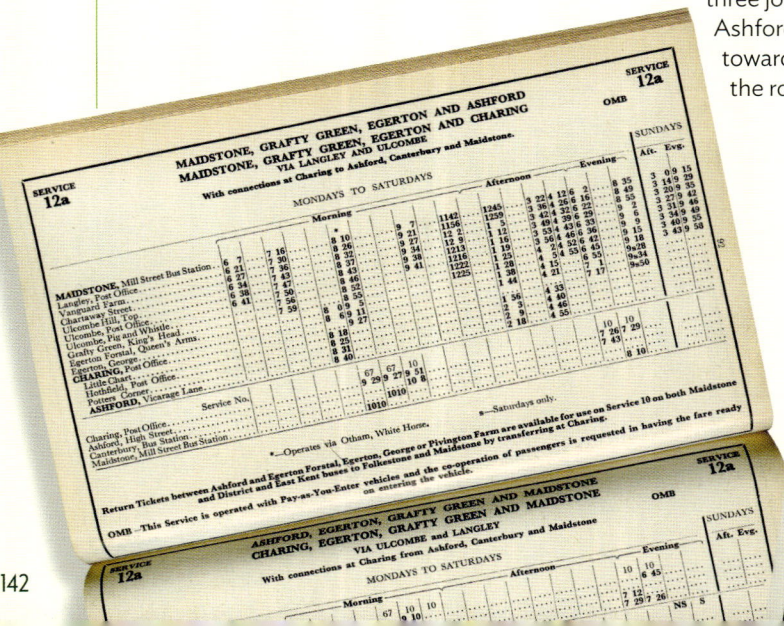

A lesser known fact is that in the 16th and 17th centuries Ulcombe had a bell foundry run by three generations of the Hatch family. One of the bells that they recast there in 1625 hung in the central tower of Canterbury Cathedral. This tower is known as **Bell Harry**, after the original bell, given in 1288 by Prior Henry of Eastry, and which hung on the roof of the tower as it then stood.

On the left 5398, a 1951 Leyland bodied Leyland Titan PD2/12, was passing the entrance to the East Kent garage at Ashford as it was coming up from Maidstone & District's second depot in the town, whose roof can be seen on the extreme right of the picture.

5398 originally had an open platform but, like others in the batch, platform doors were fitted in 1954, a much-needed comfort booster particularly on longer-distance journeys in the winter.

Behind it was a 36ft AEC Reliance bus and a husband and wife (?) sitting on the low wall. Note the East Kent Weymann bodied AEC Reliance bus on the left. East Kent's garage was next door.

ROY MARSHALL/OMNIBUS SOCIETY

The well-loaded Leyland Titan TD4 on the left, DL286, was climbing out of Maidstone in post-war days on its way to East Malling, West Malling, Borough Green and Sevenoaks.

It was delivered in 1935 as 286 with a 48-seat Beadle lowbridge body. In 1946 it was given the new Beadle lowbridge body shown here, and was withdrawn in 1957.

Technically, it was a TD4c with torque converter when new, but this was removed when it was rebodied post war.

M&D AND EAST KENT BUS CLUB

Sevenoaks bus station, built by London Transport in 1936, was also the terminus for Maidstone & District's bus services in the area.

There were a number of Country Area local bus services in the Sevenoaks area, plus longer distance routes north to Farningham and Dartford (401), to Bromley (402) and to Orpington (431); west and north west to Westerham, Croydon and Wallington (403); and south to Tonbridge (402, 403, 454).

Green Line 704 from Windsor, London and Bromley passed through on its way to Tonbridge and Tunbridge Wells. The 705 also came from Windsor and London but between Bromley and Sevenoaks went via Westerham and terminated here in Sevenoaks.

In the picture on the right in the bus station was an RT on the 454 to Tonbridge, a route that went via Sevenoaks Weald.

The Maidstone & District double decker, DL278, was a Bristol K5G new in 1938. It was one of 12 K5Gs that replaced 12 Bristol GO5Gs that had been delivered two years earlier but returned to Bristol in exchange for K5Gs, as the GO5Gs had proved unsuitable in service. However, the Weymann lowbrige bodies were transferred over to the new chassis.

The single decker, SO532, was a Leyland Tiger TS7 new in 1936 with a Harrington body. Here it was on a route 55 journey to Kemsing. Kent's first Women's Institute opened in Kemsing in December 1915

M&D AND EAST KENT BUS CLUB

Borough Green BG

The village of Borough Green lies at the foot of the North Downs on the A25, where the Gravesend to Tonbridge A227 road intersects the A25, and is getting on for halfway between Sevenoaks and Maidstone. It was also at the intersection of the long hourly 122 route from Gravesend to Brighton and the half-hourly route 9 from Maidstone to Sevenoaks. The 9 was operated in conjunction with Maidstone depot.

Maidstone & District's first depot at Borough Green was built in Maidstone Road in 1926 with only enough space for four vehicles, although this was later extended to house eight with a few more on open parking. A new depot and bus station was opened in 1954 on the site of the original one with a capacity for 30 vehicles, but it never operated at its full strength. The number of vehicles allocated there generally ranged between 14 and 18, depending on the time of the year.

In the 1950s it housed lowbridge Bristol K6A double deckers and a single all-Leyland Titan PD2/12 'decker for a 122 duty. Single-deck buses were Leyland Tiger TS8s and AEC Regals before AEC Reliances and semi-chassisless Beadle/AEC rebuilds were allocated. Coaches were, naturally, the ubiquitous Harrington bodied AEC Reliances.

As well as the 9 connecting Borough Green to Maidstone through West and East Malling, there was an hourly 25 that took a slightly different way via Wrotham. Operation of this was also shared with Maidstone depot.

There were a number of morning and late evening journeys to and from Sevenoaks worked by Borough Green. These were positioning journeys for the buses that would work local routes in the Sevenoaks area. These routes are shown on the map on the right. The 55 to Kemsing in conjunction with the 9 provided a 10-minute frequency from Sevenoaks to Seal.

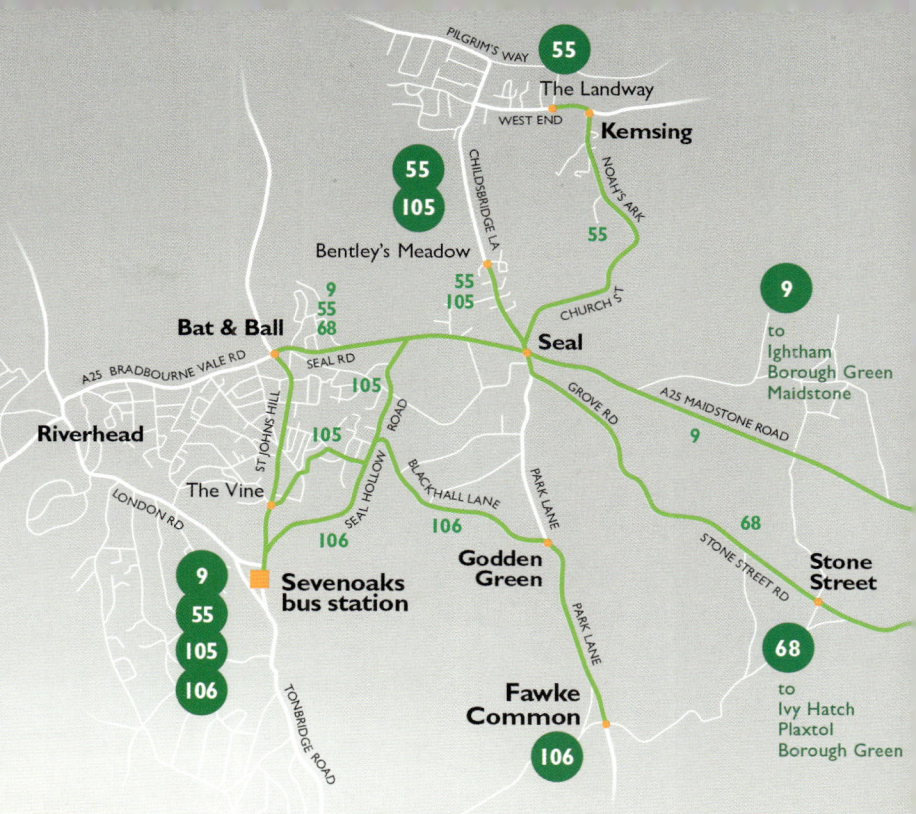

Photographed outside its home depot of Borough Green, while on its way between Sevenoaks and Maidstone on the 9, was Park Royal lowbridge bodied AEC Regent V, DL39. The journey between the two towns took one and a quarter hours.

Alongside you can see the rear of a Southdown double decker on the long 122 joint operation between Gravesend, Tunbridge Wells and Brighton.

OMNICOLOUR

Maidstone & District bus routes in Sevenoaks 1965

Isle of Sheppey – Sheerness and Leysdown SH

These depots were on the Isle of Sheppey, which was pretty well the very north of Maidstone & District's operating area, or at least level with Gravesend. The Isle of Sheppey is 35 square miles in size with, at the north western end, the mouth of the River Medway and, on the opposite side of that water, the Isle of Grain, which isn't actually an island as such; but the Isle of Sheppey very much is. The main employer on the Island used to be the Dockyard with 2,500 staff, but in 1958 it was announced that it was to be closed two years later in 1960. In the 1950s and 1960s the Isle of Sheppey was an important holiday destination, with Warner's Holiday Camp and numerous caravan parks, mostly on the eastern end of the island at Leysdown. As well as the holiday trade, farming was the other main occupation on the island.

A dark shadow has lain off the coast of Sheerness since 1944. That year the *SS Richard Montgomery* ran onto rocks, sinking with 1,500 tons of high explosive on board. Due to the unstable cargo the ship was never salvaged and still lies there today with the masts above the water line. It's checked regularly but, if the worst actually ever happened, there might well be very little left of Sheerness. One notable (some might suggest notorious) person who was born on the Island in 1913 was the famous Dr Richard Beeching of branch railway line closure fame.

Transport started on the Island with trams operated by the Sheerness & District Tramways Co. The tramway opened in April 1903 with just 2½ miles of track. The system closed during 1917 due to competition from motorbuses. Maidstone & District's Sheerness depot was the original tramway depot built in 1903, but had been acquired from Sheppey Motor Transport in 1930. It was extended in 1932, and in 1951 a further extension took place with improved engineering facilities and to give a capacity for 58 vehicles.

Leysdown garage and bus station was built in 1958 with space for four vehicles and was mainly used for overnight parking and winter storage.

Here are the ominous masts of the SS Richard Montgomery poking up out of the sea in the Thames Estuary off Sheerness. Underneath the waves are what is left of 1,500 tons of high explosive, making salvage a virtually impossible task.

CLEM RUTTER

Harrington Grenadier bodied AEC Reliance 4160 was delivered in 1965 as C60 but without a registration number - this batch of 15 coaches was stored until the spring of 1966 and only registered then before entering service.

Here, with a Wayfarer IV in the background, it was at Sheerness depot awaiting its next turn of duty on the E6 express service to London.
JULIAN BOWDEN

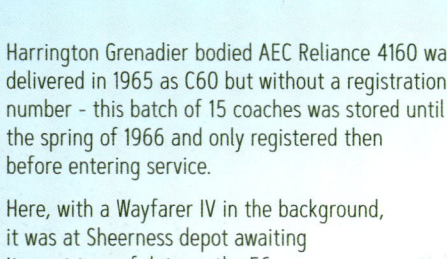

Before the new Kingsferry Bridge was opened in 1960, allowing easier access by double deckers onto the Isle of Sheppey, 17 Bristol K6As with Saunders bodies were permanently based at Sheerness.

Below, on the hourly 63A route from Sheerness bus station to the Warden holiday camps was DH232 new in 1948. All the major engineering work was carried out on the island including CoFs before 1960.
ALDER VALLEY ENTHUSIASTS' GROUP

The only access to the island was by the Kingsferry Bridge on the A249. Unfortunately, the road was crossed just south of the bridge by a very low railway bridge. Before the war it was easy to remove the top deck of double deckers so they could travel to the island under the offending bridge. After the war, when construction methods changed, a different solution had to be found. The K6As were taken to the island by being driven through a private road via Ridham Dock, close to the mud flats at low tide, to gain access to the Kingsferry Bridge just north of the Railway arch.

At all the other depots buses could be returned periodically to the Central Works at Maidstone for overhaul but, due to the logistical problems of moving double-deckers on and off the Island, overhauls were carried out at Sheerness depot. When the height restriction was removed with the new Kingsferry lifting bridge in 1960 double-deckers were free to roam to and from Sheerness more easily.

On a local journey to Eastchurch, Northern Counties bodied Daimler Fleetline 6069 was loading up in Sheerness in the picture on the left.

The very first flight by an Englishman from British soil took place at Eastchurch Airfield on Sunday 2 March 1909, when J T C Moore-Brabazon's plane achieved 50 feet of powered flight. On the same occasion he performed Britain's first plane crash but, luckily, walked away unharmed. During the Battle of Britain, Eastchurch was one of the notable bases of the Polish Air Force.
JULIAN BOWDEN

When the Medway Towns garages received new Leyland Atlanteans in 1963, several of the former Chatham & District Guy Arabs were transferred to Sheerness.

On the right was one of them, DH465, leaving Maidstone for Sheerness on the 41 route with Maidstone Corporation buses in the background. The journey was just over the hour, with the bus passing though the Kent villages of Detling, Bobbing and Iwade.

This picture was taken during the summer, and the dual-purpose AEC Reliance OMO vehicles that normally would have operated the service would have been on express relief work.

DAVID TOY COLLECTION

In the summer of 1952 Sheerness had an allocation of 55 vehicles - 17 double-deck Bristol K6As with Saunders bodies, 4 single-deck Bristol L6As, a Leyland Tiger TS7 and 7 Tiger TS8s. There were also 26 coaches - 6 AEC Regals and 11 semi-chassisless Beadles (7 with AEC running units and 4 with Leyland running units), as well as 4 of the re-bodied Leyland Tiger TS7s. The other 4 coaches were petrol-engined Leyland Tigers (2 TS7s, 2 TS1s) with 1946 Harrington bodies in their last season with the company.

The double-deck allocation didn't change until after the new bridge was opened in 1960, when a small number of Leyland Atlanteans moved to Sheerness. In time, Bristol LL5G and AEC Reliance single-deckers replaced the TS7 and 8 buses. The coaching allocation was updated with Leyland Royal Tigers and AEC Reliances in the late 1950s.

When Luton depot received new Leyland Atlanteans in the early 1960s, ex-Chatham & District Guy Arab IVs were transferred to Sheerness to replace the Bristol K6As. At first there was resistance to the Guys by the crews, as they did not have any heating. Heaters were removed from the withdrawn Bristols and fitted to the Guys, resolving that problem.

In 1957 Bristol K6A DH180 was converted to become a permanent open topper and spent most of its time at Sheerness.

In this picture on the right, now renumbered to OT8, it was at Bridge Street in Sheerness on the 52 from Rushenden to Shell Beach (or Shellness Beach as the timetables had it).

This bus lasted eight years in this guise.
DAVID TOY COLLECTION

In the mid-1950s the majority of bus services operated within the island only, and the network of routes was fairly comprehensive with most starting from Sheerness bus station. However, there were three routes that came over the Kingsferry Bridge: the 40 from Dartford, Gravesend and Chatham, the 41 from Maidstone and the 50 from Sittingbourne.

The frequency of many of the island routes increased in the summer months, mainly to the Leysdown area for the holiday camps. The area was very busy then with day trippers also arriving at Sheerness by train - the bus station was next to the train station - and continuing their journeys to Leysdown by bus for a day on the beach.

By the 1960s there were revisions to the bus network and service level due to the closure of the Royal Naval Dockyard. The 54A was withdrawn, the 63 operated Rushenden-Sheerness-Leysdown, the 52 Rushenden-Sheerness-Leysdown (Shellness Beach) and the original 63 became the 63A to Warden. The 35 was operated in conjunction with the Thames and Medway Navigation Company, with buses running to and from the ferry terminal point four times per day for connections to and from Southend.

Permanent open-top Leyland Titan TD5, OT6, was transferred to Sheerness for the summer open-top services. In the picture on the right, taken in Sheerness depot, it looked in pretty pristine condition while waiting to be fuelled at the end of the day's duties.
MICHAEL DRYHURST

Gravesend GR

Gravesend, on the south bank of the River Thames opposite Tilbury, formed one of the western boundaries of Maidstone & District's empire, and here was another place where M&D's buses met the green buses of London Transport's Country Area. In fact, only a few miles further west, at Dartford, was an eastern extremity of London Transport's red bus Central Area and some summer buses on M&D's route 40 to the Medway Towns and Sheerness actually started from Dartford.

Much of the town of Gravesend is on higher chalk that rises up from the river, and it was the Romans who first began to dig chalk here. They found a way of making a cement strong enough to bind courses of bricks and stone. The cement industry requires plentiful water supplies and chalk as its main ingredients, both of which were to be found in Gravesend and neighbouring Northfleet. In 1796, James Parker set up kilns on Northfleet creek to make his Roman cement, and this was the beginning of a large complex of cement works along this stretch of the river. By 1900, there were nine cement works operating along the Thames between Swanscombe and Gravesend, although from the 1960s onwards this industry was in decline, partly due to cheaper imports. Today the landscape is littered with vast empty chalk pits hollowed out from the bedrock.

From Gravesend there were passenger and car ferries across the Thames to the busy Tilbury Docks, a large employer from both sides of the river. Shipping was a major employer generally, with the headquarters of Sun Tugs and the Alexander Towing Company based in the town. Many of the watermen who worked on the river lived in Gravesend.

Paper making was another local industry, with the Imperial Paper Mills based below the Overcliffe alongside the river. Before it became part of the Reed Group, its blue AEC Mammoth Major lorries with their gold fleetnames would pass the side of the M&D depot at Stuart Road on their way to the newspaper industry in London's Fleet Street.

There was another paper mill at Northfleet, owned by Bowater.

In the picture on this page at Gravesend looking over the water towards Tilbury, the River Thames was as calm as a millpond.

Leyland Atlantean 5505 was coming up Crooked Lane near the start of its long journey to Sittingbourne that would take it through the Medway Towns on the way. There's a map of this route on page 155.

DAVID TOY COLLECTION

London Transport's Country Area also had a garage in the town, although technically it was at Northfleet a little to the west.

It ran the busy trunk route 480 from Denton on the eastern outskirts of the town, through Gravesend and Northfleet along the main road to Dartford (and beyond to Erith), and in the picture on the right, taken in 1966, an RML was in the distance heading towards Denton on a 480 working.

London Transport also had local routes fanning south to a number of places, some operated with 26-seat ECW bodied Guy Special GS-class buses.

London Transport had 84 of these characterful buses and, in this picture, GS53 was on its way back to Northfleet garage. A Maidstone & District Leyland Atlantean on a town route was heading in the other direction through the town centre.

RAY STENNING

Alongside the Thames were also many companies with businesses that supported the shipping industries. Gravesend had expanded after the war with new housing estates, one being built on the redundant RAF fighter base. The town also had several piers and in the summer the **MV Royal Daffodil** (2,073 passenger capacity) gave an alternative journey to the Kent Coast on its leisurely trip down the Thames.

St George's church, quite close to the river, was built in what would become known as the Georgian style, its construction partly funded by the Commission for Building Fifty New Churches, an organisation set up by Act of Parliament in England in 1710 under Queen Anne to fund the building of more churches in and close to London because of the rising population. St George's was completed in 1731.

Of course, the churchyard has the grave of the famous North American Indian Princess Pocahontas from Jamestown in Virginia, who in April 1614 at the age of 17 was married to tobacco planter John Rolfe and took the name of Rebecca. In 1616 the Rolfes travelled to London and Rebecca was presented to English society as an example of the 'civilized savage', in hopes of stimulating investment in the Jamestown settlement. She died in 1617.

Maidstone & District's garage was on Overcliffe, and this was also the main terminal point for bus services. In October 1951 the depot had an allocation of 41 buses and coaches, reducing to 33 in the winter, but some summers going back up to as many as 50 when extra coaches would be needed.

In 1951 the double decks were mainly Bristol K6As with a small number of Leyland Titan TD7s and TD5s. Single-deck buses were Bristol LL5Gs and Leyland Tiger TS8s, and coaches mainly AEC Regals, but with four of the newly-built Beadle/AEC semi-chassisless and a solitary Leyland Tiger TS7. Over the years more Bristol K6As joined the depot with Leyland Titan PD2/12s and, later, AEC Regent Vs for the longer services. AEC Reliances would later dominate the single-deck and coach allocation. During the summer peak in the 1960s (mainly Saturdays) spare buses were sent from the Medway towns to release dual-purpose AEC Reliances to work express services.

Gravesend locals

Local services operated out of Gravesend depot in the mid-1950s were the 22 to Meopham and Vigo Inn, 23 to Chatham via Cobham, 46 to Valley Drive and 46A to St Hilda's Way, 47 to Cliffe, 56 to Gravesend Airport, 108 to Chalk, 111 to Shorne Ridgeway, and 116 to Harvel via Meopham. In 1960 the 46A was renumbered 27 but continued to interwork with the 46. By this time a considerably enhanced 56 service ran to River View Estate when the new housing estate was built on the site of the aerodrome and the 108 had been withdrawn. By 1965 this was running up to every 15 minutes.

A new service to Allhallows-on-Sea, the 136, started in December 1961 via Cliffe, Cooling and High Halstow, as a replacement for the withdrawn branch railway line trains between Gravesend and Allhallows. The service had three return journeys in the morning and afternoon and two in the evening. The story of the Allhallows branch line is told on the next page.

40 Bristol K6As with Saunders 56-seat bodies entered the fleet in 1948. DH202 was one of them, shown above on Gravesend local route 46A to St Hilda's Way.

The bus was on the Overcliffe at Gravesend and in the background the roofs of the Imperial Paper Mill can be seen.
M&D AND EAST KENT BUS CLUB

On the left, Gravesend based 5599, a Mk2 Leyland Atlantean with 77-seat Weymann body, was on local route 46 at the terminus in Valley Drive in early National Bus Company ownership days.

By now it had been equipped for one-person operation and also had the farebox method of payment that had been introduced on 11 July 1971.

Passengers put their money into the top of of the machine, where the driver could check the amount paid. It was meant to speed up boarding, but it wasn't a great success.
M&D AND EAST KENT BUS CLUB

end of the line

The Allhallows branch line – the Hundred of Hoo Railway, as it was originally – opened between Gravesend and Port Victoria in 1882 (Allhallows came later), and the plan was that Port Victoria would develop as continental sea port. This never quite happened and instead a steamer would take passengers across the River Medway only to Sheerness. From Sheerness passengers could take the Medway Ferry to Folkestone and then on to the continent. Unfortunately, the Port Victoria ferry service was completely uneconomic, became intermittent and actually discontinued in 1895, although it was reinstated some years later.

By the beginning of the 20th century it was obvious that the seaport idea was not going to be the success hoped for, despite being favoured by the Royal Family, so extra halts were added to the line to drum up business, although this was a very sparsely populated area. In 1932 an extension to Allhallows was built with great optimism and the hope of luring people from the middle and working classes, for whom holidays by the seaside were increasingly becoming affordable, to this bit of coast, and thereby develop Allhallows-on-Sea into a popular resort, and even a commuter town.

The branch saw some success in its early years with day trippers; indeed, on Bank Holiday Sunday, 5 August 1934 over 9,500 passengers made the journey to and from Allhallows. And even before the Second World War the Southern Railway had plans to electrify the branch, but Allhallows as a seaside resort never really happened. Meanwhile, the Port Victoria service dwindled (there were only two trains a day in the 1930s), the pier was falling into disrepair and being patched up or reduced, and the end of that came in 1941.

After the war the picture wasn't so rosy for the remaining Allhallows service, as passenger numbers fell while costs rose, although efficiency and customer focus weren't quite the name of the game then. By the late 1950s British Railways seemed determined to close the branch to passenger traffic (it was omitted from the Kent Coast electrification plans) and, despite a number of objections, it did finally close on 3 December 1961. The line to Grain remained open as freight only, once serving oil refineries and cement works there and, after these closed, a granite distribution point.

In its last years, a rather grimy ex-SECR H-class 0-4-4 tank loco, 31308, was at the head of a push-pull train at Allhallows-on-Sea terminus in the picture at the top. You can clearly see the brake pump equipment on the left of the engine's smokebox. It was this that enabled push-pull operation.

Note also the Maidstone & District bus passing by in the background.

LAMBERHURST

The lower picture is a postcard of Port Victoria in the late Victorian era, with at least five members of staff hanging around the train.

PHOTOGRAPHER UNKNOWN

long distance

Gravesend was the starting point for a number of Maidstone & District's longer routes, and they're shown on the map on the next page.

The 57 to Hastings was interworked with the 5 from Gillingham, although in later years the 5 only started its journey south from Maidstone. The vehicle operating pattern on the 5/57 meant that a bus leaving Gravesend in the morning would not arrive back for 12 hours, so crew changes en route, at specified locations, were necessary.

Five garages operated this complex service: Gravesend (2 buses), Gillingham (1 bus), Maidstone (1 bus), Hawkhurst (2 buses) and Hastings (1 bus). Vehicles rarely returned to the same depot that they had left in the morning. This meant complicated 7-day cycle charts had to be drawn up to enable vehicle servicing and maintenance requirements to be met. One curiosity of the 57 cycle was that two of the vehicles that finished at Gravesend in the evening on the 57 had spent much of the day on the 5, so had not visited Gravesend earlier in the day at all.

To operate these longer distance routes Gravesend had the lightweight version of the AEC Regent V with a Park Royal body. The smaller wheels can be clearly seen in the main photo on the left.

The 5 from Gillingham (later, only Maidstone) and the 57 from Gravesend, both to Hastings via Cranbrook, Hawkhurst and Battle, were interworked by several garages. Gravesend based DH488 was here descending Linton Hill by the Bull Inn in April 1962 on a 5 from Gillingham. The bus would later return to its home depot as a 57.
OMNICOLOUR

Maidstone & District's lowheight Northern Counties bodied Daimler Fleetlines were used on normal height routes sometimes, as shown in the picture at the bottom of the opposite page of Gillingham's DL77 at Gravesend Overcliffe, waiting to leave on a 26 working to Faversham.
SOUTHDOWN ENTHUSIASTS' CLUB

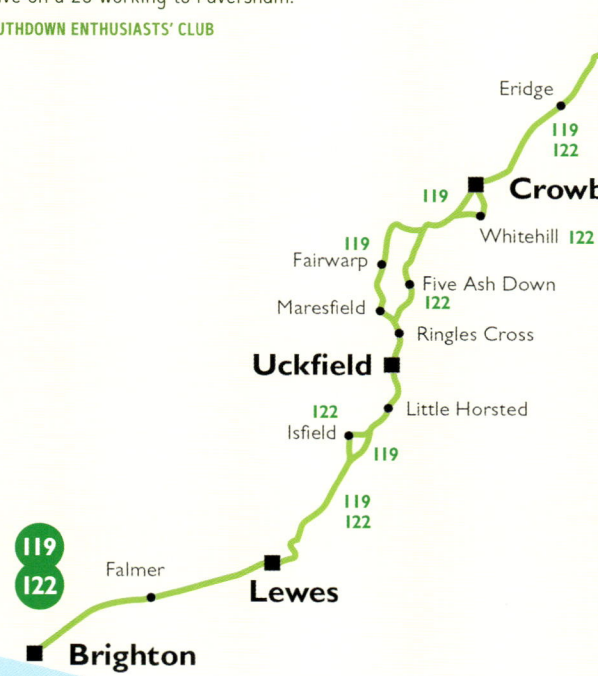

LONG DISTANCE ROUTES FROM GRAVESEND IN 1960

Here on the right in Gillingham bus station was 3080, a Leyland Panther with Willowbrook body, on its way between Gravesend and Sittingbourne, where this particular bus was based at the time.

You can clearly see the orange PAY AS YOU ENTER sticker on the front of the cream 'moustache'. The 26 route became partly one-man operated in December 1962.
DAVID TOY COLLECTION

155

M&D's longest route

The 122 was Maidstone & District's longest route, nearly 70 miles long, and it would take a bus over four hours to get all the way from Gravesend to Brighton. It was run jointly with Southdown Motor Services, as were others, and these are mentioned elsewhere in this book. It began in 1948, and after 1951 was largely run with Leyland Titan PD2/12s from both companies, although Southdown also used Guy Arabs on the route. Later, Gravesend's allocation of AEC Regent Vs could be seen on it.

This long service was hourly from both ends, starting with the first through journey leaving Gravesend at 8.03am and the last leaving at 7.08pm. From Brighton the first through journey was at 8.50am, the last at 6.50pm. There were also early morning journeys starting from Tunbridge Wells towards both Gravesend and Brighton and similar ones in the evenings. The last bus arrived into Brighton at 11.14pm.

The 122 started at the company's office at Gravesend Overcliffe and made its way out of town on the A227 to cross the main A2 at Singlewell. It then passed through the villages of Meopham, Vigo Inn and Wrotham, arriving at Borough Green depot after 51 minutes for a 3-minute stop. From Borough Green the 122 continued south through Plaxtol, Shipbourne, crossing the River Medway in Tonbridge and on to the halfway stage at Tunbridge Wells, where a crew change would take place – although it was not unknown for scheduled crew changes to take place north of Tunbridge Wells in the evening or at quieter times on the road side, as you can see on this page.

It was then on to Crowborough, Five Ash Down, with hazy views over Ashdown Forest, down into Uckfield. The route had a few steep hills and in the county town of Lewes, after leaving the bus station, there was the climb up the narrow High Street before heading down through Falmer into Brighton. Entering the seaside town on the Lewes Road, Brighton Corporation's Lewes Road garage was passed. In 1960 trolleybuses still ran in the town alongside the red and cream AEC Regents, some dating back to 1939, and new Leyland PD2/37s.

With Bristol chassis no longer available, M&D took delivery of 36 new Leyland Titan PD2 chassis in 1951. They had Leyland's own 58-seat bodywork and were used mainly on longer distance services and so accumulated very high mileages.

Not all crew changes were at bus stations or town centres on the 122. Above, two M&D all-Leyland PD2s are in the countryside with the conductor carrying all his equipment to southbound DH387, a Borough Green based vehicle. This bus spent most of its time on the route and covered a million miles in its 20-year life.
RAY SHIELDS

During 1954 platform doors were added to 28 of the batch, including DH405, shown below northbound in Uckfield Bus Station. There were often delays here because of the level crossing by the station - you can see the footbridge over the track. Years later, and years after the closure of the Lewes to Uckfield section of railway line, a new station was built on the other side of the road, eliminating the crossing.
RAY STENNING

On the right, at the start of its 70-odd mile journey over the North Downs, through the Weald and down to the Sussex coast at Brighton was DH409 on Gravesend's Overcliffe.

In the distance you can just make out a London Transport GS 26-seater heading westwards, possibly back to Northfleet garage.
CLASSIC BUS COLLECTION

At the bottom of this page you can see DH405 again, here on layover at Brighton Pool Valley bus station in its later years in company with a Southdown Park Royal bodied Guy Arab and Northern Counties 'Queen Mary' style bodied Leyland Titan PD3.

DH405 was on the 119 variation of the 122 dealt with on the next page, which interworked with the 122 to give a half-hourly service between Brighton, Uckfield and Tunbridge Wells.
ADRIAN LEWIS

For a short time in 1963 Northern Counties bodied Daimler Fleetline DL85 was used on the 122 route, as you can see in the picture on the right.

This was for fuel consumption trials. Because these Fleetlines had the Gardner 6LX engine, we must assume that the data would have been checked against the standard Leyland PD2/12 with Leyland's own 0.600 engine.
M&D AND EAST KENT BUS CLUB

Southdown 805, an East Lancs bodied Leyland Titan PD2/12, was photographed at Borough Green on its way on the final leg towards Gravesend in the picture below.

This fine looking bus had been new in 1957 and was one of the last Southdown exposed radiator Leylands to be delivered to the company.

Unlike Maidstone & District's platform doors, which were of the folding type, Southdown preferred sliding doors, although in this shot the conductor had left the door wide open.
DAVID TOY COLLECTION

Buses on the 122 had a 36-minute layover before the return journey.
In the 1950s and 1960s Maidstone & District operated mainly Leyland or Weymann bodied Leyland Titans PD2/12s on the route, although Bristol K6As had been seen in earlier times. As mentioned already, later the Park Royal bodied AEC Regent Vs were sometimes used. Buses that were permanently on the service went on to achieve very high mileages. Southdown also operated its Leyland Titan PD2s on the 122, which made it easier for driver changes between the two companies, but Guy Arabs were also used from time to time.

The addition of route 119 between Tunbridge Wells and Brighton gave two buses an hour between Brighton, Uckfield and Tunbridge Wells - its slight differences from the 122 are shown on the map a couple of pages back. This increased the number of vehicles to operate the 119/122 to 13, which operated out of no fewer than eight garages of the two operators - M&D from Tunbridge Wells, Gravesend, Borough Green and Tonbridge; Southdown from Uckfield, Brighton, Crowborough and Lewes.

Although 'officially' a double-deck route, single deckers were seen on the 122, particularly 36-footers at the end of the 1960s. Above was 3693, one of M&D's 7ft 6in wide Harrington bodied semi-automatic AEC Reliance buses, bought for use at Hastings but here heading south towards Tunbridge Wells from Gravesend.
RICHARD LEWIS COLLECTION

SO257 on the right, a Sheerness based vehicle, was one of the 25 AEC Reliances with Harrington bodies bought in 1958. Here, in the late 1950s, it was in Military Road in Chatham on a winter working of the 40 between Chatham and Sheerness. Spot the Morris Commercial Royal Mail van turning into the Brook and a Royal Navy officer marching towards the bus shelters.
M&D AND EAST KENT BUS CLUB

A few years earlier in the picture at the bottom right was SO31, a 1947 AEC Regal with a Beadle 36-seat body. In June 1958 the route was converted to one-man and by-and-large new Park Royal bodied AEC Reliances took over.
DAVID TOY COLLECTION

why a Southdown bus did a Gravesend local

To a bus watcher in Gravesend, every bus visited the town at least once, but the oddest feature was in the morning peak. The first bus up from Borough Green had always arrived before 7.30am and was not scheduled to leave again until 8.03am.

The next arrival, from Tonbridge, was just after 8, and this bus was not scheduled to leave until 9.03, so during this time it would be called into use on local service as a relief bus for schoolchildren. However, the company's schedulers later realised that if they could link the 8am arrival and departure they could make even better use of the bus that had arrived earlier.

The standard fill-in for the 7.25 arrival thus became a scheduled trip across to Cliffe via Higham and back on the 47 route, leaving at 7.45, with the strange result that Southdown buses often found themselves miles from home in an obscure part of Kent on a local service. Below, in a picture by Ray Shields, Southdown Park Royal bodied Guy Arab IV 543 was at Higham on this run.

Vehicles moved day to day between garages and companies, with bus crews normally changing at Tunbridge Wells, though the vehicles went right through. Bus movements were so complicated that even a 7-day cycle was impossible and so a cycle covering 14 days had to suffice.

Borough Green's contribution to the route was for many years DH387, and it was credited with covering over 1 million miles in the course of its 20-year life.

and over to the Isle of Sheppey

The 40 was the other longish distance, but summer only, route out of Gravesend. This went to Sheerness on the Isle of Sheppey. During the summer season it was extended to start from either Dartford or Gravesend instead of just from Chatham, and from 1960 some journeys went beyond Sheerness to Leysdown. The 40 always used to be a single-deck route, due to the restricted height on the approach to the old Kingsferry Bridge connecting the island with the mainland - see page 147.

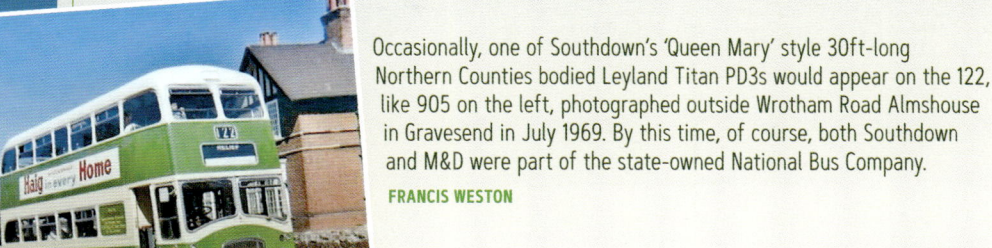

Occasionally, one of Southdown's 'Queen Mary' style 30ft-long Northern Counties bodied Leyland Titan PD3s would appear on the 122, like 905 on the left, photographed outside Wrotham Road Almshouse in Gravesend in July 1969. By this time, of course, both Southdown and M&D were part of the state-owned National Bus Company.
FRANCIS WESTON

Gravesend depot had several Saunders bodied Bristol K6As allocated to it. In the picture above, DH214 was parked up in Stuart Road, just below the depot, after returning from Harvel and Meopham on a 116 journey.

This bus was delivered in 1948 and withdrawn in 1960, although it went on for further life with Bedlington & District.

M&D AND EAST KENT BUS CLUB

Gravesend had four of the Harrington-Commer integral single-deck buses for its one-man routes, including the first in the batch, SO200. Route 22 also went to Meopham and took 23 minutes. SO200 was here on the Overcliffe in its later livery ready to make the journey.

Meopham is generally pronounced as 'Meppam.'

It's interesting to compare this Harrington body with the later style shown on the previous page, in particular the shallower roof on the later model.

M&D AND EAST KENT BUS CLUB

Working route 3 to Faversham from Maidstone in the picture on this page was DH366 (originally 292), a 1939 Leyland Titan TD5 with a Weymann body.

Faversham had an allocation of two Leyland TD5s for the longer routes, this particular bus having been transferred to the depot in early 1952 from Tunbridge Wells.

292-294 were originally ordered by Chatham & District but the order was transferred to Maidstone & District in March 1939 while still at the chassis stage. However, when they were completed, they went to Chatham & District after all.

292 passed to Maidstone & District in 1942 and was renumbered DH366 in 1950. It was withdrawn in 1955.

That rakish-looking car on the left was a Jowitt Javelin with a flat-4 engine. It was designed by Gerald Palmer, who also was responsible for styling the Wolseley 4/44 and its derivatives and the 1962 FB-series Vauxhall Victor.

DAVID TOY COLLECTION

Faversham F

Faversham is 10 miles from Canterbury and just off the Roman Watling Street (basis of the modern A2). This was where Maidstone & District met East Kent, and both bus companies had depots in the town. There's been a settlement here since pre-Roman times and the town was mentioned in the Domesday book as Favreshant. King Stephen, who ruled England from 1135 to 1154, and his wife Queen Matilda founded a Benedictine abbey at Faversham in 1148, which survived until the Dissolution of the Monasteries in 1538. It was just to the north east of the town and both Stephen and Matilda were buried there.

Faversham has one of the largest accumulations of municipal charters of any place in Britain, the first Charter of Privileges being granted to the town by King Henry III in 1252. And King James II was held prisoner here in 1688 while trying to escape to France after the arrival of the future William III at Torbay in the bloodless Glorious Revolution. This was when the Government invited William of Orange and his wife Mary over from Holland to ensure England had a continuing protestant monarchy, as both were eligible in the line of succession.

Faversham developed into an important seaport for a while and shipbuilding was practised here on a small scale. It also became a centre for brewing. The Shepherd Neame Brewery was founded in 1698 and became a significant employer over the years. In 1949 Fremlins bought out Faversham brewers George Beer & Rigden along with its production plant. Although this closed in 1954, with all brewing taking place in Maidstone, it reopened in 1961 to meet demand. There are orchards all around these parts, so fruit packing has also been important to the town's economy.

Between the 17th and early 20th centuries Faversham was known as a centre for the explosives industry, but a decline set in after an accident on 2 April 1916 which killed over 100 workers.

Maidstone & District's small Faversham depot in Preston Street, just around the corner from the railway station, opened in 1920. It replaced a small outstation and at first only held four vehicles but gradually increased its capacity to 15, then rebuilt in 1953 to take 21 vehicles. It was managed by the same District Superintendent as Sittingbourne and the Isle of Sheppey.

The depot had an 11-vehicle allocation in 1951. This changed very little over the next decade and would only increase by three for summer operations. In October that year its double deckers were two 1939 Leyland Titan TD5s and a new all-Leyland Titan PD2/3. Single-deck buses were Leyland Tiger TS8s with Harrington or Eastern Coach Works bodies, and its four coaches were three re-bodied Leyland TS7s and one AEC Regal. Faversham received three of the new Weymann bodied Leyland Titan PD2/12s in 1954 to replace the double-deckers.

Route 3 between Faversham, Sittingbourne and Maidstone became one-man operated in March 1958. SO277, one of the dual-purpose seated Park Royal bodied AEC Reliance buses delivered in 1959, was allocated to Sittingbourne from new. These buses are referred to on page 36.

Here was SO277 on the left carrying a good load as it was heading out of Sittingbourne along the A2 London Road, just passing the junction with Victoria Road.

DAVID TOY COLLECTION

In this postcard of Sittingbourne High Street from the earlier half of the 20th century the photographer was standing on the pavement outside The George, one of the coaching inns mentioned in the text.

The Bull, also mentioned in the text, is just beyond the building that juts out on the left and The Red Lion, formerly The Lion, a bit further up on the right.

The terminal point for services was Court Street, where there was a joint booking office with East Kent. Faversham had a small number of duties on the 26 to Gravesend and other longer services, including the hourly 3 to Maidstone via Sittingbourne. The 11 to Ashford, which began at Oare, was a 50 minute journey on a somewhat irregular frequency during the week but hourly on Saturdays.

Faversham had a number of local services from the smaller villages around, many on a very limited frequency. For example, in 1955 you could get a bus into Faversham from Grafty Green on the 28 for shopping in the morning or afternoon, returning at midday or 4pm, and around 6pm on a Saturday or Sunday. By 1965 this had been reduced to run only on Tuesdays and Saturdays. The 69 from Stone had just three journeys each way running Saturdays only in 1955, but 10 years later it was down to two. The depot's shortest route was the 103 to Bensted House Hospital that took only five minutes and ran five times per day.

East Kent's small depot was an outstation of Herne Bay and had around six vehicles. Connections at Faversham could be made to East Kent's route 3 to Canterbury and 37/38 to Whitstable and Herne Bay. The 3 was a double-deck service run with Guy Arabs, while the 37/38 were run with Dennis Lancets.

Sittingbourne S

Sittingbourne is about 7½ miles to the west of Faversham. In horse-drawn stagecoach days the town had been an important posting stage on the coach journey to Dover, and The George, The Bull and The Lion were all hostelries catering to the coach traffic. The Lyon, as it was known then, hosted King Henry V of England in November 1415 on his way back from the Battle of Agincourt in France, the famous English victory in the Hundred Years' War.

Between Faversham and Sittingbourne is mainly orchard farmland with fruit picking and packing being important. In the 1950s and 1960s the main industries were Bowater's paper mills at Kemsley, the brick factory owned by Marley and cement works.

Maidstone & District's Sittingbourne depot had been acquired in 1931. It had previously been a covered market and originally it could hold 22 vehicles. It was completely rebuilt in 1960. In 1951 it operated 21 vehicles; the allocation only increased by three for the summer timetable. The fleet size here stayed static well into the late 1960s. Double deckers in October 1951 were mainly Leyland (seven Titan TD5 and two new Titan PD2/3s) with two lowbridge Bristol K6As. Single-deck buses were three Bristol LL5Gs, two Leyland Tiger TS7s, one TS8 and two Dodge 84s. There were also two AEC Regal coaches.

Sittingbourne had several duties on the 26 to Gravesend via the Medway Towns, the depot's longest route, starting from early in the morning. It also had a hand in the 3 to Maidstone, including some short workings. Together with Sheerness depot (see page 146) Sittingbourne worked the 50 which ran via Kemsley Paper Mills and Iwade every hour. There were a number of local routes with varying frequencies, ranging from the half-hourly 124 from nearby Murston to rural routes from villages up in the Downs to the south, like the 117 with a bus into Sittingbourne in the morning from Wormshill and back at 5.20pm on a Saturday only.

David Toy remembers one particular bus route in the Medway Towns with great affection...

and the rebodied buses that ran on it.

travels to my Aunt's

Being brought up in the Medway Towns, I have many early memories of Maidstone & District, and I can just remember the brown and green of Chatham & District. Particularly vivid memories are of the journeys I used to make to see my mother's sister, Aunt Win, who lived in the small Medway Valley village of Upper Halling. Aunt Win went on to become the oldest person in the village and finally passed away a day before her 99th birthday. On visits to see her we would take walks through the woods and fields and I remember that until the fire roads were put in, you could still see small parts of a Lancaster bomber that had crashed after running out of fuel returning from a raid during the Second World War.

Maidstone & District ran the very infrequent route 120 to the village from Chatham. In the 1950s the population would have been under 2,000, and the bus service had odd school journeys and operated an afternoon service on a Tuesday, Thursday and Saturday. Later the service was reduced to the school journeys and a Saturday only service. I remember the re-bodied Guy Arabs that operated the route and the slow journey though the Medway Towns during the summer before the M2 was opened.

To get to the village on days that the 120 didn't run, I had to go on the Gillingham to Maidstone via West Malling route 20 (usually run with lowbridge Bristol K6As) or the 39 Lower Halstow to West Malling. Both of these went through Halling, which meant a mile walk to Upper Halling. This was not good in adverse weather and especially on my little legs at that time!

It was due to these journeys that I first became interested in buses and went on to spend my life within the industry.

Although David remembers the rebodied wartime Guy Arabs on the 120, above is a Weymann rebodied wartime Bristol K5G, DH451, loading up in Chatham ready for a return trip to Upper Halling.

This bus originally had a Bristol utility body when new in 1942.

The story of the wartime rebodies begins on page 16.
KEITH HARWOOD

And here on the left you can see David's Aunt Win standing in the front garden of her cottage in Upper Halling.
DAVID TOY COLLECTION

joint operations

Maidstone & District ran a number of routes jointly with neighbouring operators Southdown and East Kent, all three being subsidiary companies of the BET Group.

joint with East Kent

There were two joint routes with East Kent, the 10 from Maidstone to Folkestone and the 67 from Maidstone to Canterbury. The 10, briefly described under Maidstone, was a long standing operation between the two companies to the Kent channel port, the route more or less paralleling the main Southern Railway line for most of its journey. Taking just over two hours end-to-end, it was popular and in the summer months duplicates were often needed on this double-deck service.

The 10 had seen various types of buses on it over the years, and in the mid-1950s Maidstone & District's Bristol K6As gave way to Leyland PD2/12s with either Leyland or Weymann bodies. This continued into the 1960s, although an Atlantean also worked on the 10 from time to time.

It wasn't a common practice to see an Atlantean on route 10, but on the far left was DH613 leaving Maidstone on a working of the 10 to Folkestone.
DAVID TOY COLLECTION

The late-1930s East Kent Leyland Titan TD5 on the left had this Park Royal body fitted in 1949. Here it was on the 10 in 1953 in Maidstone's Mill Street bus station.
MICHAEL H C BAKER

On a warm day East Kent 1953 Park Royal bodied Guy Arab GFN 910 was returning to Canterbury on joint route 67 on the right. East Kent's Guy Arabs were a common sight on the 67 until the route was converted to one-man operation.
M&D AND EAST KENT BUS CLUB

DH429, a 1953 Weymann Orion bodied Leyland Titan PD2/12 with platform doors, was looking in pristine condition after a recent repaint when photographed in Canterbuty bus station, also on the 67 joint with East Kent.

It would take around an hour and a half to get back to Maidstone.
THE BUS ARCHIVE/ROY MARSHALL

In contrast, East Kent had been running Leyland Titans, first TD4-types, then PD1s, but as the 1950s rolled forwards East Kent's Guy Arabs became the norm. This meant passengers enjoyed either the roar of the East Kent Gardner 6LW engine or the whistle from an M&D O.600 Leyland. Later, East Kent AEC Regent Vs became a common sight on this service.

The 67 to Canterbury took the same roads as the 10 from Maidstone as far as Charing, but then struck out north eastwards to make its way via Chilham and Chartham to the cathedral city of Canterbury. By the 1960s this route had become an AEC Reliance stronghold by both companies. End-to-end time was just over an hour and a half.

joint with Southdown

As well as the 119/122, dealt with on pages 156-8, there were joint workings with Southdown on the 18 from Brighton to Heathfield and Hawkhurst (dealt with on the next page), and the two routes between Eastbourne and Hastings - the 15 inland via Hailsham and Herstmonceaux, and the 99 mainly along the coast via Pevensey and Bexhill.

the Heathfield Pool

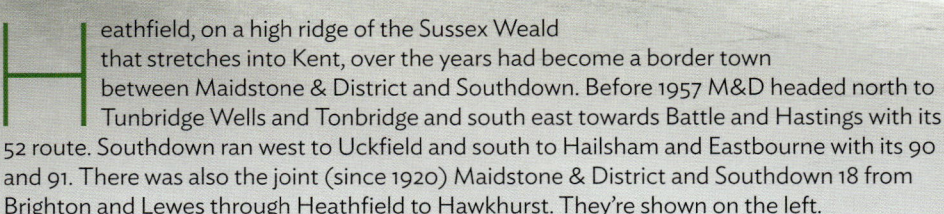

Below are the bus routes that were replaced by the Heathfield Pool services in 1957. Only the 52 was run by Maidstone & District on its own, the 90 and 91 being Southdown routes and the 18 a joint operation with Southdown.

Heathfield, on a high ridge of the Sussex Weald that stretches into Kent, over the years had become a border town between Maidstone & District and Southdown. Before 1957 M&D headed north to Tunbridge Wells and Tonbridge and south east towards Battle and Hastings with its 52 route. Southdown ran west to Uckfield and south to Hailsham and Eastbourne with its 90 and 91. There was also the joint (since 1920) Maidstone & District and Southdown 18 from Brighton and Lewes through Heathfield to Hawkhurst. They're shown on the left.

It's a beautiful part of South East England with steep wooded valleys and pretty villages. The 18, for example, passed through Burwash, where the poet and novelist Rudyard Kipling lived in an imposing stone mansion, Batemans, from 1902 until he died in 1936. A few miles south east from Heathfield the 52 left the main road to go through the village of Brightling. It was here that towards the end of the 18th century and into the 19th century 'Mad Jack' Fuller lived as the local Squire and Member of Parliament and local philanthropist. Eccentric and generous, he is mainly remembered for some follies he built on his land and the pyramid mausoleum in Brightling churchyard, in which he asked to be placed after death, seated at a table. He founded and supported many institutions and even bought Bodiam castle for 3,000 guineas at auction to save it from destruction.

There was also a single-track railway line, steeply graded and twisty at its northern end, that ran from Redgate Mill Junction just south of Eridge down through Mayfield and Heathfield to Polegate (in the 1950s most trains ran from Tonbridge through Tunbridge Wells to Eastbourne). This sleepy backwater of a branch was known as the Cuckoo Line.

Tradition says the first cuckoo is heard on 14 April, and at the Heathfield Cuckoo Fair held sometime after mid-April each year, a lady would release a cuckoo from a basket, it being supposedly the 'first cuckoo of spring'. Steam trains ran on the Cuckoo Line practically to the end of its days in 1965, although 'Oxted' 3-car diesel-electric multiple units were increasingly used in the last

Before May 1966 the Heathfield Pool services were crew operated. All-Leyland Titan PD2/12 DH414 on the far left was leaving Brighton on a short working to Woods Corner on the main road just this side of Brightling.
M&D AND EAST KENT BUS CLUB

In Brightling churchyard in the view on the left is 'Mad Jack' Fuller's pyramidal mausoleum.

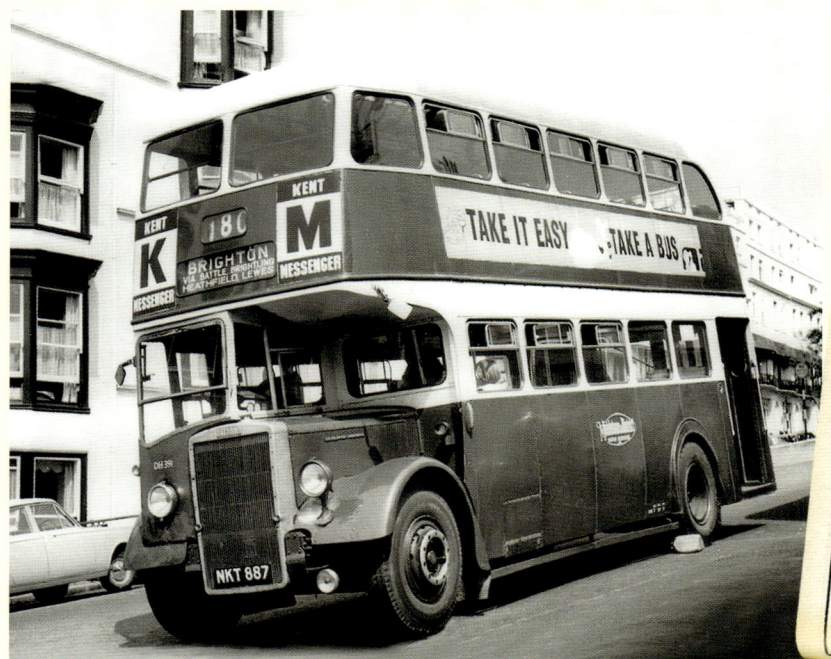

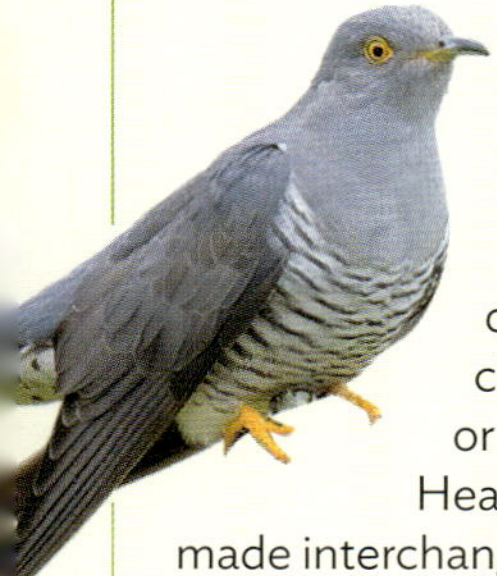

year or two. A shuttle service between Hailsham and Eastbourne using a diesel-electric multiple unit continued to run until 1968.

The Heathfield scheme was aimed at making operational efficiencies and giving passengers a bigger choice of journey possibilities, either on through services or more frequently by co-ordinated connections in Heathfield, all with through fares available. Southdown had made interchange between services an art form, and there were many points all over its territory where passengers could make a simple change from one bus route to another, such as at Golden Cross and Chelwood Gate, and these were promoted in its timetables.

A lot of planning went into the Heathfield scheme and it was approved by the South Eastern Traffic Commissioners on 21 May 1957 to begin on Sunday 2 June. The complex workings of the routes were known as the Heathfield Cycle and this was a masterstroke of bus scheduling. All buses used for this operation were regarded as for common use, irrespective of owning operator.

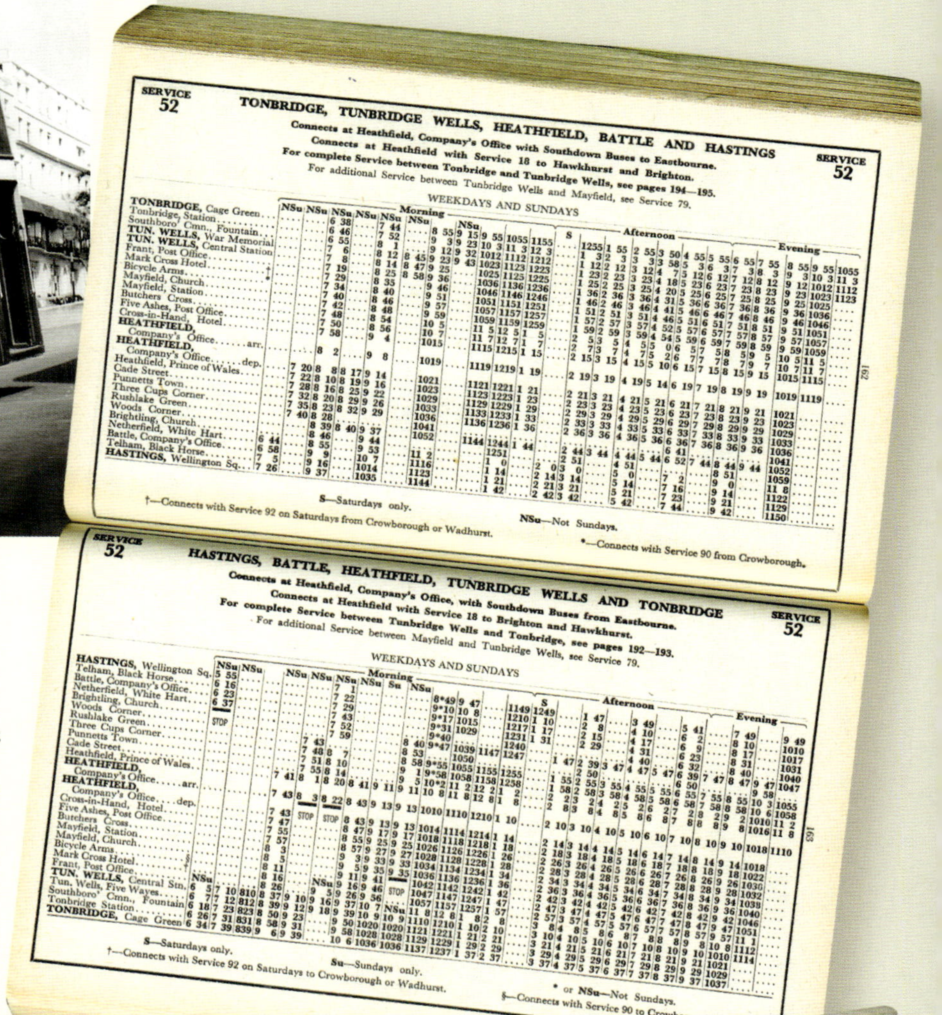
SERVICE 52

TONBRIDGE, TUNBRIDGE WELLS, HEATHFIELD, BATTLE AND HASTINGS

Connects at Heathfield, Company's Office with Southdown Buses to Eastbourne.
Connects at Heathfield with Service 18 to Hawkhurst and Brighton.
For complete Service between Tonbridge and Tunbridge Wells, see pages 194—195.
For additional Service between Tunbridge Wells and Mayfield, see Service 79.

WEEKDAYS AND SUNDAYS

S—Saturdays only. NSu—Not Sundays.
†—Connects with Service 92 on Saturdays from Crowborough or Wadhurst.
*—Connects with Service 90 from Crowborough.

SERVICE 52

HASTINGS, BATTLE, HEATHFIELD, TUNBRIDGE WELLS AND TONBRIDGE

Connects at Heathfield, Company's Office, with Southdown Buses from Eastbourne.
Connects at Heathfield with Service 18 to Brighton and Hawkhurst.
For complete Service between Tunbridge Wells and Tonbridge, see pages 192—193.
For additional Service between Mayfield and Tunbridge Wells, see Service 79.

WEEKDAYS AND SUNDAYS

S—Saturdays only. Su—Sundays only. * or NSu—Not Sundays.
†—Connects with Service 92 on Saturdays to Crowborough or Wadhurst.
§—Connects with Service 90 to Crowborough.

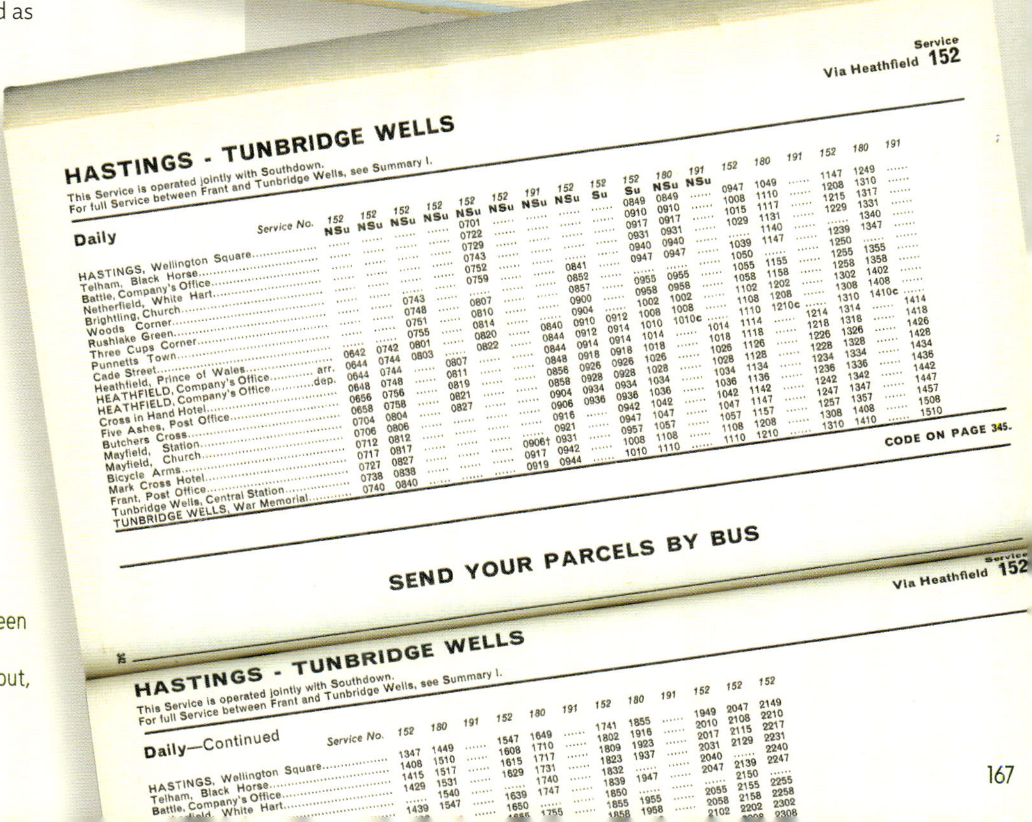
Service Via Heathfield 152

HASTINGS - TUNBRIDGE WELLS

This Service is operated jointly with Southdown.
For full Service between Frant and Tunbridge Wells, see Summary I.

Daily

CODE ON PAGE 345.

SEND YOUR PARCELS BY BUS

Service Via Heathfield 152

HASTINGS - TUNBRIDGE WELLS

This Service is operated jointly with Southdown.
For full Service between Frant and Tunbridge Wells, see Summary I.

Daily—Continued

It was a busy moment in Tunbridge Wells at the top of the opposite page, with Bristol K6As on town routes, a Commer/Harrington integral single decker going the other way and Park Royal bodied AEC Regent V DH484 waiting to leave on the long 152 route. The 22 AEC Regent Vs were M&D's last front-engined double deckers and they worked alongside Leyland PD2/12s on the longer services like the 152. It would be nearly two and a half hours before it reached Hastings.
M&D AND EAST KENT BUS CLUB

Hastings depot had several all-Leyland PD2/12s from the 1951 delivery allocated to it for longer routes out of the seaside town. Above, DH391 was parked in the notorious Wellington Square with chocks safely under the rear wheels due to the steep incline. It was waiting to leave on the 180 to Brighton.
M&D AND EAST KENT BUS CLUB

The upper timetable from summer 1955 shows Maidstone & District 52 being hourly southwards as far as Woods Corner, but only 2-hourly between there and Hastings. The lower timetable from summer 1965 shows the replacement Heathfield Pool joint 152 offering an hourly service throughout, every other hour requiring a simple change of bus in Heathfield.

The map on this page shows the network of bus services in the Heathfield Pool, covering the same roads as before but in this revised pattern. In essence each route except the 192 ran 2-hourly, but clever timetabling meant that there was an hourly service between most places, either by direct bus or changing in Heathfield.

The hourly 192 dovetailed between the combined hourly 190/191 to give a half-hourly frequency between Heathfield and Eastbourne. The diagrams on the right explain the pattern of through and connecting services on alternative hours.

As elsewhere, as the 1950s turned into the 1960s, Maidstone & District and Southdown were facing rising costs. Add in increased affluence with more and more people turning to private motoring, and all too soon passenger numbers were declining. Economies were inevitable. One-man operation came to the Heathfield Pool on 14 May 1966, with 36ft long single-deckers from both companies being used on all services, downseated to 45 due to legislation precluding more seats on a one-man bus.

Although frequencies remained the same, the 180 journeys that had terminated at Wood's Corner in the winter timetable went to Rushlake Green instead to turn round from 11 September the same year. This was simply because previously a conductor had been able to guide the driver in turning the bus round at Wood's Corner and, of course, this was no longer advisable with just a driver to perform the manoeuvre.

It wasn't until National Bus Company days that the Heathfield Pool began to untangle in 1971, but it had lasted for 14 years and had been remarkably successful in its day for such a complex scheme.

One-man operation began on 14 May 1966, and both companies used 36ft long single deckers on the services. Southdown's were Leyland Leopards and on this page Marshall bodied 118 from 1963 was photographed at Brighton's Pool Valley bus station, having arrived from Hastings on the 180.
SOUTHDOWN ENTHUSIASTS' CLUB

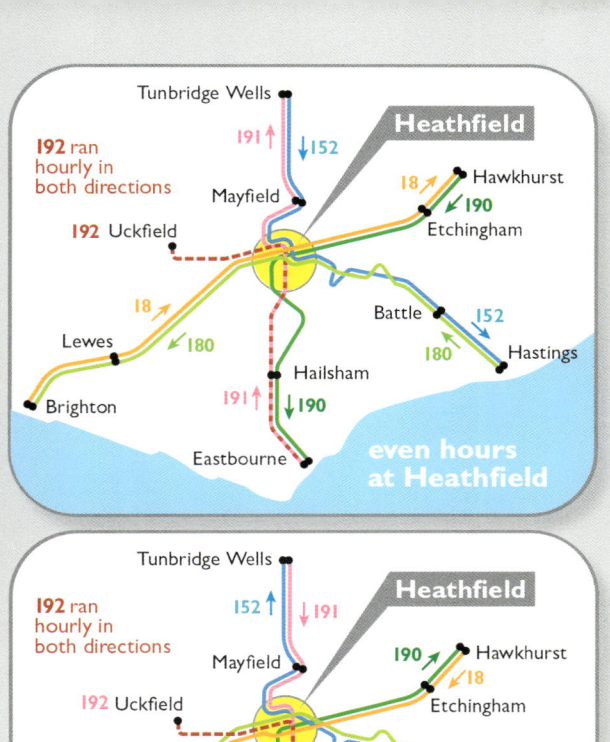

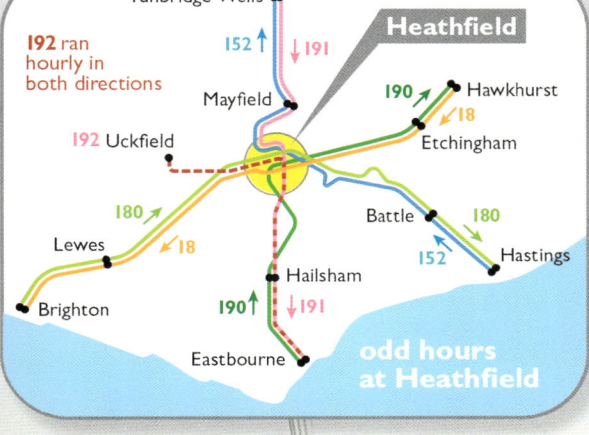

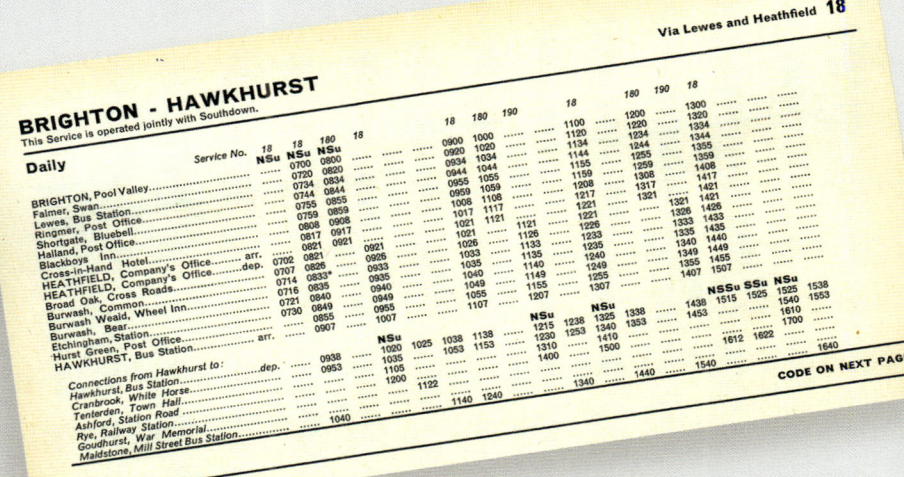

Above you can see how although the 18 was only 2-hourly, you could still get from points between Brighton and Heathfield to places between Heathfield and Hurst Green hourly by catching the alternate hours 180 from Brighton (that continued beyond Heathfield to Hastings) and changing at Heathfield to a 190 that had come up from Eastbourne.

Here is Maidstone & District S51, a one-man 36ft BET-style Weymann bodied AEC Reliance of 1965, distinguishable from the company's similar Marshall bodied Reliances from the same year by the smaller grille without the Marshall's tapered shape. The bus was passing through Framfield on the last few miles of its journey to Uckfield from Eastbourne via Heathfield in 1966.

RAY STENNING

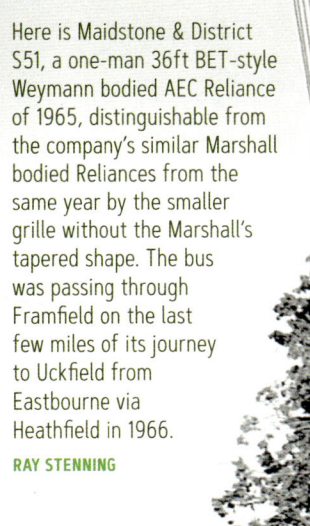

On the right, under repair in Luton garage, was Leyland Atlantean 5527 that had been new in 1960.

Early Atlanteans had a one-piece hinged engine bustle, like here. It didn't give full access to the engine bay and this made some repairs difficult to carry out.

With a jack under the angle drive, a number of repairs were being carried out around the unit.

A single-deck Daimler Fleetline was in the next bay beyond.
M&D AND EAST KENT BUS CLUB

keeping the wheels turning

As with all bus companies, Maidstone & District depended on the backroom staff of the engineering department to keep the vehicles on the road and all spick and span.

Day-to-day maintenance was carried out in Maidstone & District's local depots, including cleaning and washing of the depot's vehicles. The system in bus garages changed very little over the years. Buses would run in off service from the early evening and be fuelled ready for the next day. Washing would normally take place next, either by hand or by machine. The bus would then be parked ready for cleaning staff to get to work on it. Any defect found by the drivers would be written on a defect sheet for the engineering staff to repair. In each depot there were normally a number of skilled people, including mechanics, electricians, panel beaters, body repairers and, in the larger garages, coach painters.

Depots carried out regular safety inspections on vehicles and performed any repairs that became necessary, which would include repairs to the braking system, clutch changes, engine and gearbox changes as well as repairs to engines to an agreed level - things like changing head gaskets, pistons and liners, fuel pumps and injectors. Most of this would be carried out over an inspection pit. In the large depots at Gillingham, Luton, Tunbridge Wells and Hastings there was the facility to repaint and carry out body repairs. A high standard had to be kept as the Ministry of Transport vehicle inspectors would regularly carry out inspections on the company's fleet and issue PSV71 prohibitions if faults were found.

When the company decided to have a central overhaul works there was debate on whether the works should be built in Maidstone or Gillingham. In the end, Maidstone, as the headquarters of the company, was chosen. Postley Works in Maidstone opened in 1923 and became the centre for unit overhaul, preparation for CoF (Cerificate of Fitness) and major body repairs.

The works had two main sections - mechanical and body - each with its own manager. Any major modifications to vehicles in the fleet were also carried out in Postley Works. The mechanical section was split into several divisions - engine, gearbox and rear axle overhaul sections; machine shop; small unit overhaul; fuel pump overhaul shop; an electrical overhaul and battery shop; and, at one time, a blacksmith's shop. Ticket machines were also maintained in the works.

Over the years the components of the body section changed. The work required a saw mill, blacksmith's shop, glass cutting shop, panel shop, and also a trim shop which took care of the company's bus seats. The saw mill, which used ash for the wooden framed bodies, disappeared as metal framed bodies became more common. Glass was later supplied cut to size by manufacturers. In the 1960s a glass-fibre shop was set up to manufacture body sections and corner panels. The fibreglass shop produced the company name signs to be positioned above the company premises. The bus stop flags were also made from fibreglass from the late 1950s, in white, with the route numbers as an insert that could easily be changed. At one time the works had its own drawing office, where items of bodywork were designed or modifications made. Head office company cars were also maintained in the works.

Engine overhaul was on a flow line basis. The engine was stripped, components checked, washed and new parts ordered. The main block was put onto a stand that could rotate 360°. The mechanic could then rebuild the engine with access to all parts without having to move the engine until it was complete. A new or a reground crankshaft would be fitted with new pistons and liners. Crankshaft regrinding was carried out in the works, too. The fuel pump and injectors would be

Postley Works and the larger garages had facilities for chassis washing, one of the dirtiest jobs to do. At the top, SO238, a Beadle bodied AEC Reliance single-deck bus, was on the chassis wash.
SOUTHDOWN ENTHUSIASTS' CLUB

Immediately above you can see engines in Postley Works in overhaul cradles, which could be turned through 360°. After overhaul, engines would be given an eight hour test.
NA3T

Two dual-purpose single deckers and a Harrington Grenadier bodied coach were being prepared for their Cerificate of Fitness test in Postley Works in the view on the right. Note the Morris Minor van.
BRUCE JENKINS

On the left, mechanical work was being carried out on Bristol K6A DH137 in preparation for its Certificate of Fitness examination.

The engine had been removed for overhaul and it looks as if the fitter was changing the steering joint ends.
NA3T

Interesting that M&D thought nothing odd about using photographs of its workshop facilities to advertise the company's private hire service, as you can see below.

This one appeared on the back of a days out programme brochure.

overhauled in the pump shop. Fuel pumps would be stripped and new components fitted and then put on a test machine for recalibration. From another section re-conditioned cylinder heads would be fitted if the heads had to be skimmed, another process carried out in the works.

During overhaul in the works, early AEC Reliance 410 engines were modified by having a larger liner bore, from 105mm to 112mm, and this brought them up to the standard of a 470 engine, also raising the bhp figure from 105 to 112. Starters and dynamos, and later alternators, would be stripped in the electrical shop and when overhauled bench-tested to ensure that they were up to the required performance. The completed units would then go to the store where they would either be issued to reconditioned engines or sent to depots as replacements for failures in service. When complete, the engine would have an eight-hour running-in on a test bed with maximum power tests.

During the 1950s and early 1960s, up to seven engines a week of various types would be overhauled in Postley Works. The comprehensive machine shop was able to carry out many functions, including skimming brake drums, re-bushing spring hanger brackets, metal spraying and the turning of components to bring them back to their original size.

During the time period covered by this book all buses and coaches had to have a CoF which, on a new vehicle, was for seven years. At that point the bus or coach had to be recertified by a Ministry of Transport certifying officer, who would then issue a new certificate for another five or six years. The standard of presentation at M&D was very high and all vehicles received a six year certificate irrespective of age. CoF preparation was a major part of the central works function and up to nine vehicles per week would be going through this process within the mechanical, body and paint shops.

In the engineering shop the mileage of the major units would be checked and replaced with reconditioned units if they had met the overhaul mileage.

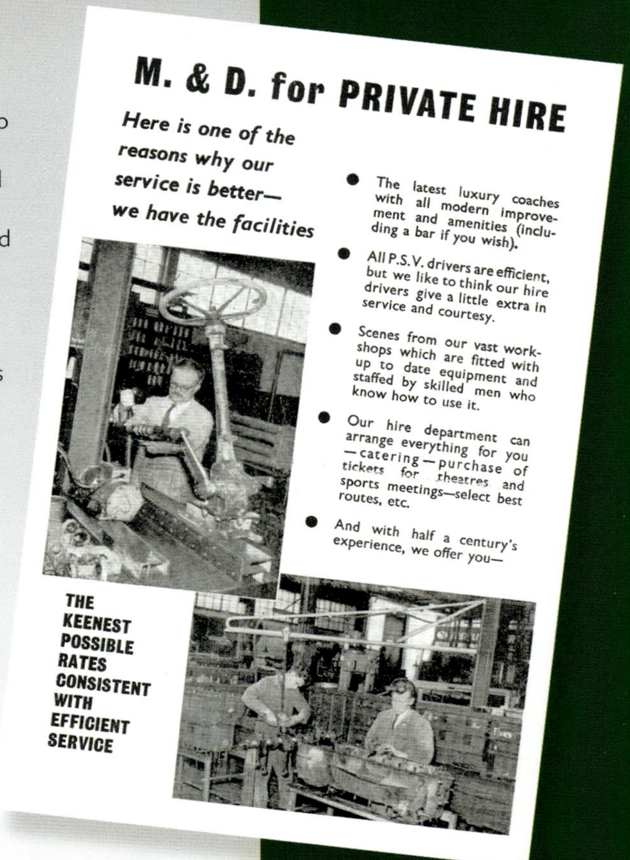

On the right is Harrington Cavalier bodied AEC Reliance coach 4028 (delivered as C28) up on a hydraulic lift in Postley Works and looking all nice and shiny.

There was a trend that started in the late 1960s for moving fleetnames to a more forward position on the bodyside, rather than the traditional position of midway along the bodywork.

It did give a slightly more modern slant to the brand, but here it seems to have been taken a step too far and looks a bit odd being right at the front on the offside.
BRUCE JENKINS

In the bodyworks section of Postley Works on the right, two dual-purpose single-decks were being repaired and prepared for repainting.

Body panels would be changed as required, the vehicle on the left with rather a lot it would seem.

Beyond them, sideways on to us, was one of Maidstone & District's Duple Commander III bodied Leyland Leopards and in the background the same Harrington Cavalier bodied AEC Reliance as in the top picture, up on the hydraulic ramp.
BRUCE JENKINS

Great pride was taken in getting the beautiful, shiny, smooth gloss finish which Maidstone & District expected for its vehicles coming out of the paintshop. This required the specialised skill of an experienced coachpainter and the eagle eye of a supervisor.
NA3T

At the top of the opposite page you can see Harrington Cavalier coach 4028 again, up on the ramp with someone working on the underside of the coach.

From this angle you can appreciate the satisfying elegance of the Cavalier's lines and proportions - a true beauty.
BRUCE JENKINS

Before computer-cut, self-adhesive vinyl technology made logo application so much easier, waterslide transfers were used, whereby the design was printed on to a clear carrier film and transferred on to the vehicle carefully, as you can see the gentleman doing at the bottom of the opposite page. A coat of varnish was usually applied afterwards.
NA3T

The steering and braking (new brake linings and skimmed brake drums) would also be overhauled, as well as the electrical items. When finished the chassis would be given a coat of silver paint. The body would have the under structure checked and repaired where necessary and then re-panelled. A new set of seats would also be fitted and the bus would be re-painted. The bus would then be presented to a certifying officer for a new certificate. The certifying officer could, if he wished, have the outer panels removed to inspect the under structure but with the standard of M&Ds presentation and its facilities this never happened to the company. During the busy periods some CoF preparation would also have been carried out in the larger garages.

Other than at CoF, the repaint cycle was three years which kept the fleet in a prime condition. The painting was by brush; spray painting had been tried and was not found to be successful. The CoF programme required the movement of many vehicles and good planning. To keep maximum availability, the coach fleet was always programmed when possible during the winter months.

The central works also carried repairs to the fleet that had been involved in major accidents where the repairs were too excessive for a depot to cope with. The central stores would purchase parts from manufacturers and suppliers, as well as keep reconditioned units from the works, and there was a regular delivery programme to depots with the stores lorry.

In the early 1950s several pre-war double deckers were converted into service vehicles. They had the front section of the roof removed for tree cutting. The rear lorry section came from earlier conversions. Leyland Titan TD4 no. 312 on the right had started life in 1936 as a bus with a Weymann body.
JULIAN BOWDEN

Below, with a body off a previous conversion, this Leyland Titan TD4 was now no. 310. It had been converted from a bus in 1950 and equipped for towing and the carrying of heavy spares.
DAVID TOY COLLECTION

The company bought two AEC Matadors that had originally been with the Ministry of Defence and were new in 1940. They were converted in 1961 to become recovery vehicles with new cabs, bodies and recovery equipment. E2 was in that guise in the picture below on the right.
DAVID TOY COLLECTION

To keep a bus company the size of Maidstone & District going, all sorts of things had to go on behind the scenes and some of these required non-PSV vehicles, commonly called service vehicles.

Quite often these would be converted from old buses or coaches.

behind the scenes

The driver trainer in the picture above, 702, had originally been DH382 when it began its life with Maidstone & District in 1951 at Tunbridge Wells.

It later spent several years at Sittingbourne and by the time it was converted to a trainer in September 1970 it would have clocked up a very high mileage.

M&D AND EAST KENT BUS CLUB

The 1928 Leyland Titan TD1 on the left originally had an open-top body by Short, which was was cut down to become a lorry in 1939.

The method of operation for cutting down trees demonstrated here does look rather precarious, but health and safety was a different game in those far-off days.

SURFLEET

a tale of two superintendents

When Alan Price started as a BET management trainee with M&D in September 1959 he knew his three years would start with a spell away from head office visiting two contrasting operating districts.

Alan tells the story.

Arthur Stossel Grist

I had no idea just how great the contrast would be or how much the superintendents who ran those districts would influence me. After a day or so at Knightrider House, M&D HQ, I was told that contrary to usual practice, I would be joining Mr Grist, the district superintendent of Tunbridge Wells area. Maidstone depot was behind head office. The fleet there made little impact on me, but two vehicle types stuck in my mind. First, some really dreadful lowbridge Weymann bodied Bristol K6As, particularly DL6 - it even had a reclining windscreen, making an already cramped cab minuscule. I drove it in service later and the crash gearbox *sans* clutch stop was another less than attractive feature. The other vehicle was the famous Knightrider. In very respectable plain blue livery, this Harrington bodied Commer contained 16 leather armchairs, full-size travelling rugs, coir foot warming mats and a bar, but no toilet. How coaching priorities have changed! In theory this was a high-class private hire vehicle, but I only recall it acting as a carriage for directors and senior management.

So on my first Wednesday with the company I found myself being driven to Tunbridge Wells by the senior traffic assistant, Eric Shipp. Although I'd seen Maidstone Corporation trolleybuses in the town, it was the first time I had seen the Corporation's then depot. Standing in the entrance as a threatened replacement for any vehicle running in with a fault was not the to-be-expected wartime Guy, but one of the Daimlers with Northern Coachbuilders body bought during the O'Donnell interregnum in the second half of the 1940s. After his departure to Northampton, the purchase of Daimlers ceased at Maidstone, although Terry O'Donnell did remain true to them in the Midlands.

On his journey to Tunbridge Wells to take up his position there, Alan recalled seeing a KKK-reg Weymann bodied Bristol K6A on the 33 and a JKM-reg Saunders bodied one on the 7. The reverse is true in the main pictures on these two pages.

DH283, the Weymann on the 7 to the left, was in Lower Stone Street bus station in the centre of Maidstone, while Saunders bodied DH217 was on the 33 in Tonbridge Road, opposite Maidstone West station, in the shot below.

M&D AND EAST KENT BUS CLUB

One M&D vehicle Alan remembered at Maidstone was the really dreadful (his words) DL6. Top right you can see the recessed screen of this lowbridge Weymann bodied 1950 Bristol K6A to which Alan refers. The bus had been repainted grey ready for sale.

MIKE HODGES

Beyond Barming the Medway Valley countryside was even more impressive than it is today! Around Teston we passed a KKK-registered Bristol/Weymann running in from 'The Wells' (Tunbridge Wells) via Matfield and Paddock Wood on what was then route 33. Then beyond Mereworth we passed a JKM-registered Saunders bodied Bristol on route 7. Both vehicles still had the by then obsolete blinds that showed the route number in a circle, but were not to last in the fleet much longer.

I got on OK with Eric Shipp, who proved to have had a long career as a district superintendent himself. Having first come to prominence at the old Dartford depot, he'd been the district superintendent at Gravesend from around the time of the surrender of routes and vehicles to London Transport, when the London Passenger Transport Board was set up. Having rebuilt the operation, he had stayed at Gravesend until during the Second World War, when he had followed the redoubtable Sam Pettican at Gillingham. Eric spoke well of the Leyland vehicles of the late 1930s, but guardedly about the Bristols, which were the workhorses of the fleet then.

After setting Eric on his way back to Maidstone, Mr Grist took me to deposit my bag at my new digs. On the way we passed, much to my surprise, London Transport's Tunbridge Wells depot; it ran Green Line coaches on the 704 to Windsor via Sevenoaks, Bromley and London. The boundary settlements of the 1930s had left London Transport with two Green Line routes projecting well into Maidstone & District territory - this one to Tunbridge Wells and the other which only ever ran to Wrotham but had shadowy rights much further into Kent. After lunch I was entrusted to Mr Tansley, Arthur's very dedicated chief clerk, and began my serious training.

Arthur Stossel Grist was a dedicated servant of M&D. He'd joined the company in the early 1920s from the London Brighton & South Coast Railway. He'd had a long spell as the travelling right-hand man of George French, the man who most of the rank and file still regarded as the father of Maidstone & District. Complete with motorbike, Arthur had been, in the eyes of many, the far too all-seeing mobile inspector.

Company legend told how a Maidstone crew on a Tilling Express on route 6 had come to Goudhurst Duck Pond from Hastings (the service ran through in those days), only to see the offending motorbike inadequately

179

One of Tunbridge Wells depot's buses used on the 91 route to East Grinstead was DL33, the 1951 lowbridge Leyland bodied Leyland Titan PD2 shown in the picture below.

With the remnants of snow still on the ground, it was at East Grinstead Station waiting to return to Tunbridge Wells by way of Forest Row, Hartfield and Groombridge.

The ex-SECR H-class 0-4-4 tank locomotive at the high-level platforms of East Grinstead's two-level station was fitted for push-pull work and was on the less frequent parallel railway service between the two towns.

To the left of the bus were the low-level platforms, rarely used at that time.

M&D AND EAST KENT BUS CLUB

hidden by the water. It was the work of a moment to stand the vehicle in the pond! 30 minutes later at Stile Bridge they were stopped by a smiling Arthur who, making no reference to the condition of the bottom two thirds of his trousers, checked the bus with unusual ferocity even for him, giving them both an Irregularity Report for minor offences.

His attitude to man management can best be summed up by a remark he made to me when I was guardedly questioning some disciplinary decision he had made. *"When it says Price is a bastard on the back of the lavatory door you will know you are doing your job. When somebody has inserted likeable between a and bastard you will know that you have earned the respect of your staff."* Oddly enough I recall no particular union difficulties at The Wells, although I gather they developed a fearsome reputation after Arthur's time!

I think there was a grudging recognition that the man was both his own man, totally genuine by his own standards, and that unexpected consequences would arise if he were crossed.

Arthur Stossel Grist managed the Tunbridge Wells area from 1947 to the early 1970s. His philosophy throughout was if it moves and has two legs, then it's our duty to make certain that going by bus or coach is the most viable option. To this end he insisted all services provided attractive frequencies, including evenings and Sundays. *"Once they use the car for preference we will never get them back,"* he'd say. He chased education and other season ticket business. He ran attractive excursions. His staff were polite and friendly or he would know the reason why. As the commuter estates around Tonbridge developed, he spent hours calculating how many passengers were to be expected and making sure that the first thing the new householders saw was an M&D bus and/or timetable.

Arthur had a very firm policy on complaints. The number was few enough to enable a personal visit from the company to the complainant, often by Inspector Russell, who had become an inspector with Redcar when a teenager. However, if the address was at all prestigious, Arthur at his most emollient, called in person.

Arthur's expansionist policies led him to accept any vehicles the company was prepared to give him. Harry Redstall, the engineer, did wonders with the cramped facilities available to him, but Tunbridge Wells engineering was good without reaching the heights achieved by, say, Luton and Silverhill. The fleet contained some less usual vehicles amongst the Bristol double decks, AEC single decks, OMO buses and coaches, such as Leyland bodied lowbridge Titan PD2s for the 91 route and Park Royal bodied AEC Regents for the Tunbridge Wells share of the long Ashford – East Grinstead 97 route, which called at most points vaguely in between.

Eight lowbridge Park Royal bodied AEC Regent Vs came in 1956, mostly used on the delightful cross-county route 97. DL42 was arriving at Tunbridge Wells Central station at the end of its long journey in the picture below. This route used to go all the way through to East Grinstead via Holtye Common
M&D AND EAST KENT BUS CLUB

The semi-chassisless bus developed by Saunders-Roe in conjunction with Maidstone & District, SO68, was based at Tunbridge Wells depot. It had a 5-cylinder Gardner engine and remained unique in the fleet. Alan talks about it on this page.
M&D AND EAST KENT BUS CLUB

Another resident of The Wells was SO68, a Saro integral saloon with an early Gardner HLW engine. Legend had it that it was the prototype of a fleet of M&D 'designed' (I suspect, read 'specified') single decks, and that it had been the consequence of a visit to Postley Works of an early Midland Red S type – probably an S15. In any event, SO68 was normally allocated to a very odd infrequent service, which started at a pub called The Kicking Donkey right out in the wilds between Ticehurst and Etchingham. Warrens of Ticehurst also used the same lanes and it was felt that SO68 would give a good account of itself should a 'cornfield meet' occur.

At that time there was no depot at Tonbridge, so Tunbridge Wells depot was host to a number of Dennis Pigs/Falcons, which operated local services in that town. These were and always had been one-man buses. Indeed, the area was generally proud of the fact that there had always been one-man buses at The Wells.

Alan mentions circular route 93 on the right, and there's a map of it on page 136. The 93 crossed over or passed underneath the Oxted to Tunbridge Wells/Uckfield railway line four times and the Redhill-Tonbridge line also four times.

In the picture above, taken in 1967, S213 was about to dive under the Oxted-Tunbridge Wells/Uckfield line by Cowden Station, the entrance to which is behind the bus on the left. This line was under threat of closure at the time but, luckily, only the bit between Uckfield and Lewes closed.

This was one of the Weymann bodied AEC Reliances Alan also refers to, delivered in 1956.

RAY STENNING

Arthur was particularly proud that his depot at Edenbridge was the first proper all one-man depot, although he was concerned that timekeeping on its 93 circular (Edenbridge-Four Elms-Chiddingstone Causeway-Penshurst-Tunbridge Wells-Cowden-Hever-Edenbridge) was not up to his usual standards. The outstation at Oxted, mentioned on page 135, was a matter of additional pride (the driver was based at Edenbridge and lived in Oxted). Generally, Edenbridge had Weymann bodied OMO buses, but tended to exchange vehicles with the Beadle bodied examples at The Wells.

Hawkhurst, on the other hand, had a very mixed fleet, providing vehicles not only for the 84 and other routes to Tunbridge Wells but also routes to Maidstone, Rye, Hastings, and Brighton. Hawkhurst had been rebuilt post-war as a rural interchange. Its island platform provided excellent railway-standard waiting facilities for passengers travelling from, say, Bodiam to Cranbrook, or Maidstone to Ticehurst, although connections were generally quite convenient. Heathfield was another major interchange. Arthur had a number of M&D crews outstationed at this Southdown dormy shed, where a streetside interchange provided opportunities to travel conveniently from places like Battle to Burwash or Five Ashes to Lewes. This is described more on page 166.

Both Southdown and M&D placed great store on a whole series of these interchange points, which meant that with regular headway services it was practical to travel from almost anywhere in Kent and East Sussex to anywhere else. Hawkhurst and Heathfield also provided a way of covering staff shortages at The Wells. This was done in two ways. Their staff were brought in to cover Tunbridge Wells shortages, and some of the mass of schooldays-only journeys around such places as Paddock Wood and Matfield were covered by Hawkhurst based vehicles. This also had the effect of relieving the chronic overcrowding of Tunbridge Wells depot. At night a very skilled man called, I think, Driver Ballard shunted the vehicles in such a way that they were accessible in run-out order in the morning.

To give an idea of how tight things were, it was normal practice to turn the mirrors in before reversing each vehicle tight to the next. This almost led to my premature departure one night, when I got trapped between the just-still-moving only Atlantean and another vehicle. Officially, the Atlantean from the company's first highbridge batch was at The Wells as part of availability trials with those at Silverhill and Hastings. However, I suspect that it suited Arthur to have it on his patch so that he could show it to his mentor George French, the long-retired former general manager of M&D. I remember the sprightly old man inspected it in total silence.

On the right, brand spanking new Metro-Cammell bodied Leyland Atlantean DH521 was being inspected in Tunbridge Wells depot.
M&D AND EAST KENT BUS CLUB

14 all-Leyland Royal Tiger coaches entered the fleet in 1952, although Arthur found them rather troublesome when used abroad on Leroy Tours continental touring work.

Below, CO285 was showing off its then strikingly modern lines in Woodbury Park Road in Tunbridge Wells, not far from the Maidstone & District depot.

In this instance it was not about to strike out to explore far-off continental countries, but merely setting out on a delightful local afternoon tour.
M&D AND EAST KENT BUS CLUB

After a further long silence he announced, "It will not do, Grist! Our engineers will never maintain that driveline! But worse, it is too big! You will have to cut frequencies to justify it. Cutting frequencies is the first step on the way out."

On the Wadhurst-Ticehurst-Hawkhurst corridor there were a number of large country houses in institutional use. Arthur made a practice of visiting them in search of coach business. Although inexperienced as I was, I was dubious of the outcome when we cold-called the Russian Embassy's country estate.

Some years earlier Arthur's enthusiasm had led to the company's only extensive exercise in continental coach touring. As handed down, the story went that in post-war, post-austerity Britain the English middle classes were discovering the continent and, with Arthur in the lead, M&D provided the vehicles for a local entrepreneur with a business called Leroy Tours, which marketed coach holidays as far afield as Yugoslavia and Spain, aimed at modestly incomed ladies in professions such as teaching and nursing. There's a bit more about this on page 62.

Arthur covered the work with a batch of Beadle bodied integral lightweight coaches with running units recovered from pre-war Leylands and AECs. The season was a great success, partly thanks to the running units having been prepared under the aegis of Postley Works (the George French designed Central Works), where they were reconditioned to impeccable standards.

The next season, unfortunately for Arthur, a nemesis appeared from head office, in the shape of underfloor-engined Leyland Royal Tigers, on paper in all respects much more suitable for the work. They boiled up all over Europe and Leyland, as had become usual, was unable to cope. The only effective help came from the Swiss firm Saurer. Arthur talked his way out of trouble with Leroy but the next season head office unsuccessfully challenged Leroy over who should hold the road service licences. Arthur, without naming names, dismissed the whole affair as an example of the result of the desire for personal prestige triumphing over common sense.

Such was the world of an old-style BET district superintendent (area manager) who regarded head office as a series of support services he could draw on at will, and as a place which also housed his nominal superiors whose primary function was to keep the owners happy while he got on with running day to day operations and development policy. His approach led to increasing numbers of vehicles being stationed in his area, with a posh new depot, albeit short-lived, at Tonbridge and the old Redcar Depot in Upper Grosvenor Road in Tunbridge Wells being reopened.

Meanwhile, two hours' bus ride away in the Medway Towns, Tony Snell, a superintendent from a different era, was following an altogether different approach . . .

Tony Snell

Tony had been imported from Crosville to be superintendent of the Medway Towns as a whole. This was just after Chatham & District at Luton and Maidstone & District at Gillingham had been brought within the same operational pattern. Given the brief he had, he did a very good job. In contrast to Arthur's dynamic enthusiasm, Tony was calm and emollient. He was also rotund, of medium height and, in those days of polite euphemisms, was what was still then called a confirmed bachelor. Most importantly, he was just right for the Medway Towns after the upheavals of the merger.

His approach to the role of superintendent could not have been more different to that of Arthur. In principle, he saw his role as that of managing the orderly contraction of head office-designed services. This contrast had the interesting effect of producing a situation where, much to his chagrin, buses saved in the Medway Towns area were immediately reused in the Tunbridge Wells area. To be fair, Tony carried burdens that Arthur had avoided.

Before his arrival, the basic town service pattern (the 140 group of routes) had been redesigned under a transient career diplomat, who years later admitted to me that he knew that the pattern was too complicated and the timings too tight, but claimed, *"it was the only way to save buses."* How often was this situation to be repeated up and down the country in the coming years?

Below, in Gillingham bus station, was one of the 1948 Saunders bodied Bristol K6As on the left. The middle double decker was DH75, a 1944 Guy Arab II originally with a Weymann utility body rebodied by Weymann in 1952. The Weymann bodied lowbridge Bristol K6A to the right of it was new in 1949.

Then, just visible on the furthest right, was SO248, one of the 24 Harrington bus bodied AEC Reliances delivered in 1958. The next batch of Harrington bus bodied Reliances the company bought, in 1963, would conform more closely to rather square BET pre-curved design.

THE BUS ARCHIVE/ROY MARSHALL

At the top of the lefthand page on a local service to Borstal was a Bristol K5G, DH310, advertising Mackeson's beer. This bus, with an earlier style Weymann body, was bought in 1939 for the subsidiary Chatham & District fleet as its no. 898. It was transferred to the main Maidstone & District fleet when Chatham & District was absorbed by M&D in 1955.

Also in Chatham on the right, but on a rather rainy day, was DH121 advertising Ty-Phoo tea. It was turning round in Military Road before picking up for the run to Maidstone.

This Bristol K6A was delivered in 1945, originally with a Park Royal utility body which was replaced in 1953 with this attractive 4-bay Weymann style.

M&D AND EAST KENT BUS CLUB

Each day and every day was saved by one of the unsung heroes of the industry, Inspector Ford, who at the end of a hotline to Tony Snell, stood at the main kerbside urban route focus in Chatham's Military Road, instantly cutting and pasting these services day in and day out. Thus he ensured that reasonable actual headways were maintained on the routes radiating from that point, although what actually happened had little resemblance to what appeared on the running boards provided by head office!

The other main burden Tony carried was a very different union situation. At Tunbridge Wells Arthur's general approach was to say, in effect, to his platform staff union, *"If we don't sort this out, it will get into the hands of the two Smiths"* - J K Smith, the union paid officer, ex-Silverhill and very sharp, and Stanley Smith, the traffic manager, ex-PMT and full of guile - *"and we will get a result neither of us wants."* Tony, on the other hand, negotiated within the brief he had been given by head office. On the whole, this worked with Michael Coveney, the union leader at Luton (Chatham), but at Gillingham, with shop stewards Briggs and Salter, impasse tended to follow impasse.

When I went from Tunbridge Wells to the Medway Towns the backbone of the 'Towns' fleet was still the ex-Chatham Traction 'big Guys', supplemented by ageing Bristol K5Gs, rebodied wartime Guys, and a selection of K6A Bristols. There was one doored double decker, an all-Leyland PD2 for Gillingham's one working on route 5 which went, ultimately, to Hastings. At the time it was understood that Gillingham would work only one double deck with doors, in practice on one double journey a day to Maidstone and back on the 5, which was a major factor in producing a situation where most journeys on the 5 trunk route were in fact provided by Gravesend depot by extension of its 57 route from Gravesend to Maidstone, then all the way to Hastings.

At this time, with the main service pattern recently replanned for better or for worse by head office, Tony was devoting a great deal of his time, and that of his enthusiastic assistant superintendent Tony Baker, to the diminution of the extensive pattern of works services. Then these were provided almost entirely by Gillingham depot using, theoretically, a dedicated double deck fleet of rebodied wartime Guys and newer Bristol K6As, which were coming to the end of their life in the fleet, although at that date the worst Bristols at Gillingham, the 'salmon can' Weymann Orion bodied HKE-series, were regarded as part of the main service fleet.

The works cars could be recognised at a glance. The main double-deck fleet had a fair-sized front blind box, with the route number displayed either in a separate route number box or on the main blind which, in any event, displayed a final destination and via information. The works cars merely displayed a final destination with part of the destination box masked or blacked out. These works blinds were still around six years later, in spite of the two Tonies' attempts upon the works services themselves.

There were, my memory tells me, 66 of these one-line destinations arranged mainly, but not exclusively, in alphabetical order, which produced a very long blind indeed. Now anyone who has set a traditional roller blind knows that the longer it is the harder it is to turn, and that the handles are not always in the most convenient places to get at them. Imagine the joys of arriving at, say, Fort Horsted, and having to wind one's way through 50 or so destinations to, say, Strood Old Gun.

To be fair, a few destinations were repeated at intervals, but the goodwill generated by that assistance was dissipated by including Maidstone, in spite of the fact that these cars were not officially allowed to pass over Blue Bell Hill between the Medway Towns and the county town!

Tony Snell, in line with conventional wisdom of the next 25 years, argued that because these works journeys added to the peak vehicle requirement, they were too expensive to operate, hence all the effort to eliminate them, despite opposition, firstly from the travelling public, and secondly from Briggs and Slater and the union branch. The Grist-Shipp school of thought argued, admittedly a lot less fluently than Tony, that they and peak hour enhancement generally inhibited the spread of the motor car and were therefore in the long run worth every penny.

With Tony Baker I was soon involved in the detail of this approach. But things were not as simple as Tony Snell had found them when, as I understand it, he had carried out similar policies at Crewe for Crosville.

DH79, on the left, was on one of the works services Alan talks about on this page, though it doesn't have the restricted blind display he describes.

This bus was a 1944 Guy Arab II rebodied by Weymann in 1952. The original utility body was also built by Weymann.

You can just make out an early post-war Wolseley car in the background, either a 4/50 or 6/80.

M&D AND EAST KENT BUS CLUB

Standing in Nelson Road outside Gillingham bus station, below, was DH195, showing the restricted blind display that Alan refers to on this page for buses used for factory services, though here being used on a normal stage route.

This Weymann bodied Bristol K6A was part of a batch of 41 delivered in 1946 and 1947, and was used as a publicity bus in the early 1950s to promote Hastings as a holiday destination.

M&D AND EAST KENT BUS CLUB

The line of M&D buses on the right was in Barrier Road in Chatham, with Weymann rebodied utility Bristol K6A DH106 leading. The side of Chatham Town Hall would be behind the photographer, and by the bus is the charming waiting shelter provided by the company on the corner of Dock Road.
M&D AND EAST KENT BUS CLUB

This is Dock Road below with the Town Hall ahead and that same waiting shelter just in view. DH467 waiting at the stop was former Chatham & District 936, a Weymann Orion bodied Guy Arab IV delivered in 1954.

At the takeover by M&D in 1955 there were eight more on order, but these were delivered straight to M&D as its DH468-475
SOUTHDOWN ENTHUSIASTS CLUB

```
Duty 10 — Weekdays AM.
Sign on
Dep. 4.30 Gill. Depot to Rochester Airport
Far Gate via City Way Arr. 5.00am.
Light to Pobjoys Back Entrance.
Dep. 5.10 to Hobourn Aero, via Cookham Wood
Arr; Hobourn Aero, 5.35am.       Run 5 late throughout
                                  — so no complaints
Dep. 5.37am to Dockyard Pembroke Gate
arr. 6.00.
Service 143 via Chatham Hill to Rainham Mark.
Dep. 6.30am to Rochester Esplanade via New Rd
Arr. 7.00am.
Light to Chatham Stn connect with 7.15
train from London       A Pig this one
Arr. Dockyard before 7.30.  with a standing load
                             of hungover sailors
Dep. Chatham Military Rd 8.10
to Higham School.    Posh girls
8.40 26 Relief to Gillingham Depot —
Run to service running times.
BREAKFAST..........
```

In the Medway Towns the pattern of operations was extremely complex, and even Tony Snell accepted that it was not practical to withdraw heavily used journeys, particularly if they did not parallel a service route. Let us illustrate the above with part of a sample AM works duty board in slightly abbreviated form. It might read something like this on the left . . .

After breakfast this crew would do a 'rounder' on, perhaps, a 26 to Sittingbourne Station, while the normal service crew had their breakfast, and then perhaps the first half of a school lunchtime 'kids' special' from the school in Maidstone Road in Rainham to the already vast commuter estates. After this, around 1pm, they were free to go home. Not quite so wasteful as it appeared at first sight! The first problem for Tony Baker and me was that some of these journeys were busy and some were not, but the lightly-loaded journeys often got the 'car' to where it was needed for the heavy journey.

So to save a 'car' probably meant re-jigging several workings and even diverting a service 'car' off its normal route. The shop stewards would immediately announce the proposed arrangements to be impractical and somehow the affected passengers became both aware of what was proposed and cross about it.

The union had a strong vested interest in these arrangements. The road staff at Gillingham were divided into a number of specialist 'keys'. These were groups of drivers and conductors who worked, often very well, a particular group of operations. Although, luckily, this was not to the levels of exclusiveness which were almost bringing operations at Oxford into total disrepute when I arrived there about nine years later.

Alan mentions the KKK-reg full-front AEC Regal coaches delivered in 1950 used by Gillingham depot.

Apart from the full-width cab with radiator disguised behind a simple slatted grille, the 32-seat Harrington coachwork was broadly the same as the half-cab version bought the same year.

On the left was one of the full-front coaches, CO113, alongside its half-cab sister CO110. Both were working the E7 Medway Towns - West of England express route that Alan also talks about, although in this case only as far as Portsmouth.

Southdown and Royal Blue were also involved in the South East - West of England express network that, with changes at key points, offered a large number of journey possibilities.

M&D AND EAST KENT BUS CLUB

As a matter of fact, when, after discreet negotiations with Messrs Briggs and Slater, of which management knew little, and which even after 40 years had better remain decently obscure, I was the first trainee to drive on service at Gillingham. I did a fair proportion of my work on the 'sports key'. I found that the early finishes had attracted the younger, fitter element among the staff who worked as a team. The name indicated that they had other interests in the afternoon, although how many were genuine sportsmen, I remember not.

The union situation at Gillingham depot was the item in the business mix in the Medway Towns which took most of the management's time, Luton depot being largely left to the firm influence of its depot engineer.

Coaching at Gillingham was another matter which contained the seeds of endless debate. As I remember events, the seasonal 'coastal express key' was particularly contentious. During the summer months Maidstone & District operated a series of coastal express services numbered from E7 (to Bournemouth) to E21 (to Hastings). At one time these had generally started from Gillingham bus station, but over the years many of their starting points had migrated to Gravesend or Maidstone, or even Sheerness.

The later, attractive Harrington Wayfarer IV bodied AEC Reliance coaches were also used on the E7. On the left was one of those Wayfarer IVs, C9, again on a Portsmouth run of the E7. It was one of 20 delivered in 1961, the last Wayfarers delivered to Maidstone & District.
M&D AND EAST KENT BUS CLUB

Just as Alan's story opened with a Weymann bodied Bristol on the 7 in Maidstone's Lower Stone Street bus station, we end it similarly.

This time it was DH 152, another of the 1945 Bristol K6As that had their Park Royal utility bodies replaced by these attractive 4-bay Weymann bodies in 1953.

El Cid, with Charlton Heston and Sophia Loren and directed by Anthony Mann, was showing at the Granada cinema, which suggests the picture was most probably taken in 1961.
GEOFFREY MORANT courtesy of Richard Morant

At the time I was with Tony, the Gillingham 'coastal express key' claimed the right to re-man coastal express services which entered Gillingham bus station. These senior drivers who, to be fair, were prepared to revert to the mundane when the coastal express services were not running, quite liked the idea of being in Bournemouth on Saturday, Worthing on Monday, Broadstairs on Tuesday, and so on. They were not, therefore, agreeable to change. In fact, the first industrial dispute I found myself involved in handling was when they made clear they were not going to accept change without a fight.

M&D hardly provided a front line fleet for them to operate on these services, although Gillingham had Harrington Wayfarer bodied Reliances for its share of the London services and for the service car on the often duplicated Bournemouth run. But most of its coach fleet consisted of Regals disguised with a full front, those of the KKK and WKM series.

what did I learn?

So what did this management trainee learn from his time with these two very different superintendents managing, admittedly, very different areas in totally different ways? First I learnt that in bus operation the quality of the product was everything and that the morale of the road staff was the critical factor in successful operation. Second, I realised that there was no one right way to manage the provision of services, and third, that the management information available at that time was capable of meaning all things to all men.

When I wrote this 40 years later, what did I feel looking back? First, the BET group was right to devolve decision making as near as possible to where the facts arose, and second that perhaps the emphasis on the ordered contraction which pervaded the next 25 years should have been better tempered by the emphasis on quality and seeking new markets - the sort of things that men like Grist and Shipp brought with them from their experiences combating the relative decline in demand in the 1930s.

along the Medway Valley

You can really feel the heat of an August day in this gem of a picture from 1966, taken by Geoffrey Morant; maybe fancy a nice refreshing pint in The Chequers. Fremlins, one of Kent's two major brewers and based in Maidstone, was taken over by Whitbread in 1967 but soon run down.

The location here is Aylesford near Maidstone. Maidstone & District S287, a 1960 AEC Reliance with Weymann so-called dual-purpose body (a bus shell with high-back seats in it) is climbing through the delightful old part of the village, on its way from Maidstone to Chatham on the pleasant if rather out of the way route 29 around the base of the North Downs, more-or-less following the River Medway.

At Sandling, across the river from Allington on the northern edge of Maidstone, this bus would have turned off the busy A229 at the Running Horse, a massive pub with a thatched roof, reputed to be one of the largest such things in the land. Allington Locks, incidentally, marks the end of the tidal section of the River Medway.

In this photograph the bus had just passed Aylesford's picturesque, arched, medieval stone bridge over the Medway, shown on the left and featured in the opening minutes of the film *Half a Sixpence* and, no doubt, on countless picture postcards, chocolate boxes and jigsaws.

The steps on the left by the Ford Anglia led to the medieval church of St Peter & St Paul, much restored in Victorian times, but still with a fine Norman tower. The actress Dame Sybil Thorndike was the daughter of one of the vicars here and was married in this church in December 1908.

On the horizon to the right you might just make out a cluster of oast houses, common all over Kent, where hops would have once been dried out (kilning) for the process of beer-making.

Soon after here the bus would pass through Eccles, shown on the blind, then Burham. Burham is home to the Golden Eagle pub that used to have a large collection of cigarette cards, some featuring buses from 287's era. It is said that a Routemaster was plunged into an old quarry here for the TV show, **The Young Ones**.

The 29 route carried on through the Medway gap where, over time, the river has worn through the chalk hills. The gap was once host to many cement works, all shut now due to cheaper imported cement from Greece. The bus would enter the Medway Towns in Rochester at its suburb of Borstal. Here was the first of such institutions, hence all of them being called Borstal.

After passing the charming, historic heart of Rochester our bus will have ended its journey in busy Chatham. Later, in National Bus Company days, the route became the 155 and for a while regularly had double decks on it, adding to the pleasure of what was a very enjoyable ride. You can see a double decker in Aylesford in the time period of this book on page 99.

August Bank Holiday 1956

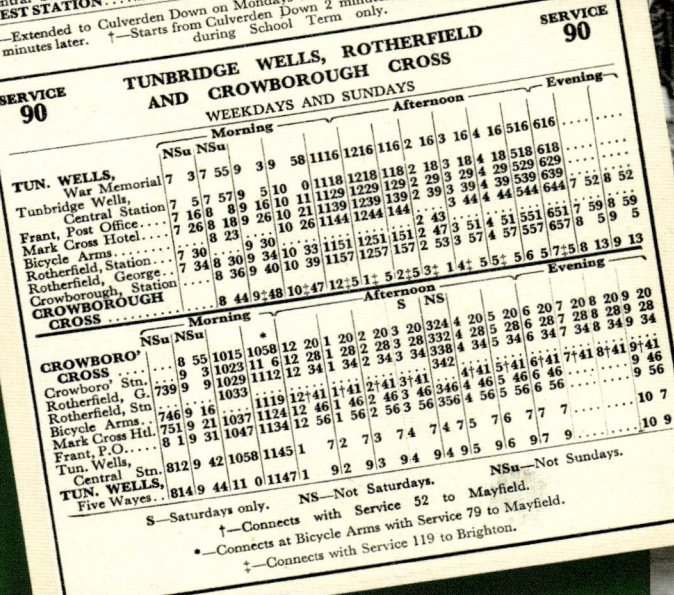

Yes, the picture on the right really was taken on August Bank Holiday. On Monday 6 August 1956 a freak hailstorm assailed the Kent town of Tunbridge Wells and this bus got stuck in the white stuff almost up to its headlights, as you can see!

The bus was one of Maidstone & District's 11 1955 Harrington/Commer Contender 42-seat integral buses (SO200-210) delivered between September and November the previous year. The bus was near the famous Pantiles, just down the hill and not far short of its destination of Tunbridge Wells War Memorial.

Leon Coast inherited this picture from an uncle in Redhill and here is the story behind it. The picture hung for many years in Uncle Ted and Auntie Julie's front room in Redhill, and Leon would gaze at it for two weeks every summer when he made the relatively short journey there from Bexhill for summer holidays.

Uncle Ted was a railway enthusiast *par excellence*, but also an observer of road transport in general, and this photo of a Maidstone & District bus reminded Leon of home if ever he began to get homesick. Not that he did, for most of the days would be spent working outwards from Redhill Station, either by train or London Transport bus, where a 2/6d Green Rover ticket provided a particularly economic passport, even on paper-round pay, to the 1,400 plus miles of green country bus routes.

The picture's full provenance came to light much later when Leon inherited the photo. It had been bought from a local paper by a relation of Uncle Ted as a memento of an afternoon they'd all spent in chapel together. We must thank the Kent and Sussex Courier's intrepid all-weather photographer for recording this event.

Attending chapel would have been quite natural for Uncle Ted on a Bank Holiday Monday, and an excuse for a steam train ride, on this occasion all stations from Redhill to Tonbridge, changing there for the Hastings line to Tunbridge Wells where, no doubt, his journey was completed behind one of his (and Leon's) favourite locos, that most powerful of all 4-4-0s, a Schools class. The characteristic, narrow-bodied 6-car 'Thumper' diesel-electric multiple unit trains were still a year away.

But on this Bank Holiday Monday, the town was two feet or more deep in hailstones for the best part of the afternoon. At the Baptist chapel Leon's uncle was attending, the minister's words were drowned out by the sound of hailstones hitting the roof!

Above is how the timetable appeared in the 1955 timetable book, while below on the right you can see the truncated service with connections at Mark Cross Hotel or Bicycle Arms in the 1965 timetable book.

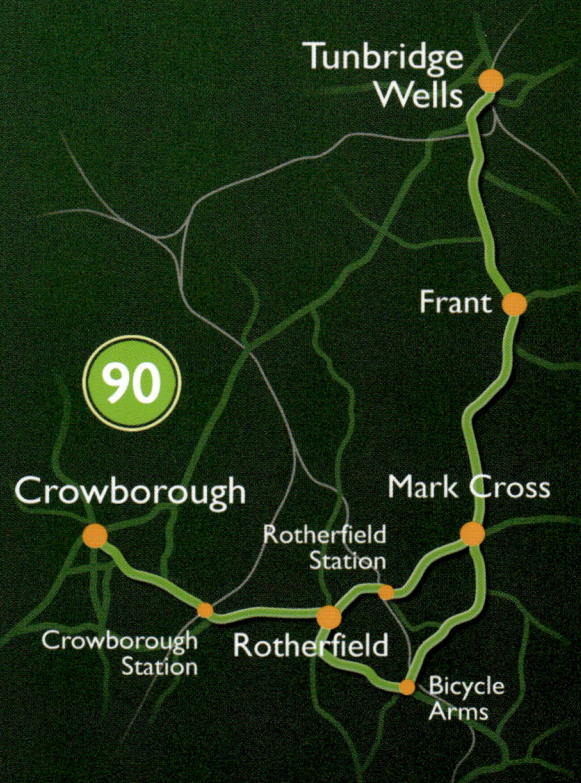

It's fascinating how the choice of apparel for the day was quite varied among the shovellers. The bus driver is suitably attired in open-neck shirt and summer jacket for the sunshine that might still have lit the leafy lanes around Rotherfield and Mark Cross, delightful Sussex Weald villages passed on his way into Tunbridge Wells on route 90 from Crowborough Cross.

However, other events that year would cause a degree of curtailment to the operation of the 90 route, namely the Suez Crisis and the need to save fuel. Within a couple of years, a footnote in its timetable for the 90 requested passengers travelling to Tunbridge Wells from the Crowborough and Rotherfield end of the route to *"change cars"* and use routes 152 or 191 to complete their journeys from either Bicycle Arms or Mark Cross Hotel, leaving very few through journeys on the 90.

The Heathfield Pool co-ordination in 1957 of the six joint M&D/Southdown routes that passed through Heathfield probably also influenced this decision. This scheme was part of both companies' aims to avoid duplication and reduce costs, although in the case of the Heathfield Pool there was an intention to give more frequent through-journey possibilities thanks to planned interchange at Heathfield. There's more on this elsewhere in this book.

The shops have all changed since this picture was taken, although unchanged to the left of the photographer - out of shot where the pavement widens - is the church of King Charles the Martyr, dating from 1678 and with a superb ceiling by Sir Christopher Wren's chief plasterer, Henry Doogood. Queen Victoria regularly attended services here whenever she was in the town.

Maidstone & District at war

a personal story

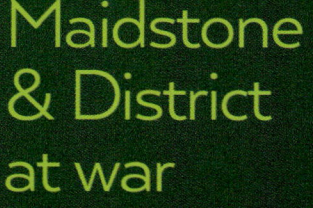

This is a tribute to those Maidstone & District staff working on the home front during the dark days of the Second World War.

It's a tale about Keith Webb told by his son Tony, and recalls those now far-off years when Britain for a while stood alone against the forces of evil, and bus men and women had a vital role to play in the struggle towards victory.

As a schoolboy in Maidstone in the period 1939-1945, my first recollection of my father during those wartime years was him being away from home for the two weeks when Maidstone & District was instructed by the Ministry to deploy its fleet of Leyland Tiger saloons that had been converted to ambulances - each with a capacity of eight stretchers - to form a mobile column at various ports along the South Coast to receive casualties from the evacuation of Dunkirk in June 1940.

Maidstone & District fleet livery had changed little at the beginning of the Second World War, with the dark green overall colour still dominant. However, the roofs were now painted matt grey instead of silver, and white was seen on the edge of wings and other places to aid visibility in the blackout. Of course, headlight masks had been in place for a while. A little-known fact today is that bus crews had a personal issue of military-style steel helmets finished in matt grey. Crews had to carry these at all times when on duty, as well as their civilian respirators, or gas masks, as they were more commonly known.

formation of the Home Guard

Also in June 1940 Maidstone & District and other bus companies launched an appeal to employees to form Local Defence Volunteer units to defend bus company depots and property. It was intended that these bus company units should operate in a static role only. The Local Defence Volunteer movement, known by its initials LDV and irreverently as **Look, Duck, Vanish**, was the basis of what became the Home Guard on 23 August 1940.

At that time the units of all bus companies in Kent were formed into one battalion known as **The Maidstone & District and Allied Companies Battalion**. This title proved too unwieldy and was changed on 17 September 1940 to **The First Battalion, Bus Companies' Home Guard,** then changed again in the November to **26 Bus Battalion**, under Lt Col H O Hollas.

Shortly after, this battalion was structured into three Home Guard Transport Columns - West Kent, East Kent and North Kent. Their role was now a mobile force to be deployed all over the United Kingdom in the transportation of Home Guard Units or battle casualties. Members of the battalion were issued with a tiger's head sleeve motif to be worn below the title HOME GUARD on their battledress, as opposed to their contemporaries in the infantry battalions who sported the While Cliffs and Dover Castle as their motif.

the Battle of Britain

Sunday 15 September 1940 dawned clear and bright, and remained so all day. The Webb family spent the entire morning from 9am in the cellar of their small terraced house in Maidstone, while intense air battles raged overhead. It was certainly unwise to venture outside. But, thankfully, this day was the turning point of the Battle of Britain and resulted in Churchill's famous remark that, "Never in the field of human conflict was so much owed by so many to so few."

German Heinkel He 111s in formation during the Battle of Britain.

Around noon that day there was a lull in activities and time to snatch a bite of lunch before father reported for duty at Knightrider Street garage in the town. His first journey that afternoon was driving the 10 to Ashford and Folkestone, and he later told me about seeing a Messerschmitt 110 fighter bomber which had just made a wheels-up crash landing close to the main A20 road at Lenham.

coaching during the war

During those wartime days the movement of civilians was restricted for those wishing to enter coastal areas, and was only allowed with the production of an identity card that proved the person's place of residence. Drivers of public service vehicles and other essential services had been issued with an identity card with endorsement, together with a certificate of occupation. Throughout the war buses ran to time as much as possible, since getting the nation's wartime workforce to factories and places of employment on time was essential. This included Maidstone & District's express E1 between Maidstone and London's Victoria Coach Station.

It was mid-October when father was keyed to take the early morning coach to London. On arrival at Victoria he managed to narrowly avoid the consequences of a parachute mine that had exploded nearby. He brought home a chunk of metal from the mine, which he claimed was still hot when he picked it up. I kept it.

As war drew on I remember my father suffered bad headaches, which he attributed to driving in blackout conditions, but in no way did it deter him from doing his shifts. There was a war to be won and everyone had a duty and determination to do their bit.

Although not quite in the same style as it is today, private hire still carried on during the war. For example, entertainers like Arthur Askey, Issy Bonn, Elsie and Doris Waters (Gert & Daisy), and bands all had to be conveyed to remote army camps in Kent as part of ENSA (Entertainments National Service Association, sometimes referred to as **Every Night Something Awful**!). Entertainment was vital for the morale of troops during the war, especially for personnel sent to Kent military bases awaiting mobilisation and action across the channel or further afield in the theatre of war.

There were also pick-ups from military establishments to dance halls and late night returns to be provided. Plus, at this time, prisoners were conveyed from Maidstone and Canterbury prisons to Brixton in South London. The upside of that particular trip was a good free lunch for my father at Brixton before returning home.

Operation Steinbock

At the beginning of 1944 the smell of victory was strong, but this seemed in doubt with the start of Operation Steinbock by the Luftwaffe on the night of 21/22 January 1944. This was Germany's nocturnal offensive aimed at destroying both military and civilian targets in Southern England.

Father got caught up in the action at Hunton Hill between Paddock Wood and Maidstone during the first phase of this operation. It was the only time during the war that he, together with his conductress and passengers, had to temporarily abandon the bus to the relative safety of a roadside ditch until safe to proceed. He described this to me as a gigantic firework display when all hell was let loose!

Doodlebugs

By Spring 1944 aerial activity had lessened, although from June 1944 London and the South East was assailed by the pilotless V-1 flying bombs, known as Doodlebugs. At its peak, more than 100 V-1s a day were being fired at South East England. Overall, 9,521 came our way, lessening in intensity as launch sites on the other side of the channel were overrun, with the last in October 1944. The awful thing about a flying bomb was that all the time you could hear the monotonous drone of the engine, it was in the air and you were probably safe as it went overhead. As soon as the engine cut out, it just glided or fell to earth and, as you could never tell where that would be, you just had to wait for explosion, and pray it wouldn't fall on or near the bus.

But by September 1944 invasion of our shores was no longer a threat and the Home Guard was stood down, just eight months before the final end to hostilities in Europe in May 1945.

Keith Webb took a driving test for Maidstone & District in Maidstone in 1928 but failed. He was contacted by the company to take another the following year; only this time he passed and was offered a job at the former Gravesend & Northfleet Electric Tramways depot in Northfleet, which had recently been acquired by Maidstone & District.

Keith moved to Northfleet and was married in the December. His son Tony was born in 1932, but in 1934 Keith was transferred to Maidstone depot, so the family moved to Kent's county town.

Keith claimed he was the last driver at Maidstone & District to work with a conductor, Reg (Dave) Davis, and both used to be on the route 109 day-in, day-out, during 1967/8 until Keith's retirement.

Keith Webb died in April 1993 and was buried at West Malling. A Maidstone & District inspector attended the funeral and the vicar mentioned his last journey on the 109 - a suitable ending for a veteran driver of his day.

A cutaway drawing of one of the dreaded Doodlebugs - the V-1 unmanned flying bombs.

Elsie and Doris Waters entertained the troops as Gert and Daisy.

reading the Rule Book

The 1965 Rules and Regulations book, illustrated on these pages, was in eight sections with 133 rules related to the duties and conditions for a driver, conductor and an OMO driver.

Part 1 gave the basic information, including giving examples of what staff could be dismissed for...

> Employment with the Company will be automatically terminated in the case of any driver or conductor who:—
> (a) Takes leave without permission.
> (b) Fails to complete his scheduled duty without good reason.
> (c) Fails to pay in receipts in accordance with regulations.
> (d) For any reason, walks off the job.
> (3) That they agree to work in harmony with all other employees of the Company.
> (4) That loss of monies received on behalf of the Company be made good by deduction from wages.

Remember that in 1965 there was no company sick pay scheme for the road staff.

Part II covered public service vehicle regulations and this went into considerable detail. This wasn't just about drivers' and conductors' legal responsibilities but what passengers were not to do, like, for example, *"not throw any article from the vehicle or attaching to or trail from the vehicle any streamer, balloon, flag or other article in such a manner as to overhang the road."* Or how about this: *"throw any money to be scrambled for by any person on the road or footway"*?

Part III set out the general rules for drivers and conductors which included civility and courtesy to passengers, drinking and general conduct while on duty, and lots more besides. Uniforms were to be worn when on duty and kept in a clean and tidy condition, and drivers' and conductors' badges always had to be worn.

The conductor was responsible for the destination screens on the bus and had to ensure that they were correctly set. Conductors also had the responsibility of time-keeping on the service. This section covered the regulations on standing passengers. Eight were allowed, unless the bus had a special permit to have a higher number set by the Traffic Commissioner. Drivers had to report any defects on the bus on the defect sheet on return to the depot (the rule book stated that no defect should be discussed with a passenger).

Other items covered by this section included the use of bell signals, relief vehicles, bus stops, deviation from an authorised route and changeovers. It also reminded crews about the need to lower the bulkhead blinds immediately after dark.

Interesting was rule 20: *"A serious view will be taken of any driver or conductor found to be signalling to any other driver or conductor by gesture, lights or other means to indicate the presence of an inspector or other official in the vicinity."* They must have found ways to get around that one undetected!

Part IV was the Special Regulations for Drivers which had 27 sections and included instructions on driving techniques, breakdowns, speed limits, vehicle safety, express service, private hires and tours.

All drivers and conductors were issued with a rule book, and this they had to carry with them when on duty. A conductor also had to carry a timetable and fare book.

Maidstone & District set high standards, and the contents of the small 100-page Rules and Regulations book had to be known by all road staff.

PART VI.
ACCIDENTS—SPECIAL REGULATIONS (DRIVERS AND CONDUCTORS)

106.—Avoidance of Accidents.
Accidents do not happen—they are caused, and it is at all times the duty of every driver and conductor to exercise his skill and vigilance in an all-out endeavour to avoid them. Accidents are the source of untold misery and suffering, endless expense and inconvenience, and may be a reflection on your efficiency as a driver or conductor.

The following are a few points which should be carefully observed, as the failure to do so is a frequent cause of accidents.

Drivers:
(i) Never drive at an excessive speed.
(ii) When overtaking, allow ample clearance and sound the horn. Special care should be exercised when passing cyclists or pedestrians.
(iii) Never overtake another moving vehicle at crossroads, or where it is not possible to see that the road ahead is clear. Never make a third line of traffic by overtaking another overtaking vehicle.
(iv) Do not follow other vehicles too closely.
(v) Pay particular attention to any warning of vehicles in front when ...
(vi) Always ...
fog ...

This Book is the property of
THE MAIDSTONE AND DISTRICT MOTOR SERVICES, LIMITED
Knightrider House, Knightrider Street
MAIDSTONE

and must always be carried whilst on duty and produced on demand to an authorised Official of the Company. On leaving the Company's employ this Book must be handed in, together with any other equipment, and if not returned will be charged for (2/6).

Issued to ......STEVENS H.G.......
Grade ......DRIVER......
Depot ......HAWKHURST......
Date ......25.11.65......
P.S.V. Badge No. ....
Signature ....

The loss of this book must immediately be notified to the depot office.

Please keep in a clean and tidy condition

On the right is rule 58 in part IV (the section started at rule 44), needed because of the severe slopes at these locations.

Part V, special regulations for conductors, was the largest, with 37 rules, many with sub-divisions. Conductors were instructed to check their ticket machine and equipment before leaving the depot and be in possession of a waybill and emergency tickets. Instructions were given on the collection of fares, types of tickets, what to do with defaced tickets, joint services, and time and duty cards.

Conductors were responsible for paying in their daily takings and, if this was short at all, the amount would be deducted from their wages. This was treated very seriously and could lead to disciplinary action. Other items for the conductor included instructions on parcels and luggage, lost property, disorderly conduct of passengers and safety of passengers in the event of a breakdown.

In Part VI we learn all about avoidance of accidents – instructions to drivers on driving in a safe manner and conductors on safety within the bus – and what to do in the event of one. For example, staff were told, *"never visit the homes of persons injured in an accident in which they were involved. Their intentions may be perfectly genuine and an expression of sympathy, but in many cases they will be wrongly interpreted as an indication of their responsibility for the accident."* Plus ça change there then.

Part VII covered the special regulations governing features peculiar to the company's territory and organisation. Rule 116, shown on the right, gave a list of bus routes that were restricted to operation by single deckers (saloon vehicles, as Maidstone & District referred to them in the rule book) or either single-deck or lowbridge double deckers. This was pretty important information for drivers and for the staff who detailed the duties, to avoid getting stuck, de-roofing a bus or damaging buildings.

There were another 14 places where drivers had to take special care, and below are a couple of examples:

> **121.—Services 22, 116, 122—British Railways Weak Bridge No. 117.**
> The drivers of any 'bus passing over the British Railways bridge number 117 on services 22, 116, 122, between Tollgate and Camer Corner are to note that the speed of their vehicle must at no time exceed 5 m.p.h. The bridge must not be used by the Company's vehicle when any other vehicle of any type is also passing over the bridge.
>
> **122.—Services 20, 120, 140, 141—Darnley Road, Strood—Arched Bridge.**
> All vehicles negotiating this bridge in either direction must keep to the centre of the roadway and approach the bridge at moderate speed in case of the need to stop.

There were detailed instructions for express coach drivers about how to enter and leave London Victoria Coach Station, as well.

The last section in the rule book, part VIII, gave details of the company's disciplinary procedure. This was an agreement with the trade unions. The interview would be held by the Area Manager and the employee could appeal to the disciplinary committee if the award was above a 'Final Warning'. The last and final stage was an appeal to the General Manager.

All eight sections covered all aspects of the crew's duties and conditions and would have taken some time to digest.

> **58.—Use of Chocks—Hastings and Chatham.**
> 'Buses are to be halted north of the entrance to Castle Hotel, Wellington Square, to avoid obstruction to the Hotel entrance. After the vehicle has taken up its position on the departure stand, chocks must be placed beneath the wheels. They must be removed immediately the 'bus is ready to move away from the terminus, and placed adjacent to the Post Office telephone box on the east side of Wellington Square to avoid vehicles running over them or any subsequent injury to pedestrians who might fall over them.
> 'Buses parked in Barrier Road, Chatham, must have chocks placed under the rear wheels. These must be removed immediately the 'bus is ready to be moved off.
>
> **59.—Fire Extinguishers.**
> When a fire extinguisher has been used, the fact must be reported to the depot foreman immediately, and a...

> **PART VII.**
> **SPECIAL REGULATIONS GOVERNING FEATURES PECULIAR TO THE COMPANY'S TERRITORY AND ORGANISATION (DRIVERS AND CONDUCTORS)**
>
> **116.—Restriction of Certain Types of Vehicles to Certain Routes, Low Bridges, etc.**
> Several serious accidents have occurred by the use of a vehicle on a route where, owing to a low bridge or other hazard, it is not suitable for the operation of that type of vehicle. It is most important, therefore, that DRIVERS AND CONDUCTORS, AS WELL AS ALL EMPLOYEES CONCERNED WITH THE DETAILING OF VEHICLES, pay particular attention to the following instructions and to any other instructions which may be issued on this subject from time to time.
>
> All vehicles proceeding "light" between MARINA and BEXHILL DEPOT must proceed via SEA ROAD, STATION ROAD, BUCKHURST PLACE and TERMINUS ROAD.
>
> The short route via Sackville Road must NOT be used, owing to the restricted height of the arch over the road.
>
> SALOON VEHICLES ONLY must be employed on the following services except where it is possible to operate larger type vehicles over sections of the route:—
> 6. MAIDSTONE and HAWKHURST or KILNDOWN.
> 6A. MAIDSTONE and WINCHETT HILL.
> 28. FAVERSHAM and GRAFTY GREEN.
> 55. SEVENOAKS and KEMSING.
>
> 60. FAVERSHAM and LENHAM.
> 61. MAIDSTONE and BEARSTED.
> 68. SEVENOAKS and BOROUGH GREEN.
> 72. ST. LEONARDS and HASTINGS (Parker Road).
> 74. ST. LEONARDS and HASTINGS (Parker Road).
> 78. TUNBRIDGE WELLS and WADHURST.
> 90. TUNBRIDGE WELLS and CROWBOROUGH CROSS.
> 93. TUNBRIDGE WELLS, EDENBRIDGE and TUNBRIDGE WELLS.
> 100. TONBRIDGE (Trench Wood Estate) and DOWGATES CLOSE.
> 105. SEVENOAKS and SEAL.
> 106. SEVENOAKS and KEMSING.
> 118. FAVERSHAM and THROWLEY FORSTAL.
> 130. TONBRIDGE (Station) and SEVENOAKS WEALD.
> 131. TONBRIDGE (Station) and UNDERRIVER.
> 134. HASTINGS (Station) and FAIRLIGHT GLEN.
> 155. HASTINGS CIRCULAR (via Castle Hill).
> 161. HASTINGS (Mount Road) and ST. LEONARDS (Harley Shute Estate).
>
> SALOON or LOW BRIDGE DOUBLE-DECKS only must be employed on the following services:—
> 9. MAIDSTONE and SEVENOAKS.
> 10A. MAIDSTONE and HOLLINGBOURN.
> 20. GILLINGHAM and MAIDSTONE.
> 24. MAIDSTONE and HORSMONDEN.
> 25. MAIDSTONE and BOROUGH GREEN.
> 91. TONBRIDGE and EAST GRINSTEAD.
> 101. TUNBRIDGE WELLS and LEIGH.
> 109. WEST MALLING and ASHFORD ROAD (Yeoman) via EAST MALLING.
> 149. MAIDSTONE and WEST MALLING AERODROME.
> 156. BEXHILL and ORE.
> 159. ST. HELENS and COODEN.

> **PART VIII**
> **DISCIPLINARY PROCEDURE (DRIVERS AND CONDUCTORS)**
>
> **131.—Issue of Irregularity Report.**
> ... inspector reporting a driver or conductor for any ... issue ... form, setting out details of the ... the driver or conductor concerned ... being reported...

a thorn in the side

John Dengate began a daily route to Hastings from Northiam and Beckley in 1919. This terminated among Maidstone & District vehicles in Wellington Square.

But while the M&D men enjoyed a cuppa between duties, Dengate drivers set off around the town with a £30 float collecting provisions for villagers along the route. Later, village shopkeepers availed themselves of this service and eventually Dengate had the contract to deliver the county paper to outlying shops and mail to village post offices. The sacks were padlocked to the front seats by the Hastings Postmaster. In peak periods, passengers sat with the sacks on their laps under the watchful eye of the driver!

A Northiam to Rye route began in 1922, extended in 1928 to start from Newenden and finally Hawkhurst in 1930. This was in friendly competition with the Weald of Kent Transport Co., both companies accepting each other's return tickets. When Maidstone & District acquired the Weald business in 1933, becoming its route 31 in competition with the Dengate service, reluctantly it was obliged to accept Dengate's return tickets. However, M&D refused Dengate entry to its bus station in Hawkhurst when that opened in 1950.

Separate termini were also the order of the day in Rye, after John Dengate refused to pay a 10/- annual Southern Railways levy to terminate in Station Approach. Dengate chose Rope Walk instead, equally convenient for the station, market and town centre.

Declining passenger numbers in the 1960s saw finances becoming an increasing problem. The end came to Dengate's in 1967, following MOT failures. The examiners, far from happy, ordered the whole fleet to be taken to East Kent's garage in Rye and a sad litany of GV9 stop notice failures followed, with only the two modern coaches passing.

A Bedford OB was merrily working the Hastings service until late in the afternoon of the fateful day, Wednesday 15 February 1967, when it too was called in for inspection at Rye. The very last John Dengate and Son Ltd journey was the 10pm Hastings to Beckley.

The Traffic Commissioners asked Maidstone & District to step in and cover Dengate's bus routes, which it did with vehicles from Rye and its two garages in Hastings. After waiting so many years, M&D had finally got the monopoly it always wanted, albeit temporarily, but quickly found the routes hopelessly uneconomic and advised the Traffic Commissioners it would withdraw in April, later extended to May.

Pam Dengate sold the stage and excursion licences to Davies of Rye, who formed a new company, John Dengate and Son Ltd - Bus and Coachmen. The new company resumed operations on both routes on 16 May 1967.

In December 1973, after previously being opposed by M&D and East Kent at every turn to expand its operations, Davies Coaches sold the bus operations of Dengate to M&D. Victory for M&D, if that's what it was, may have been sweet but it took an awful long time!

Above is an early postcard view of Wellington Square in Hastings with Dengate no. 11, a 1935 Dennis Lancet with Thurgood body, among three pre-war Maidstone & District Leyland heavyweights, including one of the 1939 Titan TD5s with Weymann open-top bodywork.

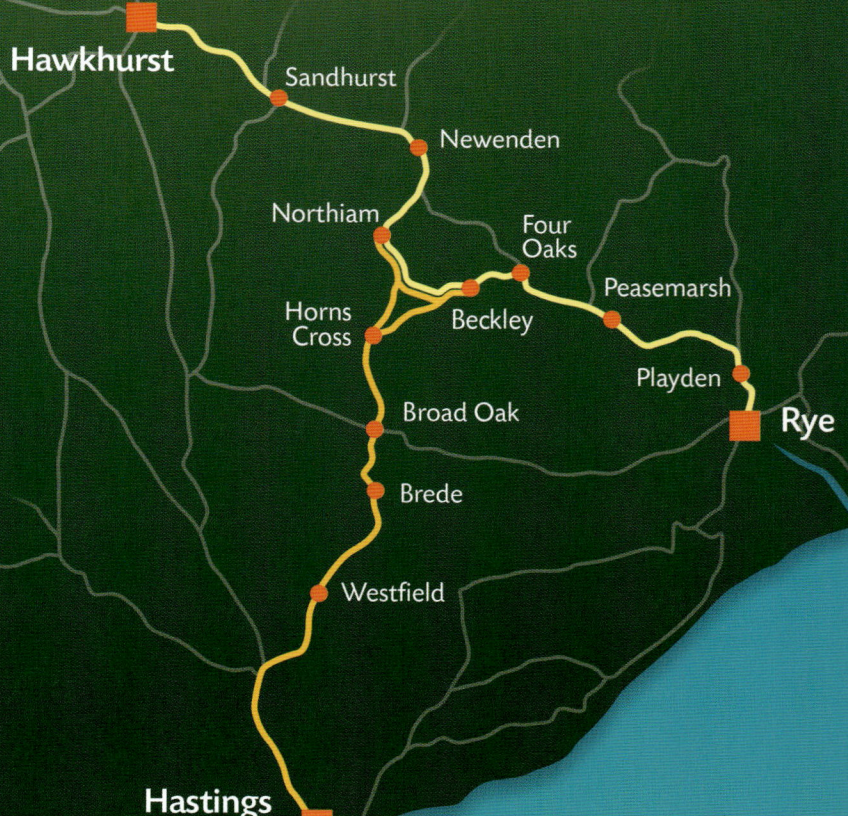

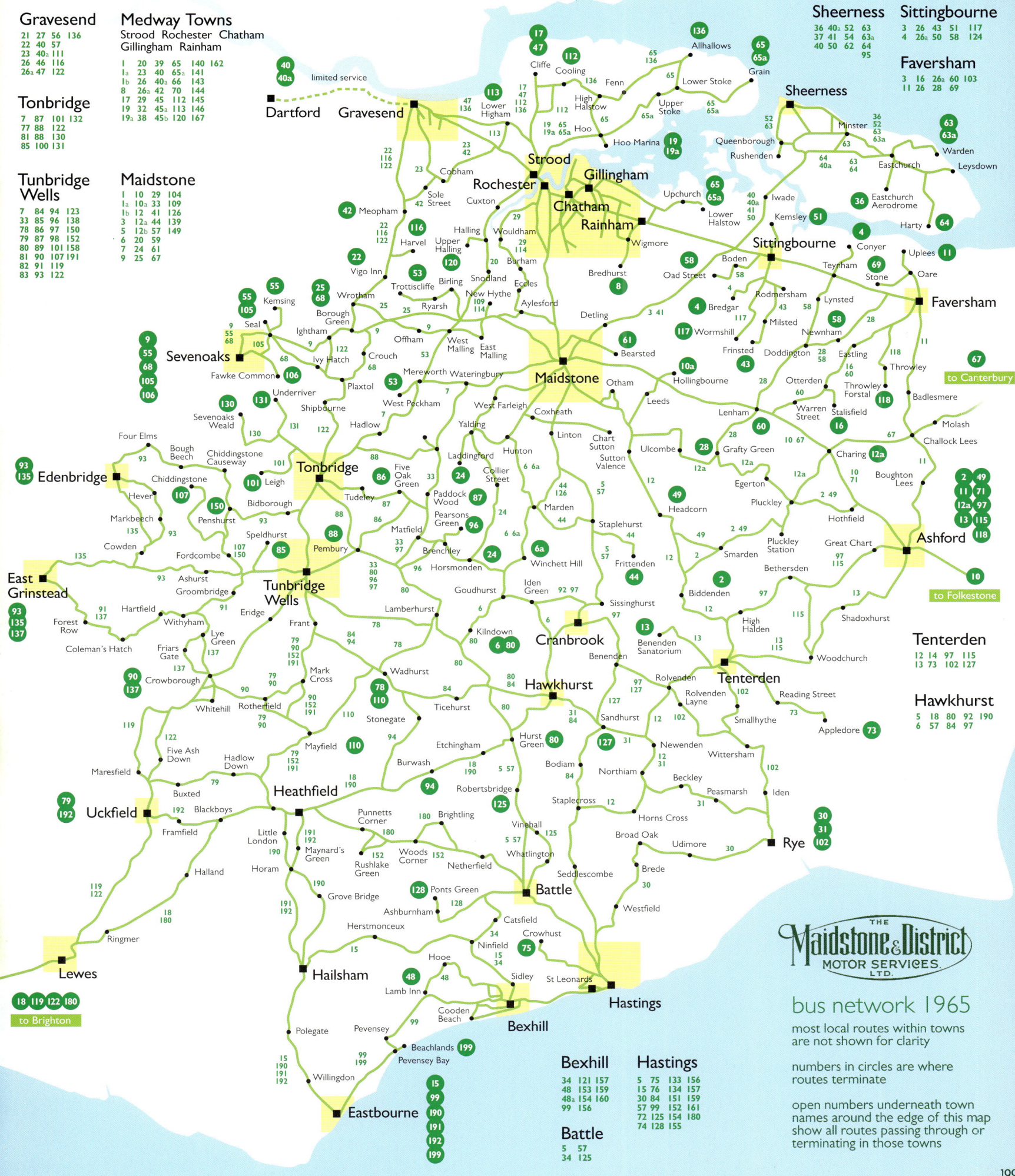

Maidstone & District new vehicle deliveries 1946-1973

FLEET NUMBER	REG NUMBER	CHASSIS	ENGINE	BODY	LAYOUT	YEAR	
DH 163-175	HKL 846-858	Bristol K6A	AEC 7.7	Weymann	H56R	1946	
DH 176	HKL 859	Bristol K6B	Bristol AVW	Weymann	H56R	1946	
DH 177-182	HKL 860-865	Bristol K6A	AEC 7.7	Weymann	H56R	1946	
DH 183-203	HKR 35-55	Bristol K6A	AEC 7.7	Weymann	H56R	1946/7	
SO 4-35	HKL 814-845	AEC Regal O662	AEC 7.7	Beadle	B36F	1946/7	
CO 1-31	JKM 401-431	AEC Regal O662	AEC 7.7	Harrington	C32F	1947/8	
DH 244-249	JKM 101-106	AEC Regent III 0961	AEC 9.6	Weymann	H54R	1947	bodies new in 1942
DH 204-243	JKM 901-940	Bristol K6A	AEC 7.7	Saunders	H56R	1948	
CO 32-61	JKM 432-461	AEC Regal O662	AEC 7.7	Beadle	C32F	1948/9	
CO 62-84	KKK 801-823	AEC Regal III	AEC 7.7	Harrington	C31F	1948/9	bodies new in 1936
CO 85-96	KKK 824-832/7/4/5	AEC Regal III	AEC 7.7	Harrington	C32F	1948	
CO 97	KKK 836	AEC Regal III	AEC 7.7	Harrington	FC32F	1949	
CO 98-112	KKK 833/838-851	AEC Regal III	AEC 7.7	Harrington	C32F	1948/9	
CO 113-116	KKK 852-855	AEC Regal III	AEC 7.7	Harrington	FC32F	1949	
DH 250-291	KKK 856-897	Bristol K6A	AEC 7.7	Weymann	H56R	1948/9	
DL 2-22	LKT 964-983	Bristol K6A	AEC 7.7	Weymann	L53R	1949/50	
SO 36-51	LKT 984-999	Bristol L6A	AEC 7.7	ECW	B35R	1949/50	
SO 52	MKN 201	Bristol LL6A	AEC 7.7	ECW	B39R	1950	
SO 53-66	MKN 202-215	Bristol LL5G	Gardner 5LW	ECW	B39R	1950	
TS 1-4	LKP 42-45	Dennis Falcon	Gardner 4LK	Dennis	B20F	1950	
CO 200	MKT 800	● Beadle-AEC	AEC 7.7	Beadle	C35F	1950	
DH 379-414	NKT 875-910	Leyland Titan PD2/12	Leyland O.600	Leyland	H58R	1951	
DH 415-419	NKT 911-915	Leyland Titan PD2/3	Leyland O.600	Leyland	H56R	1951	
DL 23-34	NKT 916-927	Leyland Titan PD2/12	Leyland O.600	Leyland	L55R	1951	
LC 1	NKN 650	Commer Avenger	Commer petrol	Harrington	C16F	1951	Knightrider
SO 67	NKT 928	● Beadle-AEC	AEC 7.7	Beadle	B39F	1951	
CO 201-240	NKT 929-968	● Beadle-AEC	AEC 7.7	Beadle	C35F	1951/2	
CO 241-259	OKP 969-987	● Beadle-Leyland	Leyland 8.6	Beadle	C35F	1952	
CO 260-271	OKP 988/9/90-8/989	● Beadle-Leyland	Leyland 8.6	Beadle	C26F	1952	
CO 272	PKE 272	Leyland Royal Tiger PSU1/15	Leyland O.600	Harrington	C37C	1952	
CO 273-286	OKO 25-34 ◆	Leyland Royal Tiger PSU1/15	Leyland O.600	Leyland	C37C	1952	
CO 287-300	SKE 983-996	Leyland Royal Tiger PSU1/15	Leyland O.600	Harrington	C37C	1953/4	Wayfarer II body
DH 420-439	RKP 901-920	Leyland Titan PD2/12	Leyland O.600	Weymann	H58R	1953	
SO 68	RKE 540	Saunders-Roe	Gardner 5HLW	Saunders-Roe	B43F	1953	
921-928	RKK 992-999	Guy Arab IV	Gardner 6LW	Weymann	H58R	1953	last new buses delivered to Chatham & District
929-936	TKM 354-361	Guy Arab IV	Gardner 6LW	Weymann	H58R	1954	
CO 301-303	SKE 997-999	● Beadle-Leyland	Leyland 8.6	Beadle	C26F	1954	
CO 304-350	TKM 304-350	AEC Reliance MU3RV	AEC 470	Harrington	C37C	1954/5	Wayfarer II body
CO 354-376	WKM 354-376	● Beadle-AEC	AEC 7.7	Beadle	C37C	1955/6	
CO 351-353	TKM 351-353	● Harrington-Commer	Rootes TS3	Harrington	C41F	1955	Wayfarer II body
DH 468-475	VKO 992-999	Guy Arab IV	Gardner 6LW	Weymann	H60R	1955	Orion body
SO 200-210	UKN 200-210	● Harrington-Commer	Rootes TS3	Harrington	B42F	1955	
DH 476-489	VKR 468-481	AEC Regent V MD3RV	AEC 470	Park Royal	H59RD	1956	
DL 35-42	VKR 35-42	AEC Regent V MD3RV	AEC 470	Park Royal	L56RD	1956	
SO 211-222	XKT 988-999	AEC Reliance MU3RV	AEC 410	Weymann	B42F	1956/7	
SO 223-239	YKR 223-239	AEC Reliance MU3RV	AEC 410	Beadle	B42F	1957	
CO 377-389	377-389 BKM	AEC Reliance MU3RV	AEC 470	Harrington	C37F	1957	Wayfarer IV body
CO 390-409	390-409 DKK	AEC Reliance 2MU3RV	AEC 470	Harrington	C41F	1958/9	Wayfarer IV body
SO 240-264	240-264 BKM	AEC Reliance 2MU3RV	AEC 410	Harrington	B42F	1958	Wayfarer IV body

layout codes
before seating capacity
- **H** highbridge - centre gangways both decks
- **L** lowbridge - sunken side gangway upstairs
- **LD** lowheight - centre gangways both decks within lower height
- **B** single-deck bus
- **C** single-deck coach
- **CH** double-deck coach
- **DP** dual purpose bus/coach
- **FC** full width front on front-engined chassis

after seating capacity
- **F** front entrance
- **R** rear open platform
- **RD** rear with doors
- **C** centre entrance
- **D** dual doors

● these were semi-chassisless vehicles
● these were chassisless vehicles
◆ registration numbers allocated out of sequence OKO 25-26, 23-24, 21-22, 27-34

FLEET NUMBER	REG NUMBER	CHASSIS	ENGINE	BODY	LAYOUT	YEAR	
DH 490-523	490-523 DKT	Leyland Atlantean PDR1/1	Leyland O.600	Metro-Cammell	H78F	1959	
DH 524-525	524-525 DKT	Leyland Atlantean PDR1/1	Leyland O.600	Metro-Cammell	CH60F	1959	
DL 43-56	43-56 DKT	Leyland Atlantean PDR1/1	Leyland O.600	Weymann	L73F	1959	
SO 265-283	265-283 DKT	AEC Reliance 2MU3RV	AEC 410	Park Royal	DP40F	1959	
CO 410-424	410-424 FKL	AEC Reliance 2MU3RV	AEC 470	Harrington	C41F	1959	Wayfarer IV body
SO 285-304	285-304 GKK	AEC Reliance 2MU3RV	AEC 410	Weymann	DP40F	1960	
DH 526-550	526-550 HKJ	Leyland Atlantean PDR1/1	Leyland O.600	Metro-Cammell	H77F	1960	
DH 551-570	551-570 LKP	Leyland Atlantean PDR1/1	Leyland O.600	Metro-Cammell	H77F	1960/1	
SO 305-319	305-319 LKK	Albion Nimbus NS3N	Albion EN250	Harrington	B30F	1960	
S 320-349	320-349 NKT	AEC Reliance 2MU3RV	AEC 470	Weymann	DP40F	1961/2	
C 1-20	101-120 PKP	AEC Reliance 2MU3RV	AEC 470	Harrington	C41F	1961	last Wayfarer IVs
DH 571-585	571-585 RKJ	Leyland Atlantean PDR1/1	Leyland O.600	Metro-Cammell	H77F	1961	
S 350	350 RKR	AEC Reliance 2MU3RV	AEC 470	Weymann	DP40F	1962	
S 1	984 TKO	AEC Reliance 2U3RA	AEC 590	Willowbrook	B54F	1962	first 36ft bus
C 21-30	21-30 TKR	AEC Reliance 2MU3RV	AEC 470	Harrington	C37F	1962	Cavalier body
DH 586-632	586-632 UKM	Leyland Atlantean PDR1/1 Mk2	Leyland O.600	Weymann	H77F	1963	
S 190-199	190-199 XKE	AEC Reliance 2MU2RA	AEC 470	Harrington	B42F	1963	7ft 6in wide
S 2-5	2-5 YKK	AEC Reliance 2U3RA	AEC 590	Willowbrook	B53F	1963	
SC 31-32	31-32 YKK	AEC Reliance 2U3RA	AEC 590	Willowbrook	DP49F	1963	
DL 57-91	57-91 YKT	Daimler Fleetline CRG6LX	Gardner 6LX	Northern Counties	LD77F	1963/4	
C 33	3294 D	AEC Reliance 2U3RA	AEC 590	Harrington	C47F	1964	Grenadier body
C 34-37	AKP 251-254B	AEC Reliance 2U3RA	AEC 590	Harrington	C47F	1964	Grenadier body
S 6-25	BKT 821-840C	AEC Reliance 2U3RA	AEC 590	Marshall	B53F	1965	
S 26-37	DKE 251-262C	Leyland Panther PSUR1/1R	Leyland O.600	Willowbrook	B53F	1965	
S 38-40	DKE 263-265C	Leyland Panther PSUR1/1R	Leyland O.600	Willowbrook	B45F	1965	
S 41-60	EKJ 101-120C	AEC Reliance 2U3RA	AEC 590	Weymann	B53F	1965	
SC 38-57	BKT 801-820C	AEC Reliance 2U3RA	AEC 590	Weymann	DP49F	1965	
C 58-72	FKL 121-135D	AEC Reliance 2U3RA	AEC 590	Harrington	C47F	1965	Grenadier body
DL 92-111	FKL 101-120D	Daimler Fleetline CRG6LX	Gardner 6LX	Northern Counties	LD77F	1966	
SC 73-76	HKR 173-176D	AEC Reliance 2U3RA	AEC 590	Marshall	DP49F	1966	
SC 77-80	HKT 577-580D	AEC Reliance 2U3RA	AEC 590	Marshall	DP49F	1966	
SC 81-82	HKT 591-592D	AEC Reliance 2U3RA	AEC 590	Marshall	DP49F	1966	
S 61	HKK 61D	Leyland Panther PSUR1/1R	Leyland O.600	Willowbrook	B53F	1966	
S 62-80	JKK 162-180E	Leyland Panther PSUR1/1R	Leyland O.600	Willowbrook	B53F	1966/7	
S 81-110	JKK 181-210E	Leyland Panther PSUR1/1R	Leyland O.600	Willowbrook	B45F	1967	
2801-2818	OKO 801-818G	Leyland Leopard PSU3A/4RT	Leyland O.600	Willowbrook	DP49F	1968	
3111-3120	LKT 111-120F	Leyland Panther PSUR1/1R	Leyland O.600	Strachan	B45D	1968	
3121-3140	LKT 121-140F	Leyland Panther PSUR1/1R	Leyland O.600	Strachan	B48F	1968	
4601-4612	NKL 205-212F	Leyland Leopard PSU3A/4RT	Leyland O.600	Duple	C45F	1968	Commander III body
6112-6131	MKO 112-131F	Daimler Fleetline CRG6LX	Gardner 6LX	Northern Counties	LD77F	1968	
4613, 4622	RKM 613,622G	Leyland Leopard PSU3A/4RT	Leyland O.600	Duple	C44F	1969	Commander IV body
4614-4621	RKM 614-621G	Leyland Leopard PSU3A/4R	Leyland O.600	Duple	C44F	1969	Commander IV body
4623-4628	VKN 623-628J	Leyland Leopard PSU3A/4R	Leyland O.600	Duple	C48F	1970	Commander IV body
3801-3830	SKO 801-830H	Daimler Fleetline SRG6LX-36	Gardner 6LX	Marshall	B45D	1969/70	
3401-3420	UKE 401-420J	Leyland Leopard PSU4A/4R	Leyland O.600	Marshall	B45F	1970	
3421-3440	AKM 421-440K	Leyland Leopard PSU4A/2R	Leyland O.600	Willowbrook	B45F	1971	
3441-3456	EKJ 441-55K/EKL 456K	Leyland Leopard PSU4B/4R	Leyland O.600	Marshall	B45F	1972	
3457-3475	GKE 457-475L	Leyland Leopard PSU4B/4R	Leyland O.600	Marshall	B45F	1972/3	

As the 1970s unfolded, vehicle buying policy was controlled centrally by National Bus Company head office; also vehicles began to be transferred between NBC subsidiaries, so in essence these Leyland Leopard buses delivered in between 1970 and 1973 were the last true traditional Maidstone & District purchases.

the final years

Although the telling of our tale ends at the end of the 1960s, Maidstone & District as a company continued for more than a couple of decades, at first as a subsidiary of the state-owned National Bus Company and later back in the private sector, owned by its own management for a few years, then as part of British Bus, one of the large bus operating groups that formed in the aftermath of the privatisation process. But it was a different Maidstone & District for a different era with an altogether different personality.

National Bus Company

Maidstone & District had in our period been part of the largely independent British Electric Traction Group. The other big largely independent group was Tilling. When the Tilling companies came under state ownership in 1948, these were put under the auspices of the British Transport Commission, later the Transport Holding Company. After Labour came to power in 1964, Prime Minister Harold Wilson appointed Barbara Castle to be Transport Minister in December 1965. A charismatic, formidable, controversial and determined politician - not for nothing she was sometimes called the Red Queen - she proposed forming regional transport authorities, which would take over the THC subsidiaries and municipal transport undertakings in their areas, and would also have the power to acquire private bus operators.

However, in November 1967 British Electric Traction, possibly thinking the writing might soon be on the wall and seeing a continuing downturn in business, unexpectedly offered to sell its bus operations to the government. BET was paid £35 million for 25 provincial bus companies with over 11,000 vehicles. This deal meant that the state now operated a high proportion of scheduled bus services in England and Wales. So, abandoning the regional authority plan, the government instead published a white paper proposing the merger of the THC and BET organisations into a single National Bus Company. This formed part of the Transport Act 1968, and thus the National Bus Company came into being on 1 January 1969.

As far as Maidstone & District was concerned, all too soon changes were afoot. In 1971 it made a financial loss. To reduce overheads, NBC decided to have a single senior management and finance team for both M&D and adjacent East Kent, with control transferred to the Canterbury office. Gradually the new NBC corporate identity began to eradicate Maidstone & District's traditional appearance, but the story of changes within the company and with its neighbouring fellow NBC companies is not the focus of this book. It was still an interesting company and the management faced the difficult times of the 1970s and early 1980s with fortitude and considerable acumen. It really was a changed world but Maidstone & District no longer looked like the Maidstone & District this book is about.

With the National Bus Company's corporate identity, a bland uniformity spread across the land, possibly reaching its nadir with noisy, industrial-looking Leyland Nationals in unrelieved poppy red or leaf green. Oh, how plain and dull they looked!

Maidstone & District's first Nationals appeared in 1973, and 3514 above was delivered the following year. It was photographed at the Lime Hill Road stop in the Green Line coach station in Tunbridge Wells on its way to Gravesend soon afterwards. This coach station used to be for the exclusive use of Green Line 704 from Tunbridge Wells to Windsor by way of Sevenoaks, Bromley, London and Slough.

In the 1970s the long 122 route (see pages 156-8) was split at Tunbridge Wells and the northern section became 322, although there was a *penchant* within many NBC companies for replacing easy-to remember, well-established low route numbers with high ones.

RAY STENNING

privatisation and a management buyout

It was a Conservative government under Margaret Thatcher that embarked on a major sell-off of state assets. When it came to the National Bus Company, understandably the NBC Board was keen to see it sold off as one entity but Nicholas Ridley, Secretary of State for Transport between 11 June 1983 and 21 May 1986, had a vision of lots of entrepreneurial smaller companies running buses. NBC was instructed to break up the bigger companies into smaller units, although Maidstone & District's Hastings operations had already been made a separate company in 1983. Also, East Kent was disentangled from Maidstone & District.

In 1975, Maidstone & District was selected to trial batches of the MCW Metropolitan, Volvo Ailsa B55 and Bristol VRT series 3 for potential future NBC buying policy. They entered service first at Hastings Silverhill, eventually transferring to the Medway Towns.

On the left is preserved Ailsa 5385. The excessively large fleetnumber was for the less-than-brilliant cameras at Chatham's less-than-charming Pentagon bus station to be able to see which buses were entering the bus station.
CHRIS SAMPSON

Bids from management teams were encouraged and were actually incentivised. It was a nailbiting time for local management teams wishing to buy the bus companies they already ran, and this was the case with Maidstone & District. Luckily, the bid was successful and on 7 November 1986 M&D was sold to its management. NBC leaf green livery was kept, although the white relief was later changed to cream.

back in a group

After the first few years of owning their own bus company, some management buyouts found they hadn't always enough financial muscle or wherewithal to reinvest in the business as much as might be prudent, or sometimes the offers being made by the nascent groups that were forming were just too tempting to resist. Altruistically, many had the future good of their companies at heart, and realised belonging to a group would give better security to their businesses and staff.

Maidstone & District sold out to British Bus on 13 April 1995. British Bus grew out of a company called Drawlane. Drawlane had begun as a holding company formed by businessmen Ray McEnhill and Adam Mills called Endless Holdings, based in Salisbury. They formed it to buy NBC companies when they were being privatised, London Country South West being an early purchase. British Bus expanded quite a bit, and by July 1994 had acquired the small Proudmutual Group that owned neighbouring Kentish Bus. Kentish Bus was the new name adopted at privatisation by what had been London Country South East.

Thus, with the purchase of Maidstone & District, British bus owned operations in the South East covered a swathe of territory from Guildford in the west to Ashford in the east. Soon, John Piper, who for a while had been joint managing director for London & Country (the new name created by one of your authors, Ray, for London Country South West), became managing director of Kentish Bus and was then given responsibility for Maidstone & District, too. In 1996 the Cowie Group acquired British Bus (the how and why is complex), but Cowie, not the best name for a company with ambitions for international expansion, renamed itself Arriva, and in April 1998 Maidstone & District became Arriva Kent & Sussex, which was then subsumed into a larger area division of Arriva called Arriva Southern Counties.

the old Maidstone & District returns?

But this is jumping ahead, for soon after John Piper took charge and before Arriva decided it needed to have a nationwide corporate identity, something of the old Maidstone & District briefly reappeared! And hereby hangs a story with a personal involvement. Co-author Ray Stenning, well known for creating rather a lot of bus company liveries, having learnt that Maidstone & District was in the British Bus fold and that John Piper was in charge - and having worked with John on a number of projects - decided to create a modern version of the M&D scroll fleetname ... you know ... just in case ... sort of ... as it were! Here are his words:

"I put it in a drawer (this was pre-computer days when we did everything with pen on paper) until the phone call came. And it did. So I set to create a modern reinterpretation of the traditional Maidstone & District livery and, with an over-the-moon delighted John Piper and team, for a brief flowering something of the good old Maidstone & District was back. But all too soon the Arriva corporate look consigned this to posterity. The weird irony of all this is that I was also responsible for the initial new Arriva livery that killed off the new M&D one. The fates work strangely and cruelly sometimes!"

Above is a former Maidstone & District Northern Counties bodied Leyland Olympian preserved in Ray Stenning's all-too-brief M&D 'comeback' livery.

Not only was there a proud, modern re-interpretation of the familiar M&D scroll fleetname, but you'll notice a light green pinstripe within the dark green as a subtle nod to the earlier style of lining out.

What a shame it didn't survive longer than it did, but it's a fitting note on which to close this story.

With the loyal following it had, it's not surprising that an impressive number of Maidstone & District buses and coaches have been preserved by enthusiasts and regularly get admiring glances at rallies and gatherings.

On these two pages are just a few of them, all looking resplendent in the classic Maidstone & District colours.

The line-up below was photographed by Ray Stenning at the M&D100 event in April 2011 staged at Detling Showground a few miles north east of Maidstone. This was to celebrate 100 years since the formation of the company.

Nearest the camera was BET-style Marshall bodied AEC Reliance S6 from 1965, then Harrington bodied Albion Nimbus SO308, then one of the Harrington coach-to-bus conversions, a Weymann post-war rebody of a wartime utility Bristol K and, just in view, a Strachan bodied Leyland Panther. The Panther can also be seen providing trips around the Showground in the middle picture on the right.

KO 7311 on the right, fleetnumber 461, was a Short bodied Tilling-Stevens B9A new in 1928. It left the fleet in 1937. It was photographed by Roger Davies.

The Harrington Cavalier bodied AEC Reliance touring coach at the top of the opposite page is a splendid example of the preservationists' skills. This one was photographed by Ray Stenning at one of the Brooklands Spring Gathering events, as was SC390 at the bottom.

a Maidstone & District legacy

David Toy took the picture above of preserved Maidstone & District DL39, a Park Royal lowbridge bodied AEC Regent V, which had been painted in the original lined out livery it wore when new in 1956.

This was taking part in one of the popular running days regularly held in towns in the old London Transport Country Area, this one at East Grinstead on Sunday 22 April 2018. It had route 9 shown in the blind at the front. As is explained in this book, the 9 ran from Sevenoaks to Maidstone, whereas it was the 91 that ran from East Grinstead to Tunbridge Wells. Lowbridge double deckers were used on both routes.

Below is pre-war Leyland Tiger TS7 CO558 with a Harrington body. Lovingly and beautifully restored, its survival has probably been due to it being kept on for boat-carrying duties after others in the same batch had been retired.

M&D buses & coaches seen in the trade press

Body, chassis and component manufacturers would often feature recent vehicle deliveries to advertise their wares and prove their credentials, and Maidstone & District featured from time to time.

Here on these pages are a few examples. Immediately on the right at the top is an advert by Duple for the BET-style Willowbrook dual-purpose single-deck body (Duple owned Willowbrook), here on a Leyland Leopard chassis. The 5-bay construction of the body gave it longer windows, an improvement over the original 6-bay style. This was actually 2804, a 49-seater new in 1968.

Below that are a couple of adverts that actually appeared in Maidstone & District timetable books. One can't help wondering how many ordinary passengers would be interested in buying an AEC Reliance or Beadle-Commer integral coach; also did M&D 'cheek' the manufacturers into advertising in their timetable books? - probably!

Passenger Transport was an industry trade magazine and carried a fair bit of advertising, including always on the cover. On the opposite page MCW took the front cover of this issue from 1959 and used it to advertise its body for the new Leyland Atlantean rear-engined chassis, using a Maidstone & District example.

Coachbuilder Thomas Harrington of Hove must have been proud of its long association with Maidstone & District. On the furthest right it used an image of one of M&D's Wayfarer IV bodied AEC Reliance touring coaches in a trade press advert.

Lastly, in the lower picture on the opposite page, is an advert for Beclawat sliding windows, using a Maidstone & District Harrington bus bodied AEC Reliance of 1958.

Beclawat was the name used by the British firm Beckett, Laycock and Watkinson Ltd. It made openable windows and other fittings for many transport applications. The company was established in 1912 in London NW10, and later set up companies in Australia and Canada. It moved to Newport Pagnell in 1983, and later to Elland, West Yorkshire, but closed down in 2005, although the Canadian company continued.

the origins of Knightrider House

Above is a fine study of the sole Harrington bodied 16-seat petrol-engined Commer Avenger coach delivered in 1951, known as the Knightrider and named after Maidstone & District's head office, Knightrider House. It was certainly in pristine condition here, its gleaming deep blue paintwork and brightwork trim highly polished and glinting in the sun outside the front entrance of Knightrider House.

It was officially numbered LC1, although the coach never carried this identification on the bodywork. There is more about this magnificent vehicle on page 54.

This impressive 18th century Grade II Listed building's first owner was William Shipley. William was born in Maidstone around 1715, but moved to London when he was only three to live with his grandfather after his father had died. He studied drawing in Northampton but moved back to London around 1750. In 1754, in a coffee shop in Henrietta Street in London's Covent Garden, he founded an arts society that became The Royal Society of Arts, or Royal Society for the Encouragement of Arts, Manufactures & Commerce.

On 23 November 1767 William Shipley married Elizabeth Miller, and soon after moved back to Maidstone and that's when he had Knightrider House built for him and his family.

While back in Kent, he also founded The Maidstone Society for the Promotion of Useful Knowledge, which in 1783 was instrumental in improving the sanitation of Maidstone gaol and preventing what was known as 'gaol fever', typhus in fact. He died in Maidstone on 28 December 1803 at the impressive age of 89.

the authors

David Toy

David Toy has spent 33 years as either a Chief Engineer or Engineering Director within the bus industry in both England and Scotland. For example, he has held pivotal senior roles with Brighton Corporation, with Northern, Kelvin and Western Scottish, with London & Country, at the Cawlett Group and within First Group.

David was born in Kent and completed his engineering training with the Transport division of the Reed Paper Group at Aylesford and Gravesend, both in Maidstone & District territory. Even before moving to his first management position in the bus industry at Reading in 1972, as assistant to the Chief Engineer, he had an interest in the bus industry. This interest included, of course, the Maidstone & District company.

In his retirement, David has written many articles and several books on buses and transport, and is a regular contributor to Classic Bus magazine.

Ray Stenning

Ray is the founder and head of the specialist design, marketing and advertising agency Best Impressions, which has possibly done more than anyone else over the past 40 years to change how public transport is perceived, presented and sold, through projects and schemes big and small in the bus, coach and rail sectors. Ray is committed and passionate about the role that public transport should play in a progressive society and not only practises what he preaches, he also preaches what he practises as a regular conference speaker and writer in trade magazines on his pet subjects of design, marketing and customer care.

As well as being a talented designer, Ray is also a total enthusiast. His mother claimed the first word he ever spoke was bus. He has been editing, designing and publishing the magazine Classic Bus since 2006, and has written and/or edited and published a number of books on buses and bus people over the years.

Growing up in the south east corner of Surrey, Ray's interest in, fascination for and love of Maidstone & District stemmed from forays into its territory by bicycle as a lad. Some of the photographs in this book are from when he had his first 35mm camera as a teenager. So Ray was delighted when David asked if he was interested in helping with this book, and confesses to it being a hugely enjoyable labour of love!

The pictures above show the interior of a typical Maidstone & District coach of the mid-1950s, in this case CO322, a Harrington Wayfarer II bodied AEC Reliance pristinely restored.

The photographs were taken in Winchelsea on the first public appearance of this coach after a 20-year comprehensive rebuild and restoration in which all mechanical units were removed and rebuilt and the body completely repanelled.
ROBERT GIBBONS

understanding the jargon

Like any industry and the enthusiasts who are involved with it, the world of buses and coaches has its own way of describing or classifying things. So the following explanations are intended to help anyone not so well-versed in the peculiarities of bus nomenclature.

Most buses and coaches from the earliest days had a complete chassis carrying all the mechanical parts, and a separate body that was then affixed to that chassis. Bus companies chose the chassis they wanted and approached directly, or through the chassis manufacturer, the bodybuilder to make the body type they required. There was a great variety to choose from.

chassis

Chassis suitable for double deckers were for many years traditional front-engined types with the driver alongside the engine. Then in 1958 a revolutionary, rear-engined model came on the scene with the front wheels set back to allow an entrance opposite the driver. This was the Leyland Atlantean, which Maidstone & District took to enthusiastically - see page 80.

Similarly, single-deck chassis had a vertical engine at the front, mostly with the driver alongside. This arrangement was called **forward control**. If the driver sat behind the engine it was referred to as **normal control**.

The change to having the entrance alongside the driver ahead of set-back front wheels took off in the early 1950s. With this arrangement the engine had been tilted on its side and placed under the floor amidships. Maidstone & District's first choice of chassis like this was the Leyland Royal Tiger although, once lighter-weight versions appeared, the company switched its allegiance to rival AEC and chose AEC's Reliance for the next 10 years or so for both coach and bus single deckers.

bodies

Over the years dealt with by this book, Maidstone & District opted for bodies built by a variety of manufacturers, although for coaches M&D will always be closely associated with the quality styles from Hove-based Thomas Harrington.

Coach styles mostly had names, like Harrington Cavalier or Duple Commander, but not always. For bus bodies this was less common, although you will find in this book one or two names cropping up, like Weymann Orion.

integral

These are where there is no separate chassis and the body manufacturer has produced the entire load-bearing structure and mechanical components are incorporated into it. There have been various attempts to encourage bus operators to go for these but a combination of conservatism and liking to use their preferred bodybuilders meant these types were only built in limited numbers until the Leyland National was effectively 'forced' on operators like Maidstone & District in the 1970s

M&D had flirted with a few single-deck integral designs in the early 1950s, both buses and coaches, and these you'll find within the pages of this book.